TOO YOUNG TO DIE

by
Patricia
Fox-
Sheinwold

New Revised Edition

BELL PUBLISHING COMPANY
New York

By the Author

Books

Husbands And Other Men I've Played With

Crossword Puzzle Dictionary

The Jolly Time Party Book

Essays

Seeing The Blind As They See Us
Slugging It Out In The Ring
The Day of The One Night Stands
Where You Thought You'd Never Be:
In A Gay Marriage
My Last Date With A Teen-ager
Too Much TM

Library of Congress Catalog Card Number: 79-92269

This edition is published by Bell Publishing Company, a division of Crown Publishers, Inc.
a b c d e f g h
Published under arrangement with Ottenheimer Publishers, Inc.
Printed in the United States of America.

friend is a six-letter word,
for Teresa

CREDITS

Special Thanks to:
Arthur Herzog, Jr.
Evelyn Lee Jones
Barbara Lea
Jeanne Schapiro

The author wishes to thank the following individuals
for their generous assistance:
Justin Anthony, Monty Arnold, Charles Earle, Bob
Edison, Milt Gabler, Stephen Greene, Kim Hartstein,
Marion Horvitz, Shirley Jones, Richard Katz, David
LaHeure, Elizabeth Lessen, Maurice Lockamy, Elinor
Pynes, Jack Raymond, Jimmie Rowles, Susan Senk,
Sylvia Syms, Pauline Vadas, Shayne Weir, and Ronny
Whyte,

The author expresses thanks and appreciation for the
courtesy of the following who helped provide the
photographs, some never published, that are included
in the book:
John R. Adler, Mark Beltaire, Fawn Bifoss, William
Ewald, Mr. and Mrs. Erwin Harburg, Douglas
McClelland, Loonis McGlohon, Mr. and Mrs. Burton
Tremaine, Leo Castelli Gallery, Marilyn Pearl Gallery,
Maurice Davey/Bill Stribling (UPI), Paula Vogel (Wide
World), Lincoln Center Library, Cinemabilia, Dan
Nooger (Atlantic Records), Columbia Records, RCA
Records, and Warner Brothers Records.

Table of Contents

"And into The Eighties"

Conclusion

Foreword

It would be rather easy to make a blithe assumption that film stars have more interesting sex lives than the rest of us or take more drugs, drink more booze, live in a less restrained fashion, or make any other assumption we want to. All these notions would be garnered from a casual impression of newspaper headlines, television, Hollywood gossip columns, and word of mouth. But a reasonable generalization about the lives of movie stars/entertainers had better be based on some fairly solid facts. In other words, we could write a penetrating essay on why more famous politicians come from the state of Iowa than anywhere else, only to discover that Iowa contributed not one more politician to the national scene than its own proportion of the population would warrant.

So let's lay aside our prejudices about film stars and consider these facts: From 1940 to the present there are at most about 300 entertainers whose names could be recognized by many people and identified as easily as the 30 odd stars whose biographies are outlined in this book. Now this fact alone would suggest that about 10% of all top notch entertainers died in a violent fashion and primarily of a self-inflicted nature like suicide, alcohol, and drugs. Hardly 10% of our total population die in this fashion.

About three times as many film stars die violent deaths as do top figures in the world of sports. Thus we are on fairly safe ground if we want to discuss the role of self-inflicted injury or violence in the lives and motives of well-known entertainers.

We shall eliminate from our speculations the fact that more public figures die of plane and auto crashes than the population at large since public figures must, of necessity, travel more than the rest of us. But considering the number of figures who are famous in areas other than entertainment and who died in a violent fashion, film stars are unique in their propensity for taking out aggression against themselves.

There is a fairly common notion that publicity itself has a bad effect on people's lives and that universal admiration is somehow responsible for the suicide of the well-known personality. This is just not true. Public figures in many other areas of American life simply do not have such a high proportion of self-inflicted deaths, as do the popular entertainers. We must look for the causes of violence directed against the *self* in the basic make-up of the "star" personality.

Thus it is reasonable from a statistical point of view to make some hypotheses about the role of violence directed against the *self* in the early motivations of movie stars. The popular notion that film stars tend to do bad things to their bodies does, indeed, seem to be substantiated by even the most casual numbers. Moreover we have the right to speculate about the kind of people who try successfully to become noted singers or actors since there is such a high proportion of early and violent deaths among them as compared to people famous in other fields.

Suppose we advance this notion: Hunger. The popular entertainers hunger for love, for praise, for applause, adulation, and affection. And this hunger presupposes an inner emptiness, a gnawing feeling that something desperately needed for survival is lacking. Many stars have a never-ending search for supplies of emotional nourishment. The love given by their mate can never be enough and the disappointment engendered by the spouse's lack of ability to give emotional stroking in endless supply, leads the star to find another and yet another mate who now, at last, will be the eternal source of love, appreciation, worship, and total giving. Needless to say, nobody can ever give enough, no amount of public applause lasts forever or is of sufficient intensity to satisfy, nor are the material objects that the star can buy, enough to allay such awful pangs of psychic emptiness.

When Arthur Miller wrote the play, *After the Fall*, some critics believed that a production about the life of his former spouse was simply in poor taste. Yet it is entirely possible that

6

when Marilyn Monroe's sexy appeal is long forgotten, the play will continue to be known as a valid description of a heroine's destruction, not out of *hubris*, but from an inner imbalance, hunger, and lack of self-control.

Well, how about other people who are famous in the arts such as music, both popular and classic, the graphic arts, writers of novels and plays? Generally they are no more prone to self-injury than the rest of us. So how do they differ from the entertainers?

Figures who are famous in sports, in politics, and even in the arts, differ from the charismatic entertainers in one important respect: They have patience. Although the artists may be motivated by the same hunger as the entertainers, they spend many long hours and days and years perfecting their craft. We may even include actors who have worked hard and long to become the fine artists that they are today, such as Laurence Olivier and Ingrid Bergman. These people all differ from the entertainers in their ability to restrain their needs, their hunger, in the interest of artistic production.

Another distinction between the artist and the "star" lies in the serious artist's devotion to his or her own artistic integrity. This dedication is conspicuously lacking in the entertainer. As long as the public continues to give its acclaim to the "star", he or she believes that they have done quite well and must simply go on to another box-office "success". The artist, however, is not so prone to be swayed by applause from his or her pursuit of excellence. The serious artist has other goals in addition to the craving for applause. Artistic integrity is at least as meaningful to the artist as garnering public acclaim.

Not so the popular entertainers. By and large their ability to fascinate us sprang full blown from a kind of natural facility. Their knack for public performance was not achieved by years of hard work at their craft, although the rough edges of their act may have been rounded by many appearances in front of audiences. Specifically, how many of the entertainers can read

music? How many years of voice training did they have? How long have they spent in acting classes? It is clear that capacity for sustained study, which is not immediately rewarded, is beyond the grasp of the entertainers as opposed to the serious artists. The entertainers need immediate gratification and simply cannot spend long hours improving their craft; hours which go past unrewarded by applause right then and there. Their hunger is too great. Their need is too immediate. And it is this very need for inner peace that drives them out of anguish and desperation to do away with themselves.

Impatience and the lack of self-restraint may even be a recently acquired trait. An examination of the language of Janis Joplin shows clear differences when she first started to perform as a college student and her speech during later years. In college she spoke with due regard for the conventions of grammar and syntax. Gradually her style changed into a much looser and "hip" language. Was this an affectation? It really doesn't matter. What is important is that conventional restraints were tossed aside in her all consuming hunger.

A personality change, like Joplin's, can explain James Dean. Dean was known to have worked very hard and very long at his craft and yet met a violent self-inflicted death. Here the story of his life suggests that although possessing self-restraint during the beginning of his career, the erosion of patience and the increasing inability to delay gratification, became apparent to those who knew him towards the end of his career. The same is true of John Barrymore.

As so often is the case when it comes to expressing fundamental things, the Rolling Stones said it all much better: "Ah cain't get no, satis-fac-shun . . . Ah cain't get no, satis-fac-shun . . . Ah cain't get no . . ."

Phineas Kadushin M.S.
New York City 1978

7

ABOUT THE AWARDS

Awards for performers constitute recognition from three different kinds of sources: Awards voted by professionals working in the performers' own industries, awards voted by the press, and awards based on polls of fans, or on sales of something (tickets, records, etc.).

All of the important awards for acting—the Oscars, the Tonys, and the Emmys—are based on voting by professionals in the various entertainment fields. The Oscars, or Academy Awards, were first given in 1928 for the season 1927-28. At that time there were just two performers' awards, for Best Actor and Best Actress; categories for Best Supporting Actor and Actress were added in 1936. The Tonys, or Antoinette Perry Awards—the highest honors in the legitimate theatre—were not given until 1947, for the theatrical season 1946-47. Their number has remained fairly constant: Best Leading Actor and Actress and Best Supporting Actor and Actress, in musicals and in straight plays.

The Emmy Awards for the new television industry were started in 1949 for the eligibility year 1948. There were just five awards that year, and none for acting, just one for the most "Outstanding Personality." Best Actor and Best Actress were first named for the eligibility year 1950, and now, in the late 70's, there are eighteen performers' awards, for Leading and Supporting Actors and Actresses in series and single shows, in comedy, drama, and music.

In contrast, many musical awards are based on popularity. In the late 30's, 40's, and early 50's the important awards for musical performers were the readers' polls conducted by *Down Beat* and *Metronome* magazines; there are still readers' polls by various magazines, but their significance has greatly decreased. Added to the readers' surveys were two important votings by music critics: *Esquire* magazine's critics' survey, starting in 1944 (the year Billie Holiday won a Gold Award) and the *Down Beat* International Critics' Poll, starting in 1953 (when Charlie Parker won as Best Alto Sax).

In 1958 the newly-formed National Academy of Recording Arts and Sciences gave the first Grammy Awards, for the eligibility year 1957. These awards, like those for actors, are voted by professionals in the recording industry and are considered awards for recognized quality, rather than popularity. The first NARAS Hall of Fame Awards were given in 1974.

The matter of Gold Record Awards is more complicated. Certainly they are based on popularity, for single records selling one million copies, or for albums reaching a million dollars in sales. The Recording Industry Association of America has brought order and authenticity to the claims of million-sellers, and official awards are now given only upon presentation of documented sales figures by member companies for certification by the Association. This results in some anomalies. For example, a very few companies (such as Motown and Keen) have never joined the Association; thus their artists have never received official Gold Records. It is quite common for companies to claim many more million-sellers, or "gold records", than can actually be authenticated. And sometimes a record can reach the magic million figure several years after its release.

The first official Gold Record Awards — just five — were given in 1958. It is interesting to trace the growth of this award from 5 in 1958 to 42 in 1962, to 120 in 1968, to 169 in 1970, to 249 in 1977.

RIAA Platinum Record Awards, for singles selling two million copies and albums reaching two million dollars in sales, were instituted in 1976 with 19 given that year and 73 the next year (1977).

Downtown Los Angeles 1925

UPI

"The Twenties and The Thirties"

Instant fame. Instant wealth. Instant identity.

Orange groves and avocados outnumbered automobiles.

Joy was rampant; joy powder (cocaine) was readily available for an instant *up*; the trip down was faster. Broadway beauties and country Charlies flocked to the beck-oning studios; their massive gates represented the portals of heaven.

Some made it, some didn't. Some could handle it, some could not.

Fans, floundering from Depression Blues, screamed for and demanded their idols; they took the trip vicariously.

America's royalty was born.

Wilshire Boulevard 1930

Rudolph Valentino—"America's Love God"

Rudolph Valentino

Born: May 6, 1895 Castellaneta, Italy

Rodolfo Alfonzo Rafaelo Pierre Filibert Guglielmi di Valentine d'Antonguolla is the real name of the real Rudy. He was born into a good Italian family who boasted of his grandfather's prominence as a civil engineer, famous for designing railroad bridges. Rudy's father Giovanni Guglielmi disappointed the family by joining a traveling circus before settling down to his profession of being a veterinarian. However, had he not wandered, he would have never met Donna Gabriella Barbin, a school teacher of French extraction. And the world would never have had The Great Lover, The Sheik , The Sex God, The Idol.

Rodolfo had an older brother, Alberto, and a younger sister, Maria, but it was the young Rudy who was the recipient of his mother's lavish affection and constant pampering. She adored her "beautiful baby." She regaled him with stories about his aristocratic background, perhaps one-quarter true, one-quarter not true, and one-half something they both wished to believe. His father, by contrast, was realistic, strict, and demanded absolute obedience from his children. By the time Rodolfo was eleven he was known as the town's "Bad Boy", a bully, undisciplined, pampered, and never a good student. Unfortunately for him, his father died when he was twelve and the family moved to Taranto, a village in the southern part of Italy. After expulsion from several schools his mother could no longer control him, so off to military school went the young Rodolfo. He dreamed of being a bandit, a cavalier, a romantic rogue, while Donna Gabriella dreamed of his becoming a surgeon, so she then enrolled him in another school to study medicine. Rodolfo

dropped out in the hope of becoming a cavalry officer but the family was not in a position to pay for nor support this new dream of his. He then applied to the Royal Naval Academy where he was refused admittance. Finally he succeeded in completing his studies at the Royal Academy of Agriculture with a certificate in the Science of Farming. He convinced his mother that a trip to Paris would be best for him and his new career.

In Paris, with no thought of farming, he quickly fell into the night life and gaiety of the city. It was there that his dancing career started. He met apache dancer, Jean Martin, who instructed him. It was also there that he fell into the "gay" crowd which only furthered the already sexual confusion of Rodolfo: the mother image had been firmly stamped on him. It was a confusion that plagued him his entire life. Eventually he ran out of money and returned home. In December of 1913, with a small inheritance of four thousand dollars, he set sail for New York City.

In New York, again with no thought of farming or accepting any related jobs, he worked as a busboy. But his love of dancing and the sort of life that went with it was what he settled for. He learned to tango and it was the tango that later became synonymous with Valentino when he played Julio in *The Four Horsemen of the Apocalypse*. As his dancing improved so did his position. Elevated from busboy to gigolo, he was given a free room and free meals at the posh restaurant Maxim's, in exchange for his services as a dancing partner. It was the custom in those days at tea time, the equivalent of today's cocktail hour, for wealthy unescorted ladies to patronize the restaurants—socializing, dancing, sipping wine, and hoping to arrange a liaison for the rest of the evening. Rodolfo's money had long since disappeared but the generous tips he received at the "thés dansants" were his to keep. His dancing improved to the point where he and his partner dancer Bonnie Glass could demand fifty dollars a week salary. It was the time when ballroom dancing was hitting its peak with Irene and Vernon Castle leading the way. Later Rodolfo teamed with Joan Sawyer and together they had a fairly successful vaudeville tour which ended when she married. Tired of the east, he turned his attention to the west and Hollywood.

He joined the chorus of *The Masked Marvel* and toured with it until it folded in Utah. He managed to get as far as San Francisco and it was there his luck began to change. He met an old friend from New York Norman Kerry, who promised Rudy that he would help him get to Hollywood. Kerry kept his promise but even though Rudy appeared in *Alimony* as a dancing extra in 1917, he did not get the overnight success he thought would be his. So it was back to exhibition dancing. This was a time in America when the male image was still the typical "All American" look. The time of the Latin lover had yet to come. The parts they were cast in were usually those of villains or ruthless men. For example, his small part in a film first released in 1920 as *The Married Virgin*, later as *Frivolous Wives,* depicted him as an evil Italian count. Paul Lowell, a director at Universal, told him: "You have what it takes. You'll make it big one day in Hollywood." In different words but the meaning was the same . . . when the world is ready for the suave Latin lovers you'll be it.

He met actress Jean Acker whom he married on November 5, 1919. She would always remain his close friend and it was she who was at his bedside when he died. Rudy's mother died about a month after the marriage, leaving him distraught and grieving, for she didn't live long enough to know the fame her "beautiful baby" was to achieve. Rudy had many mother

images and one was June Mathis, a script writer trying to get her anti-war film project off the ground. The book by Spanish author Vicente Ibáñez entitled *The Four Horsemen of the Apocalypse* was selling well in the United States and finally together with director Rex Ingram they convinced Metro to acquire the screen rights. They also decided that Rudolph Valentino was to play the lead, Julio Desnoyers. This collaboration produced several interesting results: One—failing Metro was prevented from folding; Two—it set Metro on the path of big films; Three—it became the first million dollar production; Four—Rex Ingram was established as a leading director; Five—Rodolfo became a star and now could live in real life and play on the screen, all of his childhood fantasies. His leading lady Alice Terry coincidentally had played opposite Rudy when they were both "extras" earlier in New York.

Wide World

Rudy in "The Four Horsemen of the Apocalypse," 1921, the film in which he made his first great success.

Rudy dances his famous "tango" in "The Four Horsemen of the Apocalypse."

Jean Acker, first wife of Rudolph Valentino

The Russian star Alla Nazimova had been looking for an Armand to play opposite her Marguerite in *Camille*. It was Rudy she wanted, but first he had to be passed on by her friend and confidante, costume and art designer, Natacha Rambova. Despite warnings from June Mathis concerning the strange and self-appointed authority Rambova, Rudy wanted the part and succeeded in getting Rambova's approval. Before he could go to work on *Camille*, he had one last picture to do for

Metro and it was the last picture that the foursome of Mathis, Ingram, Terry, and Valentino would do. He had become a prima donna, impossible to work with, and it led to Ingram's statement: "I can take any good-looking extra and make a star out of him." He chose extra Ramon Samaniegos from *The Four Horsemen*, put him opposite Terry in *The Prisoner of Zenda* and gave the world Ramon Navarro.

15

Rudy as Armand and Russian star, Alla Nazimova as Marguerite in "Camille." It was love scenes such as this that made millions of women swoon and faint . . . in the twenties.

Natacha Rambova had changed her name from Winifred Hudnut, stepdaughter of cosmetic king Richard Hudnut, while studying dancing in Russia. She was heavily involved with the occult, rich, beautiful, and talented. All of this intrigued Rudy, but the other side of her, the side that wanted absolute power over his career, eventually resulted in emotional disaster for him and an almost disaster to his career. She told him not to do *The Sheik*, not to do *The Eagle*, but fortunately he overruled her. *Cobra*, which she convinced him to do, as she scrutinized every foot of film, was one of his biggest mistakes. She decided to advance her own career and got Rudy to back her screen venture, *What Price Beauty*, for a mere thirty thousand dollars, which ended up costing a ghastly one hundred thousand.

On March 4, 1922, Jean Acker Valentino got an interlocutory decree while on May 13th, Rudy and Natacha mistakenly eloped to Mexico for a quickie marriage. Upon their return Rudy was jailed as a bigamist. He was released on bail set at $10,000 and Natacha was dispatched to the east until he was free to marry her. In March 1923 they were remarried in Crown Point, Indiana. With the overwhelming success of *The Sheik* and *The Eagle* and the failure of *Cobra* plus the humiliation now of being barred from the set, a clause in Rudy's new contract, Natacha fled to Paris. Rudy had purchased a mansion, Falcon Lair, but Natacha never put her foot inside. He named his home after a film, *The Hooded Falcon*, one of Natacha's film projects which was never produced. Rudy had become involved with his wife's seances, mystical meanderings, and even her attitude of marriage: "A real union was a spiritual one, not one of the flesh." More sexual confusion. As far as his career was concerned he was always hard driving and intense. Natacha's concern for his career flattered him and gave him confidence, but in truth it was Natacha who wanted to be furthered. Although he followed her to Paris, he then followed the advice of his friends and let her go with these words: "I'm sorry it had to happen. But we cannot always order our lives as we would like to have them."

Falcon Lair, the mansion Rudy purchased with the hope of luring back his second wife, Natacha Rambova. She went to New York, and never stepped inside it.

Wide World

Natacha Rambova, second wife of Rudolph Valentino.   *Wide World*

He never abandoned his love of the fun life, hard drinking, hard living, and the question of his masculinity never abandoned him. Reporters can report, writers can write, speculators can speculate, but only those who bedded with Valentino know the truth. What is known is—that he changed the art of love-making on the screen. He set twenty million American women free . . . to fantasize, to dream of love-making, and to become dissatisfied with their husbands or boyfriends. He made baggy pants and slave bracelets famous, hair dressing for men a must, and the lover of the day—Latin. He also caused Senator Henry L. Meyers to put into the Congressional Record in June 1922, a statement to enforce censorship of the movies immediately. The reason . . . the meaning of the word "sheik."

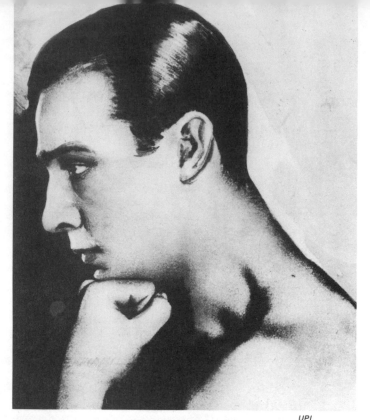

UPI

TOP: Valentino assumes "The Thinker" pose showing his muscles and famous profile. No matter how he tried to prove his masculinity, it was under attack until the day he died.
LEFT: The last picture of Pola Negri and Valentino taken together in Los Angeles. He died in New York. Miss Negri's gown for the funeral reportedly cost $3,000.00. (Left to right) Rudy, Pola Negri, actress Mae Murray, a close personal friend of Rudy's, and Prince David Mdivani.
BOTTOM: Rudy and Vilma Banky as they appeared in "The Son of the Sheik," 1926.

Wide World

Wide World

He returned to Hollywood and began dating German actress, Pola Negri. He knew that the publicity would be good for his career and image, as she was considered a hot-blooded sexy temptress. She also would include him in the partying life-style he loved and it was she who was on his arm at *The Son of the Sheik* premiere. But the film received only cool reviews, Rudy was beginning to slip so the studio decided he must tour and promote his film. He was already ailing when

the tour started and despite warnings refused to consult a doctor. He was being tortured by the press and by their references to his masculinity . . . none of which his wife Natacha helped dispel . . . even if she could.

En route to New York he was further humiliated by the Chicago *Tribune* in their "Pink Powder Puffs" editorial. It was a dreadful attack on him personally: *"The editorial regarded Valentino as the epitome of foppishness, slurred his masculinity, and charged him with the effeminization of the American male." Rudy countered in an interview with the *Herald-Examiner*, the Tribune's rival, saying: (in part) "You slur my Italian ancestry; you cast ridicule upon my Italian name; you cast doubt upon my manhood." And "If that son of a bitch [Tribune] thinks I'm a sissy, I'll let him feel my fists against his jaw. We'll soon see which one is the better man." His offer to fight was taken up by Frank O'Neil, boxing expert on the New York *Evening Journal*. They went a few rounds and Rudy vindicated himself by felling O'Neil.

But it was a sick Valentino who was finally felled in New York. Admitted to Polyclinic Hospital for a perforated ulcer he succumbed to the blood poisoning that followed. His manager, S. George Ullman said: "The psychic drain of his emotional powers had even blunted his will to live." He was a falling star, who might have risen again: he was a half a million dollars in debt, but might have recouped; he was on film as a self-assured lover, who might have been able to prove to the world what he really was, but he was dead at thirty-one. As he lay in a bronze coffin in the Gold Room at Campbell's Funeral Home, over 80,000 mourners waited to view his body as the New York police fought to keep order. Pola Negri came in from California and after she saw the man she was supposedly engaged to, she said: "My love for Valentino was the greatest love in my life. I loved him not as one artist loves another, but as a woman loves a man." A few days later there was another service for him in California where his body was laid to rest in a marble mausoleum.

* from "Valentino" by Brad Steiger and Chaw Mank, Manor Book Inc., New York, N.Y.

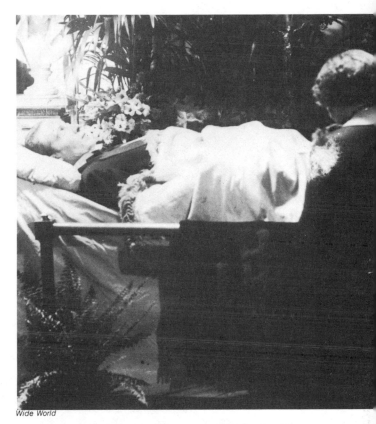

Wide World

Rudolph Valentino lies in state in New York City before his body was shipped to Los Angeles for the final interment. Miss Eva Miller was one of the first of Rudy's admirers to visit the funeral parlor.

Police attempt to keep order, as over 80,000 fans wait outside of Campbell's funeral home to view the body of Rudolph Valentino in New York City.

UPI

19

H. L. Mencken had this to say: "A man of relatively civilized feelings thrown into a situation of intolerable vulgarity."

Pola Negri arrives back in Los Angeles with the body of her fiance, Rudolph Valentino. She is being assisted by Dr. Louis Tolger.

RUDOLPH VALENTINO
Died: August 23, 1926, New York, New York

RUDOLPH VALENTINO
EARLY FILMS

1918
to
1920

Before attaining stardom, Valentino made many films. Some of the most important, all made at Metro during the years 1918 to 1920, are the following:

ALIMONY, with Josephine Whittell

THE BIG LITTLE PERSON, with Mae Murray

THE DELICIOUS LITTLE DEVIL, with Mae Murray

A SOCIETY SENSATION, with Carmel Myers

A ROGUE'S ROMANCE, with Earle Williams

OUT OF LUCK, with Dorothy Gish, directed by D. W. Griffith

ONCE TO EVERY WOMAN, with Dorothy Phillips

PASSION'S PLAYGROUND, with Norman Kerry, Katherine McDonald

THE GREAT MOMENT, with Margaret Namara

MAJOR FILMS

1921 *FOUR HORSEMEN OF THE APOCALYPSE — Metro
with Joseph Swickard, Alice Terry, Alan Hale, Nigel de Brulier
*Film was on the New York *Times* list of the 10 Best Films of 1921

1921 UNCHARTED SEAS — Metro
with Alice Lake

1921 CAMILLE — Nazimova Productions
with Alla Nazimova

1921 *THE CONQUERING POWER — Metro
with Alice Terry
*Film was on the New York *Times* list of the 10 Best Films of 1921

1921 THE SHEIK — Famous Players-Lasky
with Agnes Ayres

1922 MORAN OF THE LADY LETTY — Famous Players-Lasky
with Dorothy Dalton, Walter Long

1922 BEYOND THE ROCKS — Famous Players-Lasky
with Gloria Swanson

1922 BLOOD AND SAND — Famous Players-Lasky
with Lila Lee, Nita Naldi

1922 THE YOUNG RAJAH — Famous Players-Lasky
with Wanda Hawley, Pat Moore, Charles Ogle

1924 MONSIEUR BEAUCAIRE — Famous Players-Lasky
with Bebe Daniels

1925 THE EAGLE — United Artists
with Vilma Banky

1925 COBRA — Ritz-Carlton Pictures, Inc.
with Nita Naldi

1926 THE SON OF THE SHEIK — United Artists
with Vilma Banky

Jeanne Eagels at the beginning of her Broadway career. Circa 1917.

Jeanne Eagels

Born: June 26, 1890, Kansas City, Kansas

Born Amelia Jean Eagles, not Eagels, Jennie, as she was called by her family, was the second child in a family of six. Her father Edward was a carpenter and the last of a long line of Pennsylvania Dutch farmers. Her mother Julia Sullivan was originally from Boston but the family moved to Kansas and it was there she met and married Jennie's father.

As a child Jennie was frail, even though she was a tomboy and very mischievous. She started dramatizing her life at a very young age by explaining a broken arm from falling off of a fence as "broken when she fell from a big white horse in the circus." At age 11 she played Puck in *A Midsummer Night's Dream*—her first real stage appearance. Her schooling terminated after she made her first communion. She got a job in the stock-room at a local store for five dollars a week. Her first paycheck went for presents for her mother and father and a theatre ticket for herself. This act of generosity never stopped. Throughout her life she cared little for money and although she made millions, she died poor. After she lost her first job, she appeared at the Mackensen casting office, known for burlesque and vaudeville. They sent Jennie, now only 15, to the Dubinsky Brothers Stock Company. The company wandered all over the middle west and for six years Jennie, now Jeanne, went with them—but she always had her eye on Broadway . . . *always*. Her first show for Dubinsky was *Pickings from Puck* but it was not long before she convinced them that she should play leads . . . and she did. Jeanne was determined to get ahead and always believed in her talent. Although she was extremely poor and could rarely afford acting lessons, she spent her time watching other actors, studying them, and then practic-ing what she had seen in front of her boarding house mirror.

The Dubinsky Brothers, three in all, were good showmen and quick to pick up on the ideas of others. For example, when Sarah Bernhardt appeared in Texas there was no theatre large enough to handle the crowd so someone came up with the idea of using a huge tent. Morris Dubinsky, whom Jeanne married, seized on to this for his shows. He had a huge canvas made, purchased folding chairs, and carried the equipment from town to town. Only in bad weather would his shows go back into the regular theatres. Morris, who was old enough to be Jeanne's father, was always good to her even though he knew some day she would leave. Supposedly, they had a son whom they gave up for adoption and reportedly, they were divorced before Jeanne left the company.

En route to New York she stopped off in Kansas City and there she got her first real job, in a real theatre, working for Richard Carle in *Jumping Jupiter* for twenty-five dollars a week. Jeanne was right out of the cornfields and she knew it. This made her shy but to the cast she posed as "indifferent." She was different from the other girls, different in background and in training, but she made up for it in sheer determination. The show finally closed in Providence and now Jeanne headed for New York. There she starved until finally she landed a job in a Ziegfeld chorus. There is a legend about her leaving. She supposedly told the Master (Flo Ziegfeld) that she was a dramatic actress and even though he offered her $150.00 a week to stay, she walked out.

Jeanne was always an opportunist even if it meant side-tracking from her career. Broke and hungry, she took up with a millionaire. According to her—"just another stagedoor Johnny"—She then went to Europe as a glorified pimp for an aging actress, who was looking for her own millionaire. Jeanne's beauty and youth could attract the men and that's what her friend wanted. While in Europe she met Julian Eltinge, who became invaluable to her. He introduced her to the right people, told her what to say to them, and how to treat them. He also got her a part in *The Crinoline Girl* for seventy-five dollars a week. When the show folded, she turned to silent movies and scored a sensation as Miriam in *Outcast* which she then took "live" on the road. When she returned there wasn't a theatre available in New York and no one of importance ever saw her performances. Broke again and out of work, she went to see David Belasco. He had nothing to offer her at the time, but he did have this to say about her: "Thousands of girls have come to me in my time, hardened little wretches, shy sweet virgins, girls who would step over the bodies of their dearest friends for a chance to play in a theatre, poor girls, rich girls, daughters of society leaders—but never such a girl as this Jeanne Eagels. She is an alley cat and a little girl."

Her next opportunity came on Broadway at the Shubert Theatre . . . she finally had made it. But only temporarily as the show, *The Great Pursuit*, for Joseph Brooks closed. Finally in February of 1917 at the Knickerbocker Theatre playing opposite George Arliss in *The Professor's Love Story*, she did make it. This play made her rich and famous. However, she was not content with just the play but continued to make silent films in the daytime. She would rise early, shoot all day long, and then rush to the theatre to do her performance. She began to complain that everything hurt; she was suffering from exhaustion and now began to take sedatives. Clifton Webb and his mother Mabel became two of her closest friends. She and Webb pretended they were brother and sister. Steve and Helen (Broderick) Crawford were close friends also,

RIGHT: A portrait of Jeanne Eagels taken in 1917, the year she appeared in "Disraeli" with George Arliss.

BOTTOM: Jeanne Eagels as she looked when she appeared in "Daddies" in 1918 for producer David Belasco.

and it was at their apartment she lived when she was broke and out of work.

Her next play was again with Arliss, *Alexander Hamilton*. Playing the role of Maria Reynolds, most of the critics said she stole the show. She was now established, young, and beautiful. But she had had her share of broken love affairs, she was in pain from her old ailment, the broken arm, and turned to drugs for relief. She was the product of starvation and she was worn down from her incessant determination to be the greatest dramatic actress. This dream was finally fulfilled when Sam Harris gave her the lead in her most famous play, *Rain*. She was no longer the "Barrymore of the Corn Belt."

In his book "The Rain Girl," *author Edward Doherty says: "Harris owned the rights to *Rain* and offered it to Eagels, who accepted. Actress Pauline Armitage had dreamed of doing the role of Sadie Thompson in *Rain* and had accepted the offer from John D. Williams and Kent Thurber to play the part. Williams and

* Macrae, Smith Co. Philadelphia, Pa.

Thurber could not come up with the money needed to produce it and that's how *Rain* came into the hands of Sam Harris." In the movie *Jeanne Eagels,* starring Kim Novak, Eagels is depicted as stealing the script from Armitage. Armitage *did* throw herself out of a window, as the movie discloses, but biographers agree it was because she lost the part, but they do not blame Eagels.

A mature and successful Jeanne Eagels poses for a publicity picture after her smash in "Rain" which opened November 8, 1922 in New York City.

Rain flopped in Philadelphia. But when her second act speech was rewritten, the play took on another tone and became a sensation. The new closing words were: "Hang me and be God-damned to you." The play ran for five years in New York and then on the road. Jeanne missed only eighteen performances and eventually returned to New York for one final two-week return engagement.

While she was playing *Rain* she met her future husband, Ted Coy, at the home of actress Fay Bainter. Coy had been one of the greatest football players of his generation, handsome and sought after, but he lived in the past and dreamed of past glories. At first Jeanne was proud of him, but as he became her slave, she took to insulting him in public and later began to despise him for letting her walk all over him. Her drinking increased . . . although she did not touch a drop until each performance of *Rain* was over . . . she and Coy became heavy drinkers. He felt like an outsider in her world; a world where no one knew or cared about his goals on the football field; a world that cared only for the goals of its actors. When *Rain* closed in Los Angeles their marriage folded, too. While in Los Angeles she made a movie with John Gilbert, *Man, Woman, and Sin,* which catapulted her to national fame. She hated movies, hated making them, and yet her immortality came through the film medium, *not* from her beloved stage.

Back in New York she next went into *Her Cardboard Lover* and became involved with one of the actors, Barry O'Neill. By the time the play reached Chicago they were spending each night together . . . Barry would knock on her door after each performance and they would go out drinking and seeking amusement. On closing night he left the theatre without her and she holed up in her hotel room drinking—claiming she was ill. She did not make the Milwaukee opening the following week and refused to see the Equity representative when he called on her. Equity never doubted that she was ill but charged her with "defying them by not seeing them." This was out of line and they brought her up on charges. Had it not been for Ethel Barrymore, who interceded for Eagels, Equity would have barred Jeanne forever. Barrymore pleaded her case and the result was a fine of $3600.00 (two weeks salary) and an eighteen month suspension. This was in April of 1928.

Eagels turned to vaudeville doing bits and pieces from *Rain* and was a tremendous success. She was earning about four thousand dollars a week, spending it, and drinking heavily. By now she was being called "Gin Eagels."

She turned to Hollywood, where she made *Man, Woman, and Sin* with John Gilbert. Then Paramount Pictures gave her a contract for three movies, two of which she completed, *The Letter* and *Jealousy.* In the third one, *Laughing Lady,* Eagels had to be replaced by Ruth Chatterton. *The Letter* has gone down in the annals of filmmaking as the first dramatic smash of the talkies.

Jeanne Eagels and costar John Gilbert in Hollywood where they filmed, "Man, Woman, and Sin," 1925.

Jeanne Eagels returned to New York worn out, in pain, and by now even her mind had begun to slip. She was hallucinating from the drugs, had a chronic throat infection, neuralgia, and kidney disease. But still she was reading scripts for her return to Broadway . . . a return that never happened. The chorus girl from Kansas City died in a doctor's office among strangers. Her body went to Campbell's Funeral Home, the very one where Rudolph Valentino had lain in state, just three years before. But unlike Valentino, there were no huge crowds fighting for a last view of this great actress. Jennie, Jeanne, Gin has been called "dainty, reckless, fragile, brave, mercurial, timid, sweet, neurotic, and irresponsible." In her own words she said: "I'm the greatest actress in the world and the greatest failure. And nobody gives a damn."

JEANNE EAGELS
Died: October 3, 1929, New York, N.Y.

JEANNE EAGELS
BROADWAY PLAYS

1915 to 1920 For approximately five years Eagels appeared in minor plays on Broadway, among them the following:
THE CRINOLINE GIRL, with Julian Eltinge
THE GREAT PURSUIT, with Marie Tempest, Charles Cherry
THE PROFESSOR'S LOVE STORY, with George Arliss
ALEXANDER HAMILTON, with George Arliss
DADDIES, produced by David Belasco
A YOUNG MAN'S FANCY

1920 THE WONDERFUL THING, with Gordon Ash, Philip Dunning

1921 IN THE NIGHT WATCH, with Cyril Scott, Margaret Dale, Edmund Lowe

1922 RAIN, with Robert Kelly, Catherine Brooke, Fritz Williams, Shirley King
Eagels appeared in this play for 5 years

1927 HER CARDBOARD LOVER, with Leslie Howard

FILMS

While appearing in her early Broadway plays, Eagels also made many films for the Thannhouser studio, including:
THE OUTCAST
THE WORLD AND THE WOMAN
FIRES OF YOUTH
UNDER FALSE COLORS
THE SIGN OF THE CROSS
THE BRIDE OF THE SEA

1925 MAN, WOMAN, AND SIN — Metro with John Gilbert

1929 *THE LETTER — Paramount
with Reginald Owen, Herbert Marshall
*Eagels was nominated for an Academy Award as Best Actress

1929 JEALOUSY — Paramount
with Fredric March, Henry Daniell, Halliwell Hobbes

Young and beautiful Jean Harlow. She was fond of caressing herself and the beauty mark is painted on.

Jean Harlow

Born: March 3, 1911, Kansas City, Kansas

Harlean Carpentier was an only child of a well-to-do middle class family: A family that would control, dominate, and dictate to her all of her life. Her dentist father Dr. Montclair Carpentier, was quietly divorced from her mother, Jean Harlow Carpentier. Before Harlean changed her name to Jean Harlow, she was called "The Baby." She never know her real name, Harlean, until she entered school. After the divorce, Harlean and her mother went to live with her maternal grandparents, Sam and Ella Harlow. The grandfather was very strict to the point of refusing to let schoolmates visit his young granddaughter. He was overly protective and a bit of a tyrant. Her grandmother and mother were devout Christian Scientists and Sam tried desperately to keep his granddaughter from what he termed "their craziness." Harlean's mother was the first to break away. After a few unsuccessful years on her own in Chicago she met and married Marino Bello, supposedly a descendant of rulers and crusaders of Trieste and Sicily. In actuality he was an unsuccessful "wheeler-dealer" with a great deal of charm in the boudoir. Grandfather Sam refused to allow the Baby to live with them, but did allow her two visits, Christmas Day of 1924 and 1925. Eventually the Bellos were forced to return to Kansas City where they all lived under Grandfather Sam's roof and off of his money.

At age fifteen, The Baby was sent to Ferry Hall Boarding School in Lake Forest, Illinois. Perhaps a bit pretentious for this family, but much to Bello's liking and a way for Sam to get Harlean away from their [Bellos'] influence. The Baby coun-

Harlean Carpentier (Jean Harlow) age three, in Kansas City, Kansas.

tered with a plan of her own. She lasted less than a year and when her grandfather refused to let her come home, she eloped with twenty-one year old Charles "Chuck" McGraw, whose family subsequently had the marriage annulled. In the summer of 1927 the Bellos and Harlean moved to Los Angeles with Sam's promised monetary assistance for nine months. They lived in cheap, rented places as Bello's attempts to put deals together were as unsuccessful there as they had been in Chicago. Harlean, meanwhile, was contributing to their support with odd jobs at the studios. She had grown into a real beauty with a dazzling figure. One day agent Arthur Landau was on the lot looking for a replacement and it was Stan Laurel who pointed out Harlean to him. She was pouring herself a drink of water and her body and body movements were enough to make Landau take notice. Prior to this, she had appeared in the Laurel and Hardy film *Double Whoopee,* a few Christy comedies, in *Moran of the Marines,* starring Richard Dix, and *The Saturday Night Kid,* starring Clara Bow. But she had gone unnoticed until Landau spotted her at the water cooler. Her screen test for Howard Hughes revealed enough for him to put her under a three year contract. Her first Hughes' film, *Hell's Angels,* opened June 1930 at Grauman's Chinese Theatre. The studio immediately sent her on tour to promote the picture, but she was young and green, and the tour flopped. However, her looks and body did *not* flop. People were beginning to recognize her and The Literary Digest reported that in a national poll Jean Harlow (she had dropped the Harlean) "placed 17th out of 100, as one of the best known people in the world." The studio hired writers to assist her and things did begin to pick up. With questions and answers such as: "Miss Harlow, are today's young women immodest?" (Jean) "An immodest young woman is somebody who would look better covered up." or "Miss Harlow are you wearing a bra?" (Jean) "That sounds like a nearsighted question." Besides her looks and body another quality began to work in her

favor. In 1927, with the breakthrough of the talkies, *The Jazz Singer,* audiences were now demanding dialogue and with it, good voices. Voices such as Greta Nissen's, with its strong Swedish accent, were not acceptable and by 1929 there were no more silent films. Jean had good timing, plus a good voice, so when Landau had to replace his silent film stars Jean filled the bill. In 1931 she had five films released, *Iron Man, Public Enemy,* and in *The Secret Six,* she was billed above Clark Gable. She also had worked with Wallace Beery, who did not join her fan club. He made no bones about hating her. By the time *Goldie* came out, she was the most photographed star, had risen to great popular heights, and had become America's sex goddess. In was in *Goldie* that the word tramp was used for the first time on the screen. Another first occurred in *Platinum Blonde,* when star Loretta Young got the hero away from Harlow. In a strange sort of way this was good for her image ... the seductive one, who doesn't always win, kept her popular with women. Fan clubs began to sprout up all over the place, beauty parlors were cleaning up as they turned all of their customers into platinum blondes, while the brassiere companies floundered. The Bellos, especially Marino, had no difficulty spending her money, giving her unsound advice, and making her aware that she was unfulfilled as a woman.

Harlow with Laurel and Hardy in "Double Whoopee." Circa 1929.

(l-r) Jean Arthur, Clara Bow, Harlow, and Lorna Love as they appeared in "Saturday Night Kid" 1929.

Harlow and Ben Lyon as they appeared in "Hell's Angels" in 1930.

Harlow and Clark Gable in "Hold Your Man," 1933.

Harlow with James Cagney in "Public Enemy," 1931.

In 1932, she turned to German born, forty-two year old MGM executive Paul Bern. The marriage had a devastating effect on her and resulted in suicide for Bern. It was the Landaus, Arthur and his wife, she ran to on her wedding night after Bern had beaten her: a beating which resulted in a kidney malfunction, an ailment from which she never fully recovered. Speculation as to Bern's suicide was that he was impotent but believed the sex goddess could help him. When she couldn't, he put a bullet through his head, thus ending his self-imposed shame. He

Jean Harlow in her all white boudoir. White became her trademark, and she was known throughout the world as the Blonde Bombshell.

did not leave a grieving widow, instead— one who was full of hatred for him. For it was her husband she thought would finally fulfill her as a woman. She cut off her hair and went on a binge, sexually and alcoholically, in San Bernadino— coincidentally a city whose first four letters were the same as her husband's last name, Bern. Arthur Landau told the studio she cut off her hair because of her deep mourning. They managed to keep it a secret and also managed to construct believable wigs for her next film, *Red Dust*.

(At left) Jean and her first husband Paul Bern. (At right) The suicide note left by Bern to her, September 5, 1932. UPI

Just two months after their marriage Harlow's husband, Paul Bern put a bullet through his head. His body is being removed from their Beverly Hills home.

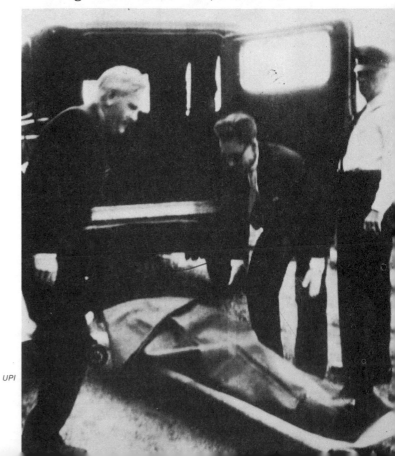

UPI

Her next binge took place in San Francisco after the completion of *Hold Your Man.* Hounded by frustration without a man of her own, humiliated at being the sex goddess sans sex, it all culminated when she discovered in San Francisco that she was sterile. Her mental distress was further complicated by living with her sexually oriented step-father and mother, who never kept their intimacies intimate, and by her marriage that had failed her. The binge in San Francisco did nothing to relieve any of this, instead it managed only to get the taxi driver of her choice into trouble. To keep the Bellos off her back, she compounded her trouble by allowing them to plunge her heavily into debt. Conversely she was a fun girl, loved by her crew members, and despite the drinking and sleeping pills, in August of 1933 when *Dinner At Eight* opened, it was considered her best performance to date.

Jean and Wallace Beery as they appeared in "China Seas," produced in 1936. Beery openly disliked Harlow and told her so.

Jean's parents, Mr. and Mrs. Bello, accompanied her to San Francisco, the place of one of her most famous "binges."

Her third husband was thirty-eight year old cameraman Harold Rosson. By eloping to Yuma, studio titan Louis B. Mayer, became enraged. As head MGM lion, sovereign over all, he took this as an insult to him . . . to the point where he began to despise her. He could not fault Rosson, who had a good reputation as a man as well as a fine cameraman. So fine was Rosson, that star Gloria Swanson refused to be photographed without him. According to biographer Irving Shulman in his book, "Harlow," Mayer ended it with this statement: "Anyway, when a good boff is married, it takes her out of circulation, unless she's a tramp. So it ruins them, like people finding out that Frank Bushman was married, killed him at the box office." Mayer never forgave Harlow and deviously set about to wreck her. It was all redundant because the Bellos and Jean's own self-hate were already doing it. The marriage to Rosson lasted eight short months and she moved back in with Mama.

UPI

Jean Harlow with her third husband cameraman, Harold Rosson. Standing is her mother and step-father, Jean and Marino Bello. The new Mrs. Rosson seems to be wearing a brassiere, to go along with her new image.

Jean enjoying a day at the races at Santa Anita in California.

Her salary demands, fostered by step-father Marino, were met with studio suspension. A break with her agent, Landau, resulted in her worst move, as she let Bello take over her finances. And then Bello did the unforgivable . . . he started romancing other women. In a last ditch effort to straighten out her life, Harlow patched things up with Landau. Bello was bought off for thirty-thousand dollars and

Jean moved into a "reasonable" house with her bitter and heartsick mother. She turned to friends for refuge from her ailing mother, who had dug deeper into the depths of Christian Science. She began a love affair with William Powell while she was filming *Reckless* and finally legalized her name, Jean Harlow, in 1936. She was desperately trying to put things in order.

35

But during the filming of *Saratoga* with Clark Gable she fell ill. Her mother nursed her, read to her from Science and Health, and refused to allow anyone to see her. When Arthur Landau finally found out how seriously ill she was—it was too late. She was suffering from cholecystitis, inflammation of the gall bladder, but the infection had spread out of control before he was able to have her hospitalized.

Jean Harlow had been a big star. For years she had been in the top ten, her hands and high heels were immortalized in cement at Grauman's Chinese Theatre, and she had been the first studio representative in Washington at the March of Dimes Campaign. Eleven years had passed since Valentino's death and Hollywood wanted a big funeral. MGM halted work for one day while the other studios observed a minute of silence. Mama would not allow her to lie in state, but would allow her closest friends to view the body. She was buried in a gown worn by her in *Libeled Lady*, Jeanette MacDonald sang *Indian Love Call*, the bronze and silver casket was lined with pale translucent silk and rested under a portrait of Sir Alfred Tennyson, with a volume of his poems opened to "Crossing the Bar." Nelson Eddy closed the Christian Science service by singing *Ah, Sweet Mystery of Life*. Hollywood had its way.

Jean loved working with William Powell and supposedly they were to marry. Powell had been married to another blonde beauty, Carole Lombard. Powell and Harlow as they appeared in "Libeled Lady" in 1936.

Harlow and Cary Grant in "Suzy," 1936.

Courtesy of Doug McClelland

Jean Harlow's dentist father, Dr. Montclair Carpentier, arrives for funeral. He and her mother were divorced when Jean was nine years old.

William Powell, rumored as Harlow's next husband, and Mrs. Jean Bello, mother, visited the crypt a year after her death. Mrs. Bello died in 1958. She had been given a pension by the studio, of $500.00 a month, after her famous daughter died.

Coincidentally, both Jean Harlow and Marilyn Monroe were to make their last films with Clark Gable. Harlow devotees remember her quote: "A brassiere is an unnecessary garment, actually unhealthy." Unnecessary and unhealthy are two words that describe her untimely death at twenty-six.

JEAN HARLOW
Died: June 7, 1937, Los Angeles, California

JEAN HARLOW
MAJOR FILMS

1930 HELL'S ANGELS — Caddo Corp. (Howard Hughes)
with Ben Lyon, James Hall
1931 IRON MAN — Universal
with Lew Ayres, Robert Armstrong
1931 THE PUBLIC ENEMY — Warner Bros.
with James Cagney, Mae Clarke, Donald Cook, Joan Blondell
1931 THE SECRET SIX — MGM
with Wallace Beery, Lewis Stone, Clark Gable
1931 GOLDIE — Fox
with Spencer Tracy, Warren Hymer, Lina Basquetta
1931 PLATINUM BLOND — Columbia
with Loretta Young, Robert Williams
1932 THREE WISE GIRLS — Columbia
with Mae Clarke, Walter Byron, Marie Prevost, Andy Devine
1932 THE BEAST OF THE CITY — MGM
with Walter Huston, Wallace Ford, Jean Hersholt
1932 RED HEADED WOMAN — MGM
with Chester Morris, Lewis Stone, Leila Hyams, Una Merkel
1932 RED DUST — MGM
with Clark Gable, Gene Raymond, Mary Astor
1933 HOLD YOUR MAN — MGM
with Clark Gable, Stuart Erwin, Dorothy Burgess
1933 DINNER AT EIGHT — MGM
with Wallace Beery, John Barrymore, Madge Evans, Lee Tracy, Billie Burke, Marie Dressler, Edmund Lowe, Joan Hersholt

1933 BOMBSHELL — MGM
with Lee Tracy, Frank Morgan, Franchot Tone, Pat O'Brien
1934 THE GIRL FROM MISSOURI — MGM
with Lionel Barrymore, Franchot Tone, Lewis Stone, Patsy Kelly
1935 RECKLESS — MGM
with William Powell, May Robson, Franchot Tone
1936 CHINA SEAS — MGM
with Clark Gable, Wallace Beery, Lewis Stone
1936 RIFFRAFF — MGM
with Spencer Tracy, Una Merkel, Mickey Rooney
1936 WIFE VS. SECRETARY — MGM
with Clark Gable, Myrna Loy, May Robson, James Stewart
1936 SUZY — MGM
with Franchot Tone, Cary Grant, Lewis Stone, Benita Hume
1936 *LIBELED LADY — MGM
with William Powell, Myrna Loy, Spencer Tracy
*Film was nominated for an Academy Award as Best Picture
1937 PERSONAL PROPERTY — MGM
with Robert Taylor, Reginald Owen, Donald O'Connor
1937 SARATOGA — MGM
with Clark Gable, Lionel Barrymore, Frank Morgan, Walter Pidgeon
1968 THE FURTHER PERILS OF LAUREL AND HARDY — 20th Century-Fox
A compilation of clips from the films of Stan Laurel and Oliver Hardy

George Gershwin. One of the few existing camera studies ever done of the famous composer/pianist. Circa 1930.

George Gershwin

Born: September 26, 1898, Brooklyn, New York

"East Side West Side All Around The Town" could have been written for Jacob Gershvin, as he was born, for that's how he lived and where he lived most of his life . . . all over New York City. His father Morris went from one business to another which accounted for the family's various moves. They always wanted to be close to Papa Gershovitz's work. Although the family wasn't rich it was far from poor, for despite Papa's assorted professions, he was a good provider. George's mother Rose Bruskin and father both emigrated from St. Petersburg, Russia and were married on the east side of New York in 1898. The immigration officials, as so often happened, changed Morris' name from Gershovitz to Gershvin, although the spelling on George's birth certificate underwent another change: It read, "Ger-

shwine." When George went into the music business he changed it to Gershwin and the family followed suit. There were four children, Ira, George, Arthur, and Frances. After George's birth the family moved back to the city from Brooklyn and from that time on they remained in New York.

George was not a particularly outstanding student, never a diligent reader, but was beset with a restlessness that got him into trouble. However, brother Ira was always there to come to his rescue. Ira, on the other hand, was a diligent student who loved books and was an avid movie-goer. Their ambitious mother decided that Ira should be a schoolteacher and that George should be an accountant. Conversely their father was an easy going, gentle soul who thought the boys should do what would make them happy. Combine the ingredients from each parent, one strong and driven, the other mild and not too ambitious, shake, mix, and the world got the Gershwin brothers.

There wasn't much music at home but George heard it on the streets, blaring from the penny arcades, (the style in those days) from free concerts or at clubs. The first piano purchased by the Gershwin family was for Ira . . . not for George. But soon he usurped it and was taking lessons at a cost of 50¢ per. Later he met his first strong influence in his teacher, Charles Hambitzer, who taught him for free. He recognized not only the talent of the young George but the seriousness of this rather headstrong pupil. Hambitzer remained a close friend, teacher, and counsellor until his death in 1918. He also was responsible for making George a concert-goer. George loved being grounded in and exposed to

George Gershwin's birthplace, 242 Snediker Avenue, Brooklyn, New York. In 1963, ASCAP presented a commemorative plaque to be placed on the site.
World Wide

the other side of music yet his love of Tin Pan Alley drew him out of school and into the famous area, 28th Street, so named by writer, Monroe Rosenfeld. His first job in 1913 was in the Catskills for about $5.00 a week and his first song, never published, was written there. Since *I Found You*, which aptly describes what he found . . . Tin Pan Alley, and his first job there in 1914 working for Jerome H. Remick's publishing house for $15.00 a week. Working in a publishing house in those days meant sitting in a small cubicle, eight hours a day, playing and pushing the songs of others. But the influences of fellow song writers was strong, especially the music of Irving Berlin and Jerome Kern. Another important influence on his life was violinist Edward Kilenyi. George studied theory and harmony with him and learned how to dissect every aspect of music. Kilenyi understood the goals of his young pupil and encouraged him to work in the field of popular music while he [Kilenyi] taught him everything he knew about the fundamentals of "his" music. Gershwin played, practiced, listened, plugged, played, and played and played. He was fascinated by black music, blues music, and spiritual music. Soon people began to be fascinated not so much by his music but by his playing. He returned to the Catskills for two more summers, 1914 and 1915, and although he kept his fingers on the keyboard at Remick's for two years, his eyes were focused on Broadway. In 1916 his name appeared for the first time on a copy of music with lyrics by Murray Roth, *When You Want 'Em, You Can't Get 'Em*. He earned $5.00 for that one. Later, after he met Sigmund Romberg, who was also taken with the young, talented, ambitious Gershwin, he accepted a Gershwin song for a Broadway production in 1916. This song brought in $7.00. Meanwhile Ira had abandoned the little red schoolhouse his mother had thought would be his home. He was writing his heart out and his

hands off as he supported himself with jobs that ranged from a cashier to a photographer's assistant, to Altman's Dept. Store to a vaudeville critic for a minor publication.

George's next job was as a rehearsal pianist for a Broadway show, *Miss 1917*, music by Jerome Kern for $35.00 a week. The show closed after a week or two, then George got another job—as a rehearsal pianist. He met Irving Caesar about this time and they collaborated on their first tune, *You-oo Just You*, which was published in 1918. Never far from the piano or the music of the piano or just music, George made piano rolls starting around 1916 for small sums of money. Because of the amount of "rolls" he turned out, he played under a couple of other names. Ira was also using another name, Arthur Francis, as he did not want to cash in on his younger brother's name, which was rapidly gaining prominence. It was Max Dreyfus, head of T.B. Harms Publishing House, who entered George's life and paid him $35.00 weekly to write songs . . . his type of songs. Mr. Dreyfus also threw in a 3¢ royalty. For George the year 1918 was just one defeat or disappointment after another while Arthur Francis had his first financial hit. But 1919 and the opening of *La,La Lucille* provided the first Gershwin score for a B'way show. Unfortunately the show closed after a few months due to an Actors Equity strike. But Gershwin had composed a song with Irving Caesar called *Swanee* and Al Jolson decided to use it in his show, *Sinbad*. The song sold over two million records, over one million copies of sheet music, and brought $10,000.00 apiece to its composers. *Swanee* caught on all over Europe even reaching Russia and the ears of one Vladimir Dukelsky, another composer, who loved the music of the young American.

The year 1919 also marked George's first attempt at the other side of music as he wrote *Lullaby* for a string quartet. *Lullaby* was brought to light by the Juilliard

String Quartet in the '60's and finally published in 1968. In a series of Sunday brunches at New York's Pierre Hotel, New Yorkers heard *Lullaby* by the Juilliard players although it had been premiered in Washington, D.C. Still in 1919 George got another first by another George . . . White. White decided to give Flo Ziegfeld a run for his money with what became the famous George White's Scandals and unlike Ziegfeld, who bought or hired "names", White liked to try unknowns. His first *Scandals* left him [White] not too happy with Richard Whiting's music so in 1920 he hired Gershwin. This started a five year partnership for the two Georges. In 1922 *Somebody Loves Me* appeared along with *Blue Monday*, a Negro opera, placed in *Scandals*. For all intents and purposes this was the first outing of Gershwin's other side, as the aforementioned *Lullaby* was not aired. Although White removed it from *Scandals* it did not go unnoticed. Later it was renamed, *135th Street*.

George composed for many other musicals while he was working with White but 1923 marks the first time he walked on a concert stage. Accompanying singer Eva Gauthier, who included some jazz in her program, George Gershwin became known as Gershwin pianist and composer. And he was launched into another world . . . the one of high society and money. He was at heart a party lover, fond of women, enjoyed nightlife but first, last, and always was his love of his art. The reading he had neglected as a child he made up for in his later life by constantly studying scores, literature of other composers, manuscripts, and books. Of the many people who entered into his life and he into theirs, notably of course, was the alliance of Gershwin and Paul Whiteman.

Paul Whiteman played Gershwin's music, believed in Gershwin's music, and together they believed that dignity and recognition should be given to America's original art form-jazz. It was Whiteman who suggested a new work, it was George who decided on the rhapsody form, and it was Ira who titled it *Rhapsody In Blue*. It took George about three weeks to write "it" and "it" cost Whiteman quite a bit of money to stage, but what "it" did for the world of music can never be measured in time or cost. On February 12, 1924 in Aeolian Hall in New York City with George Gershwin at the piano the *Rhapsody In Blue* was presented to the skeptical world of musicians, critics, and the rest of the audience. Deems Taylor (in part): "Mr. Gershwin may yet bring jazz out of the kitchen;" a thought expressed by Mr. Taylor but agreed to by others. Maybe it was jazz that brought Mr. Taylor and the others out of the basement. The word "serious" music had always been applied to the concert stage (not to be confused with the incorrect words classical music*) but anyone who dares to think that the music of Charlie Parker or Billie Holiday or Duke Ellington or George Gershwin is not serious, should go back to the basement and start over again. But that was the climate of the times when Paul Whiteman and George Gershwin walked onto the stage that February night in 1924. What was called "Whiteman's Folly" would now be sheer folly to further define or explain.

The *Rhapsody In Blue* was published by Max Dreyfus and sold several hundred thousand copies, Paul Whiteman recorded it on RCA and sold over a million records. Although Ferde Grofé, due to lack of time did the original orchestration, the later orchestration and the version found today is Gershwin's.

*"Style in art moves between two poles, the classic and the romantic. Both the classic artist and the romantic artist strive to express significant emotions, and to achieve that expression within beautiful forms. Where they differ is in their point of view. Specifically, the classic and romantic labels are attached to two important periods in European art: Classic to the 18th-century and Romantic to the 19th-century."

The Enjoyment of Music, Joseph Machlis, W. W. Norton Co., Inc., N.Y.

Artur Rodzinski, standing, and Gershwin conferring over "An American In Paris" which was played by the Los Angeles Philharmonic in January 1931, Mr. Rodzinski conducting.

"Men of Note" . . . (l-r) Fritz Reiner, Gershwin, Deems Taylor, and Robert Russell Bennett. Circa 1931.

Conductor Serge Koussevitzky and Gershwin at final rehearsal for Second Rhapsody premiere. Performed in Boston January 29, 1932 with Gershwin at the piano.

Gershwin with director, Rouben Mamoulian going over score for "Porgy and Bess", premiered September 1935. Mamoulian had directed the original stage production of "Porgy." "Bess" was added to the title in keeping with operatic tradition and to lessen confusion.

When George broke with *Scandals* he went to work for Aarons and Freedley's newly formed production company and with this duo he wrote some of his greatest musical-comedy successes. *Lady, Be Good!* opened December 1924, his first big smash hit, with Fred and Adele Astaire, lyrics by Ira Gershwin. One song was dropped from the show with George's consent . . . *The Man I Love*. In 1941 *Lady, Be Good!* was filmed by MGM but additional music for the movie was done by Jerome Kern and Oscar Hammerstein II. Their song, *The Last Time I Saw Paris* received an Oscar not Gershwin's *Fascinating Rhythm* or *Oh, Lady Be Good!* both from the original stage production. And that was the fly in the ointment. Only music written expressly for a film was eligible. This explains why none of the great Gershwin songs, composed for the stage but used in films, were eligible for an Academy Award. However, it must be noted that in later years when Gershwin songs were written specifically for movies only one, *They Can't Take That Away From Me* from the film *Shall We Dance*, RKO, received a nomination. It lost to *Sweet Leilani*, words and music by Harry Owens from *Waikiki Wedding*, Paramount Pictures.

In 1925 all of the Gershwins moved into a brownstone with George on the top floor. In 1928 George cut the cord and moved into his own apartment on Riverside Drive with Ira and his wife, Lee, in an adjacent one. There were many women in and out of his life and perhaps the most sustained relationship was with fellow artist/composer/musician Kay Swift. There were many, many friends always around, always involved in his life and work but it was always his brother Ira whom he adored and with whom he shared the deepest relationship. The Russian composer, who adored *Swanee*, finally came to this country and became another close friend. Here in the U.S. he is known as Vernon Duke! Gershwin always retained his excitement about music . . . not only his own but the music of others. He was known for his generosity in time and in help to fellow composers when they asked or needed it. He developed a love for art both as a collector and as an amateur painter. He had two one-man shows, both after his death; one in 1937, another in 1963. He adored Rouault and in his own words: "If only I could put Rouault into music." He played golf, would participate in any activity that did not jeopardize his hands, and most of his life he was in good physical condition. Therefore it came as a great shock to his friends and family when he began complaining of headaches and blackouts.

Gershwin lover of art turned from collecting to artist, aided and abetted by his famous cousin artist, Henry Botkin. Gershwin shown here with one of his first completed works.

Gershwin's portrait of his mother, Rose Bruskin Gershwin. Mrs. Gershwin died in December, 1948.

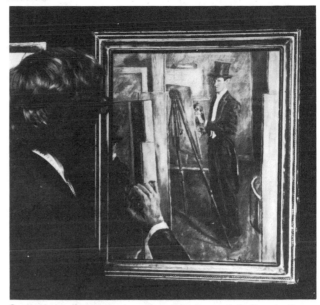

Gershwin by Gershwin . . . self-portrait. Lower left of portrait depicts Gershwin painting himself. Young viewer of painting was one of many who flocked to New York's Hallmark Gallery to view exhibition of Gershwin's work shown on the composer's 75th anniversary.

Lower left: Gershwin's portrait of his father, Morris (Gershovitz) Gershwin. Mr. Gershwin died in May, 1932.

Gershwin's portrait of friend and great composer, Arnold Schönberg, who died in Los Angeles in 1951 at the age of 77.

Alex A. Aarons (1) preferred sponsoring Gershwin music to his successful clothing business and produced "La La Lucille" in 1919. Aarons and Gershwin shown here in 1926. Gershwin, out of loyalty to Aarons wrote the music for the Aarons debacle production of "Pardon My English" 1933. It ran for only 46 performances but "Isn't It a Pity" came out of the score.

French composer, Maurice Ravel (seated at piano) requested a meeting with Gershwin as a birthday present from hostess, Eva Gauthier, on the occasion of his 53rd birthday celebrated in New York City, 1928. (l-r) conductor, Oscar Fried, Mme. Gauthier, Ravel, conductor Tedesco, and Gershwin.

Gershwin(l) and producer Edgar Selwyn in Florida, 1928. Selwyn produced "Strike Up The Band" twice. The first version closed out-of-town in 1927. The second version in 1930 ran for 191 performances. Finally in 1940 MGM filmed it with Judy Garland, Mickey Rooney, Paul Whiteman and his orchestra. Only one Gershwin tune remained for the film, **Strike Up The Band** but one song from the second version, **I've Got A Crush On You** was immortalized by the late Lee Wiley.

Top right: Gershwin was summoned by Fox Studios to work on the film, "Delicious," 1931, starring Janet Gaynor and Charles Farrell. He rented a house in Beverly Hills with brother Ira and his wife, Lee.

Bottom right: Gershwin at home in California 1931 working on "Second Rhapsody" premiered in Boston 1932.

Rehearsal for "Rosalie" 1928. (l-r) Jack Donahue, Gershwin at piano, Sigmund Romberg, who did additional songs, Marilyn Miller, and Florenz Ziegfeld. Favorite Gershwin tune from this show, "How Long Has This Been Going On?"

(l-r) Alexander Smallens, conductor of the opera, Rose Gershwin, mother of George, and Anne Brown, who played Bess in the original production. "Porgy and Bess" premiered in Boston September 1935. Two weeks later it opened in New York City.

Gershwin and close friend, Edward Warburg, then director of the American Ballet, arriving in New York after a brief vacation in Mexico. Circa 1935.

Actor Frank Morgan pours as Gershwin poses for camera while bartender relaxes in Havana's Biltmore Hotel. Circa 1936. Gershwin's "Cuban Overture" was premiered in New York City, August 16, 1932.

Protecting their (copy) rights Tin Pan Alley greats met in a special house committee hearing for revisions and additions. ASCAP members shown are (l-r) Rudy Vallee, Irving Berlin, Gershwin, and Gene Buck. 1936.

George and brother Ira arriving in Hollywood, 1936.

Gershwin (left) with musical director, for Goldwyn Productions, Alfred Newman and Samuel Goldwyn with earphones, 1937. "An American in Paris" ballet was removed from film but appeared later as the film with the same name in 1951 starring Gene Kelly.

Wide World

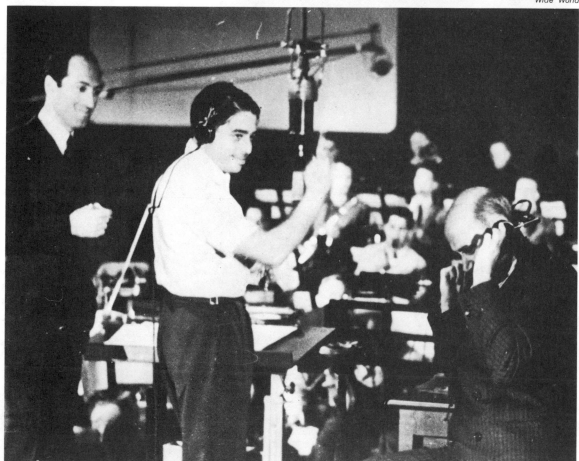

Wide World

Happier times in Hollywood's famous Cocoanut Grove Circa 1937 (l-r) Gershwin, lyricist, Dorothy Fields ("I Can't Give You Anything But Love") Doris Warner, Ira Gershwin, (standing) and Jerome Kern.

"The King of Jazz" conductor Paul Whiteman and Gershwin, Circa 1932. When "Rapsody In Blue" was premiered in 1924 Whiteman supposedly took a personal loss of several thousand dollars but it is safe to assume he made it back in the ensuing years. Whiteman died in 1967 at the age of seventy-seven.

Oscar Levant, longtime friend of Gershwin's and according to many "a permanent fixture" in the Gershwin home. Levant died in 1972 at the age of sixty-six.

He was hospitalized and given a complete check-up just a month before his final days. But the check-up revealed nothing. His friend and fellow composer, Erwin "Yip" Harburg, turned over his Beverly Hills house to Gershwin when the doctor suggested that he live alone for awhile . . . quietly. Only Ira and Lee visited him there. On July 9th he fell into a coma and was rushed to Cedars of Lebanon Hospital. It was then and only then that the fatal cystic tumor was discovered. He never regained consciousness after the operation. However, because the growth of the tumor was in a part of the brain that could not be touched, had he lived he would have been disabled and/or blind for the rest of his life. His body was sent by train from California to New York where services were held at Temple Emanu-El on Fifth Avenue. Hundreds of friends attended the service inside while thousands lined the street outside. He was buried in the Mount Hope Cemetery in Hastings-on-Hudson.

Courtesy of Mr. And Mrs. Erwin Harburg

Al Jolson (died 1950) attends services for Gershwin.

Gershwin with friend Erwin "Yip" Harburg. Harburg turned over his Beverly Hills home to Gershwin where he spent his last days. Harburg, lyricist, wrote "Over The Rainbow" with composer, Harold Arlen.

Former Mayor of New York James J. (Jimmy) Walker attends Gershwin memorial services.

Although to many George Gershwin appeared to have had an oversized ego, those who were close to him knew that in the presence of composers such as Ravel, Stravinsky, Schönberg and many others he always felt unworthy and in awe of them. Had he lived another fifty years he would have continued to work, to study, to produce, and maybe to realize how worthy he was . . . is. Or maybe, just maybe, he heard his friend Arnold Schönberg express how he and other composers felt: "I grieve over the deplorable loss to music, for there is no doubt that he was a great composer."

GEORGE GERSHWIN
Died: July 11, 1937, Los Angeles, California

The casket bearing the body of George Gershwin being removed from Temple Emanu-El in New York City. Former NYC Mayor, Fiorello LaGuardia is seen (at left foreground) holding white straw hat.

GEORGE GERSHWIN

(Dates given refer to the first public performance of stage productions, to the year of release of films, and to year of composition or publication of concert works.)

STAGE PRODUCTIONS

1918 HALF PAST EIGHT (closed before reaching Broadway)
1919 LA, LA, LUCILLE
1919 CAPITOL REVUE (one special performance)
1919 MORRIS GEST MIDNIGHT WHIRL
1920 GEORGE WHITE'S SCANDALS OF 1920
1920 BROADWAY BREVITIES OF 1920
1921 A DANGEROUS MAID (closed before reaching Broadway)
1921 GEORGE WHITE'S SCANDALS OF 1921
1922 GEORGE WHITE'S SCANDALS OF 1922
1922 OUR NELL
1923 GEORGE WHITE'S SCANDALS OF 1923
1923 THE RAINBOW (REVUE) (London)
1924 SWEET LITTLE DEVIL
1924 GEORGE WHITE'S SCANDALS OF 1924
1924 PRIMROSE (London)
1924 LADY, BE GOOD!
1925 TELL ME MORE
1925 SONG OF THE FLAME
1925 TIP-TOES
1926 OH, KAY!
1927 STRIKE UP THE BAND — first version (closed before reaching Broadway)
1927 FUNNY FACE
1928 ROSALIE
1928 TREASURE GIRL
1929 SHOW GIRL
1930 STRIKE UP THE BAND — second version
1930 GIRL CRAZY
1931 OF THEE I SING (first musical to win a Pulitzer Prize)

1933 PARDON MY ENGLISH
1933 LET 'EM EAT CAKE
1935 PORGY AND BESS (opera)

STAGE PRODUCTIONS WITH GERSHWIN SONGS INTERPOLATED

1916 THE PASSING SHOW OF 1916
1918 HITCHY KOO OF 1918
1918 LADIES FIRST
1918 SINBAD
1919 GOOD MORNING JUDGE
1919 THE LADY IN RED
1920 DERE MABEL (closed before reaching Broadway)
1920 ED WYNN'S CARNIVAL
1920 LOOK WHO'S HERE
1920 THE SWEETHEART SHOP
1921 THE PERFECT FOOL
1922 FOR GOODNESS SAKE
1922 THE FRENCH DOLL
1922 SPICE OF 1922
1920 THE DANCING GIRL
1923 LITTLE MISS BLUEBEARD
1923 NIFTIES OF 1923
1926 AMERICANA
1936 THE SHOW IS ON

MOTION PICTURES WITH GERSHWIN SCORES

1930 KING OF JAZZ (Gershwin played RHAPSODY IN BLUE with Paul Whiteman's Orchestra)
1931 DELICIOUS
1932 GIRL CRAZY (adapted from stage version)
1937 SHALL WE DANCE ("They Can't Take That Away from Me" nominated for Oscar as "Best Song")
1938 THE GOLDWYN FOLLIES
1940 STRIKE UP THE BAND (adapted from stage version)

1941 LADY, BE GOOD! (adapted from stage version)
1943 GIRL CRAZY (adapted from stage version)
1945 RHAPSODY IN BLUE (film biography of Gershwin)
1947 THE SHOCKING MISS PILGRIM
1951 AN AMERICAN IN PARIS (won Oscar as "Best Picture")
1957 FUNNY FACE (adapted from stage version)
1959 PORGY AND BESS (adapted from stage version)
1964 KISS ME, STUPID
1965 WHEN THE BOYS MEET THE GIRLS (third adaptation of GIRL CRAZY)

CONCERT WORKS

1919 LULLABY, for string quartet
1922 135th STREET, one act opera. (Original title: BLUE MONDAY BLUES)
1924 RHAPSODY IN BLUE, for piano and orchestra
1925 CONCERTO IN F, for piano and orchestra
1925 SHORT STORY, two early Novellettes for piano, transcribed for violin and piano by Samuel Duskin
1926 PRELUDES, for solo piano (FIVE performed, THREE published)
1928 AN AMERICAN IN PARIS, tone poem for orchestra
1928 "IN THE MANDARIN'S ORCHID GARDEN," concert song
1931 SECOND RHAPSODY, for piano and orchestra
1932 GEORGE GERSHWIN'S SONG BOOK, piano transcriptions of 18 songs
1932 CUBAN OVERTURE
1934 VARIATIONS ON "I GOT RHYTHM," for piano and orchestra
1936 CATFISH ROW, suite for orchestra, adapted from PORGY AND BESS

Movie mecca's famous corner, Hollywood and Vine, 1948.

"The Forties and The Fifties"

Molded fame. Modulated wealth, Muddled identity.

Oranges were crated and shipped. Avocados filled salad bowls.

Hopefuls became car hops; others hopped waiting tables or whipped up sodas.

Musicals added merryment. War films were rampant: USO not UFO. The infant eye of television opened. Some made it, some didn't. Some could handle it, some couldn't cope.

Khaki clothing gave way to hippie haberdashery. Disc jockeys mounted the airwaves.

Fans were kept in frenzy by columnists.

Another generation of America's royalty was being crowned.

Hollywood Boulevard with Grauman's Chinese Theatre on left, 1952.

Jane Alice Peters of Indiana becomes Carole Lombard of Los Angeles as she signs papers to legalize her new name.

Carole Lombard

Born: October 6, 1908, Ft. Wayne, Indiana

Jane Alice Peters was the youngest child of Frederick C. and Elizabeth Knight Peters. She had two older brothers, Frederick and Stuart, whom she tried to emulate on the baseball diamond and/or the football field. She was their very pretty, blonde "tomboy," loving sister. No matter how many times they'd chase her home, soon she would be seen scampering over the white fences of Ft. Wayne en route back to the game. A Friday night ritual of the Peters family was the movies. Jane Alice would perform the following morning, what she had seen on the screen the night before. So it seems early in life she knew what she was all about. For even in later years her love of sports and love of acting never diminished. Nor did her love for her family, as her mother was always her best friend.

In October of 1914, her parents separated so the boys and Jane Alice settled in Los Angeles with their mother. She did a small part in a film when she was twelve, but her actual career did not get underway until she dropped out of school. She managed to finish public junior high, then opted for exhibition dancing at the world famous Coconut Grove in the Ambassador Hotel. In 1925 an executive from Fox Pictures spotted her and invited her to do a screen test. The test was successful even though her first film a spy story, *Marriage In Transit,* was not. When she appeared opposite Edmund Lowe in the film, she had already changed her name to Carole Lombard. Although her performance was well received, her personal acclaim was not enough for Fox to renew her option. Early in 1927 she was again tested. This time at the Mack Sennett Studio and again put under contract. Only this time it was custard pie in the eyes . . . no spies. Every Monday morning a new Sennett comedy was started, usually with Carole Lombard, as Sennett had singled her out as a future star. The year she spent there helped develop her exquisite sense of timing and began to mold her comedic style. She met Madalynne Field, another Sennett player, who became her life-long friend, later her secretary/adviser.

Courtesy of Doug McClelland

UPI

Lombard as a silent film player for Mack Sennett in the 20's. Sennett knew she was marked for stardom.

Lombard's Christmas card 1928 which read: "Holiday Greetings from Carole Lombard."

Paul Stein, a director at Pathé, saw her in a Sennett comedy, put her under contract for one hundred fifty dollars per week and she stayed there long enough to do several films for them. She took one side step when director Cecil B. DeMille called for her, but then changed his mind. When she left Pathé in 1930 and returned to Fox, it seemed as though she was skipping about, but she was making a lot of films, gaining experience, plus working under outstanding directors.

Later she signed with Paramount for three hundred dollars per week and in about six years had upped it to thirty-five thousand dollars weekly. Before her death she was earning five hundred thousand a year as the highest paid female star—all in a period of seventeen years. She co-starred with William Powell in two films, *Man of the World* and *Ladies' Man* before their marriage. She met Powell in October 1930 and married him eight months later, June 26, 1931. Then twenty-eight months later, in August 1933, they were divorced. They remained friends and although incompatible as married partners, as film partners their compatibility was overwhelming: They co-starred in one of the great comedies, *My Man Godfrey*, for which Lombard received an Oscar nomination.

UPI

In June 1931 Carole Lombard became Mrs. William Powell. She is shown here with her husband, Powell, who was her co-star in "My Man Godfrey" for which she received an Oscar nomination.

Wide World

Carole Lombard is met at airport by her mother, Mrs. Peters, after her divorce from William Powell. Col. Roscoe Turner, noted air racer, piloted plane from Nevada to California. 1933

Lombard and George Raft in ''Bolero'' (1934)

She met Clark Gable for the first time in 1932, when they co-starred in *No Man of Her Own*. The second time they met was at the home of John Hay Whitney in 1936 and from that night until they were married in March 1939, they were a duo. Gable had to wait for a divorce before remarrying. They bought a twenty-acre ranch in the San Fernando Valley with animals for her to take care of, while he tended the land. They were one of Hollywood's happiest couples, enjoying one another's company and sometimes the company of good friends. They were not the nightclubbers usually associated with stars of their ilk, nor were they splashed across the headlines for "extra curricular activities." They called one another Ma and Pa, tended to their careers, their ranch, and each other. Together they were invited to the White House by President Franklin D. Roosevelt.

Lombard and then future husband, Clark Gable, attend the funeral of Jean Harlow. (1937)
Mr. and Mrs. Clark Gable pose with the bride's mother, Mrs. Elizabeth Peters. Carole Lombard, nee Peters, and Gable were married in March 1939.

At left the famous Fanny Brice (died 1955) shown with Carole Lombard and Clark Gable in 1937.

The beautiful and beautifully happy newlyweds, Clark and Carole Gable, shown here at their twenty-acre ranch in the San Fernando Valley, California.

Lombard's screen image began to change with *Made For Each Other*. She proved in this film, and subsequently three others, that she could do drama. Later she returned to comedy, making her last film with the master Jack Benny in *To Be or Not To Be*. Many refer to this film as both . . . a real blend of drama and comedy.

UPI

Lombard and Jimmy Stewart in "Made For Each Other" in 1939.

Lombard and Gable celebrate their first wedding anniversary, March 1940.

UPI

Lombard with Jack Benny (died 1974) in her last film, "To Be Or Not To Be" in 1942.

UPI

Lombard and Gable attend showing of "Gone With The Wind." Vivien Leigh won an Oscar for her performance and the film won an Oscar. Gable won Miss Lombard. (1939)

Lombard and Gable at the races at Santa Anita, Calif. in 1941. "Bay View," at 58 to 1 odds, had just won the coveted Santa Anita handicap.

UPI

Shortly after World War II started, Gable was named chairman of the Hollywood Victory Committee. It was he who arranged for his wife to go on a bond selling tour, a tour that was to climax in her native Indiana. There in Indianapolis she sold over two million dollars ($2,107,513.00) worth of bonds and left Indianapolis after a patriotic speech, her last: "Before I say goodbye to you all— come on—join me in a big cheer—V for Victory!" She and her mother boarded TWA's flight #3 for Los Angeles but after a refueling stop in Las Vegas, Nevada the plane crashed into the Table Rock Mountains. All twenty-two passengers died. It was two days before the body of Carole Lombard was found and identified. She was buried in Los Angeles at the Forest Lawn Cemetery three days later.

Carole Lombard and her mother, Mrs. Elizabeth Peters, arriving in Indianapolis for the bond rally.

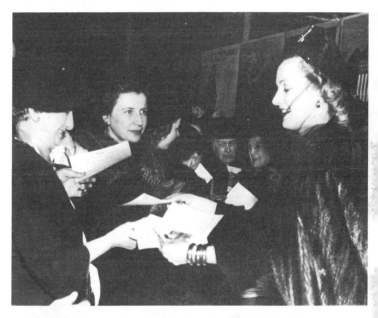

Lombard winding up tour of selling War Bonds. To her left is her mother, Mrs. Elizabeth Peters, who accompanied her daughter on the tour.

Carole Lombard Gable poses on steps with Indiana's governor H. F. Schricker on her right. Indiana honored the native born Lombard on the last stop of her War Bond Drive. On her left is Will Hays, president of the Motion Picture Producers and Distributors of America, and Eugene C. Pulliam, chairman of the Indiana Defense Savings Staff. This is the last photo of Carole Lombard, taken on January 16, 1942.

The coffin, containing the remains of Carole Lombard, is being removed from train at Pomona, Calif. to be taken to Forest Lawn Memorial Park in Los Angeles for final interment.

Soldiers prepare to lower the bodies of persons killed in the crash of TWA airliner. Scattered below the rugged face of the cliff into which it smashed, lies the wreckage of the airliner. Carole Lombard and her mother were on board.

UPI

Clark Gable, grief-stricken over the death of his wife, Carole Lombard. Gable died in 1960. Ironically he played opposite two other stars in their last films, Jean Harlow and Marilyn Monroe.

William Powell, former husband of Carole Lombard, *UPI* arrives for simple ceremony at cemetery, 1942. Only five years before, 1937, Powell attended Jean Harlow's funeral. Harlow was rumored engaged to Powell at the time of her death.

UPI

She was a fun-loving girl, a hard working career woman, a devoted daughter, and a beloved wife. President Roosevelt sent a telegram to Gable: "She is and always will be a star, one we shall never forget, nor cease to be grateful to." She was also a soldier, as she died while doing service for her country.

CAROLE LOMBARD
Died: January 16, 1942
Southeast of
Las Vegas, Nevada

Doris Jensen, a worker for California Shipbuilding Corp., inspects a model of the Liberty ship, **S.S. Carole Lombard,** named for the famous actress. The 10,500-ton freighter was to have been launched in 1944, two years after Miss Lombard's death.

CAROLE LOMBARD FILMS

1921 A PERFECT CRIME — Dwan Associates
with Monte Blue, Jacqueline Logan, Stanton Heck, Hardee Kirkland

1925 MARRIAGE IN TRANSIT — Fox
with Edmund Lowe, Adolph Milar, Frank Beal

1925 HEARTS AND SPURS — Fox
with Charles (Buck) Jones, William Davidson, Freeman Wood

1925 DURAND OF THE BADLANDS — Fox
with Charles (Buck) Jones, Marion Nixon, Malcolm Waite

1926 THE ROAD TO GLORY — Fox
with May McAvoy, Leslie Fenton, Ford Sterling, Rockliffe Fellowes

1927 THE SENNETT COMEDIES — Sennett-
to   Pathé
1929 SMITH'S PONY 1927
THE GIRL FROM EVERYWHERE 1927
RUN, GIRL, RUN 1928
THE BEACH CLUB 1928
THE BEST MAN 1928
THE SWIM PRINCESS 1928
THE BICYCLE FLIRT 1928
THE GIRL FROM NOWHERE 1928
HIS UNLUCKY NIGHT 1928
THE CAMPUS VAMP 1928
THE CAMPUS CARMEN 1928
MATCHMAKING MAMAS 1929

1928 THE DIVINE SINNER — A Trem Carr Production
with Vera Reynolds, Nigel De Brulier, Bernard Seigel

1928 POWER — Pathé
with William Boyd, Alan Hale, Jacqueline Logan, Jerry Drew

1928 ME, GANGSTER — Fox
with June Collyer, Don Terry, Anders Randolph, Stella Adams

1928 SHOW FOLKS — Pathé
with Eddie Quillan, Lina Basquette, Robert Armstrong

1928 NED McCOBB'S DAUGHTER — Pathé
with Irene Rich, Theodore Roberts, Robert Armstrong

1929 HIGH VOLTAGE — Pathé
with William Boyd, Owen Moore, Diane Ellis, Billy Bevan

1929 BIG NEWS — Pathé
with Robert Armstrong, Sam Hardy, Tom Kennedy

1930 THE RACKETEER — Pathé
with Robert Armstrong, Roland Drew, Jeanette Loff, John Loder

1930 THE ARIZONA KID — Fox
with Warner Baxter, Mona Maris, Mrs. Jiminez, Theodore von Eltz

1930 SAFETY IN NUMBERS — Paramount
with Charles "Buddy" Rogers, Kathryn Crawford, Joseph Dunn

1930 FAST AND LOOSE — Paramount
with Miriam Hopkins, Frank Morgan, Charles Starrett

1931 IT PAYS TO ADVERTISE — Paramount
with Norman Foster, Richard "Skeets" Gallagher, Eugene Pallette

1931 MAN OF THE WORLD — Paramount
with William Powell, Wynne Gibson, Guy Kibbee, Lawrence Gray

1931 LADIES' MAN — Paramount
with William Powell, Kay Francis, Gilbert Emery, Olive Tell

1931 UP POPS THE DEVIL — Paramount
with Richard "Skeets" Gallagher, Stuart Erwin, Lilyan Tashman

1931 I TAKE THIS WOMAN — Paramount
with Gary Cooper, Helen Ware, Lester Vail, Charles Trowbridge

1932 NO ONE MAN — Paramount
with Ricardo Cortez, Paul Lukas, Juliette Compton, George Barbies

1932 SINNERS IN THE SUN — Paramount
with Chester Morris, Adrienne Ames, Alison Skipworth

1932 VIRTUE — Columbia
with Pat O'Brien, Ward Bond, Willard Robertson

1932 NO MORE ORCHIDS — Columbia
with Walter Connolly, Louise Closser Hale, Lyle Talbot

1932 NO MAN OF HER OWN — Paramount
with Clark Gable, Dorothy Mackaill, Grant Mitchell

1933 FROM HELL TO HEAVEN — Paramount
with Jack Oakie, Adrienne Ames, David Mannors, Sidney Balckmor

1933 SUPERNATURAL — Paramount
with Randolph Scott, Vivienne Osborne, Alan Dinehart

1933 THE EAGLE AND THE HAWK — Paramount
with Fredric March, Cary Grant, Jack Oakie

1933 BRIEF MOMENT — Columbia
with Gene Raymond, Monroe Owsley, Donald Cook

1933 WHITE WOMAN — Paramount
with Charles Laughton, Charles Bickford, Kent Taylor

1934 BOLERO — Paramount
with George Raft, William Frawley, Frances Drake, Sally Rand

1934 WE'RE NOT DRESSING — Paramount
with Bing Crosby, George Burns, Gracie Allen, Ethel Merman

1934 TWENTIETH CENTURY — Columbia
with John Barrymore, Walter Connolly, Roscoe Karns

1934 NOW AND FOREVER — Paramount
with Gary Cooper, Shirley Temple

1934 LADY BY CHOICE — A Robert North Production
with May Robson, Roger Pryor, Walter Connolly

1934 THE GAY BRIDE — MGM
with Chester Morris, ZaSu Pitts, Leo Carillo

1935 RUMBA — Paramount
with George Raft, Lynne Overman, Margo, Monroe Owsley

1935 HANDS ACROSS THE TABLE — Paramount
with Fred MacMurray, Ralph Bellamy

1936 LOVE BEFORE BREAKFAST — Universal
with Preston Foster, Janet Beecher, Cesar Romero

1936 THE PRINCESS COMES ACROSS — Paramont
with Fred MacMurray, Alison Skipworth, William Frawley

1937 *MY MAN GODFREY — A Universal Picture
with William Powell, Alice Brady, Gail Patrick
*Lombard was nominated for an Academy Award as Best Actress

1937 SWING HIGH, SWING LOW — Paramount
with Fred MacMurray, Charles Butterworth, Jean Dixon, Dorothy Lamour

1937 NOTHING SACRED — Selznick-International
with Fredric March, Charles Winninger, Walter Connolly

1937 TRUE CONFESSION — Paramount
with Fred MacMurray, John Barrymore, Una Merkel

1938 FOOLS FOR SCANDAL — Warner Bros.
with Fernand Gravet, Ralph Bellamy, Allen Jenkins

1939 MADE FOR EACH OTHER — Selznick-International
with James Stewart, Charles Coburn, Lucile Watson

1939 IN NAME ONLY — RKO Radio
with Cary Grant, Kay Francis, Charles Coburn

1940 VIGIL IN THE NIGHT — RKO Radio
with Brian Aherne, Anne Shirley, Julien Mitchell

1940 THEY KNEW WHAT THEY WANTED — RKO Radio
with Charles Laughton, William Gargan

1941 MR. AND MRS. SMITH — RKO Radio
with Robert Montgomery, Gene Raymond, Jack Carson

1942 TO BE OR NOT TO BE — United Artists
with Jack Benny, Robert Stack

John Garfield, tough and poor, sexy and rebellious, became famous playing the same roles on the screen that had been his roles in life.

John Garfield

Born: March 4, 1913, New York, New York

Jacob and Max Garfinkle were the two sons born of David and Hannah Garfinkle. Both parents were first generation American Jews of peasant stock who migrated to the United States and landed, as so many before them, on the lower east side of New York City. Jacob became Julie and remained Julie to his friends throughout his life. The world knew him as John Garfield. Max, five years younger, became Mike. Hannah Garfinkle died when Julie was seven years old, but not before she had taught her older son to protect himself because he was smaller than the rest of the boys. And she sang funny songs to him, which may account for his comedic style in doing impersonations—first of his friends and later of his colleagues. Speaking of his mother and his life, Garfield said: "My mother dropped dead when I was seven. Not having a mother I could stay out late. I didn't have to eat regularly or drink milk at four o'clock. I could sleep out and run away, which I did." His father David was unskilled, always poverty stricken, and at a loss as to what to do with his boys . . . so they were "farmed out" constantly in their youth.

Julie (John), never understood at home, became a boy of the streets, who could take care of himself, who learned to fight, and who hung out with "gangs." From the gangs he got the attention he lacked at home. He always managed to be merry and fun-loving despite the shabbiness of his surroundings and the lack of familial guidance. After living with relatives in the Bronx, Brooklyn, and Queens, the family was reunited when David married Dinah Cohen. Julie was ten at the time, always a good athlete, until age twelve when he suffered permanent heart dam-

age after a bout with scarlet fever. It did not impede his athletic prowess but should have slowed him down. Not much of a student, he began to slip back even more after the illness until he was placed in a school for special cases, P.S. 45. Fortunately for him the principal, Dr. Angelo Patri, had evolved a new method of teaching gifted, neglected children, "special cases," and it was Dr. Patri who shaped, molded, and protected the young Julie. An uncle, who lived near the school in the East Bronx, took Julie in to live with him so that he could attend the school. Margaret O'Ryan, a teacher in P.S. 45 took him under her wing. Originally to correct a mild stammer, she soon recognized the outward confidence he had and encouraged him to study dramatics. The original intent of speaking or reciting aloud may have been to cure the stammer, but acting became Julie's way of life.

In 1928 he returned home to live with his father and step-mother and the same year Dr. Patri was instrumental in getting him into Roosevelt High School, plus a scholarship at the Heckscher Foundation dramatic workshop. In a performance of *A Midsummer Night's Dream*, actor Jacob Ben-Ami saw the young Julie and recommended the American Laboratory for his future studies in the theatre. Julie dropped out of school in his sophomore year to follow Ben-Ami's advice even though he did not have the funds to attend the Laboratory. Julie's father had little understanding of what his young son wanted to do and refused him any financial support. Again Dr. Patri stepped in and loaned him the necessary money to enroll. Julie lived at home, secured a job in the garment district, attended the Laboratory, and volunteered his services there in the evenings, doing anything and everything just to be around the other actors. He met Clifford Odet at that time, who told him he'd have to change his name and who eventually changed his own by adding an "s" to Odet.

In 1929, Julie Garfinkle stepped on the stage in a Theatre Guild production of *The Camel Through The Needle's Eye*, fluffed his lines and was covered by its star, Claude Rains. His early training and exposure was about the best any young actor could have hoped for. The Theatre Guild offered productions, The American Laboratory embraced the then new Stanislavsky Method of acting, which later became known as the Method or System, and he rubbed shoulders with future greats, Stella Adler, Morris Carnovsky, Lee Strasberg, and Clifford Odets. Later he worked for and with Eva Le Gallienne's Civic Repertory Theatre. The artistic side of the young Julie was exposed to these giants of the theatre but the other side, the uneducated side, was also exposed . . . exposed in the sense that he hadn't had very much schooling, had not been a reader and therefore was not at home with their educated and intellectual thinking. This insecurity he covered up for the rest of his life. His wife, Roberta whom he met as a young man, would always supercede him as a thinker and although their house might be stocked with books, it was Roberta, later known as Robbie, who read them unlike Julie, who professed to have read them. Later in Hollywood when Julie would hobnob with writers, whom he considered the epitome of intellect and intelligence, his own lack was constantly exposed and ridiculed. One might suspect that this feeling of insecurity was compensated for by his sexual awareness. Always a very attractive and appealing boy, he learned at a very young age that girls could not resist him. Later as a star he knew that the same appeal would appease his insecurity. For most of his life he gambled on the fact that the intelligent Robbie would under-

stand what motivated him sexually. He was correct until shortly before he died.

Meanwhile, back in 1932, he earned good money as an understudy in *Lost Boy* and finally earned a stage credit. But his first big break came at 19, when he appeared in the Chicago company of *Counsellor-at-Law* with Otto Kruger. Later in New York, when an ailing actor stepped aside, Julie took over and played the role he had done in Chicago, now opposite Paul Muni. He then toured with Muni and returned to Broadway to play an unprecedented return of the same play. It was the first time his father acknowledged his talent . . . or at least because Julie earned more in one night than his father earned in a month, the recognition was forthcoming. Universal Pictures stepped in with an offer for the film, but on the advice of playwright/director Elmer Rice, Julie turned his back on Hollywood. He apprenticed at the newly formed Group Theatre, spearheaded by Sherwood Anderson and Odets, considered a 1931 groupie cult. Way ahead of its time, its members were free thinkers, free livers, and commune dwellers. Outspoken in their political views, they opposed racist and religious bigotry but demanded absolute dedication to their cause from their members. At 22, Julie became a full-fledged member. And once again he found himself in an intellectual milieu beyond his comprehension. But by this time he and Robbie were married. In 1935 *Awake and Sing* opened and was Julie's big breakthrough. The world was undergoing some big breakthroughs of its own and the Group began to thrash about for means to advance its productions and for ways to express its political stance. Julie, in order to work, took a part in the Broadway production of *Having a Wonderful Time*, not under the Group aegis. Some of the other members opted for Hollywood and during this time once again Julie turned down another offer for the coast. He eventually signed with Warner Brothers but only after his heart had been broken by the Broadway production of

Golden Boy which he felt Odets had written for him. Instead of the lead as Joe Bonaparte, which fell to Luther Adler, Julie was assigned the role of Bonaparte's brother/cab driver, Siggie. He never got over his resentment and it was years later, and too late, when as a 39 year old he returned to Broadway to play the lead. The show had a limited run.

He left for Hollywood alone and later was joined by Robbie. In 1938 their first child, Katherine, was born along with John not Julie, Garfield—star, who now had a new contract with Warner Brothers and a lot of money. It was Fannie Hurst's *Four Daughters* with co-star Priscilla Lane that brought John Garfield, movie star, to wide public attention. The movie legend of John Garfield grew with pictures such as: *Tortilla Flat*, (1942) *Pride of the Marines*, (1945) *The Postman Always Rings Twice*, (1946) *Body and Soul* (1947, for his new independent company with Bob Roberts) and *Gentleman's Agreement* (1947). The family of John Garfield grew

with the birth of son, David Patton, in 1943 and daughter, Julia Roberta, in 1947. The off-screen legend of John Garfield grew with his countless sexcapades, shaky marriage, and many suspensions from Warner's as he refused to make inferior

Wide World

(l-r) Wife, Robbie Garfield, son David (age 10 months), Garfield, and daughter Katherine (age five), at home, in 1944.

Garfield greeting actress Faye Emerson and actor Dane Clark at studio head Jack L. Warner's party for new young players under contract to Warner Bros., 1943.

Garfield with daughter Katherine, who died in 1947. This picture was taken between overseas trips, made by Garfield, where he entertained the troops during WW II . . . one of the first to volunteer his services.

Wide World

Wide World

pictures. In 1947 he suffered a tragic personal loss when daughter Katherine died.

In 1948 the family moved back to New York, and in 1949 Julie opened on Broadway, in Odets' *The Big Knife*. Although the critics didn't rave, the public flocked to see movie star John Garfield. He quit the play after three months and returned to California to honor film commitments. Back in Hollywood, only thirty-six years of age, he collapsed one day after playing tennis: heart muscle strain was the diagnosis and "no exertion for the rest of your life" was the prescription; a nasty pill to swallow for the fun-loving, cigarette smoking, alcohol drinking, hardworking John Garfield. He resisted the advice. Garfield was the first star to entertain the soldiers during World War II, Garfield worked assiduously with Bette Davis in the famous Hollywood Canteen, Garfield whose lack of understanding "causes" was called on the carpet by the House Un-American Activities Committee, and Garfield who was supposed to take it easy, went on making films and making out. Many felt that he copped out in his testimony before the committee, many felt he had betrayed his friends, many felt he was loyal to his friends, but many felt that John Garfield never really knew what he was doing politically: that he never understood the true meaning of the causes he espoused. Whatever the truth, Julie wanted out from under of being accused a "red." The insinuations of HUAC were beginning to injure his career and he was ready to do anything to prove that he had been misled or duped, or whatever during the struggling years with his intellectual comrades. What he could not admit, either openly or to himself, was the fact that he had always feigned understanding. He had always wanted to be one of them, on their intellectual level and now he was paying for his mental game of "cover up."

Wide World

Garfield giving a farewell kiss to volunteer kitchen worker, actress Mary Gordon. The famous Hollywood Canteen, started by Bette Davis, entertained over three million servicemen during its three and one-half year run. Garfield was an active volunteer and is shown here at the closing night festivities, 1945.

Herman Hoffmann (left) Chairman of Board of Directors of the Non-Sectarian Anti-Nazi League, presents the first annual La Guardia Memorial Awards for "Work in Advancing Human Rights" April 27, 1948. Recipients (l-r) John Garfield, Israel Sachs, dept. store president, and Robert Wagner, Jr. who received the award for his father, Senator Robert F. Wagner.

Not a movie still, but a real life action shot. Garfield the first American donor, gives his blood to the Red Mogen David Blood Bank for Palestine. The organization's name means Red Star of David, an equivalent of the Red Cross. Circa 1950.

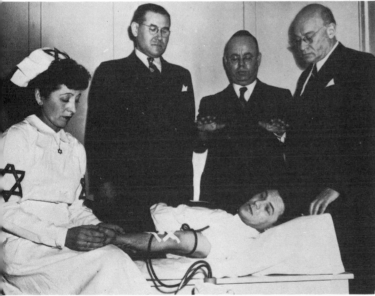

Garfield and wife Robbie with son David (age 7) and second daughter, Julie (age 4) in 1950.

Garfield testifying before the House Un-American Activities in its hunt for Communist Party connections in Hollywood. The committee described Garfield as a "friendly" witness. April 23, 1951.

His early training by his mother, "to take care of himself," reared up. He decided he was not going to be removed from his profession nor prohibited from working, so in order to affect a reconciliation with the liberals, the press, the industry, he arranged with *Look* Magazine to "tell all" in a statement after his HUAC appearance. He moved out of the apartment he shared with Robbie and the children and moved into a suite at the Warwick Hotel. Whether he and Robbie had finally split is a matter of conjecture: that he spent his last evening with former actress Iris Whitney is a matter of record. After dinner and a walk around Gramercy Park where Miss Whitney lived, Garfield complained of not feeling well and she put him to bed in her apartment. The next morning when she tried to awaken him, he was dead. It was too late to issue his "tell all" statement.

No. 3 Gramercy Park in New York City, the house in which Garfield died, 1952.

Iris Whitney, actress friend, told police that Garfield had died of a heart attack in her two-room apartment, after he had become ill the night before and she permitted him to stay overnight. They had had a dinner engagement, after which they returned to her apartment. May, 1952.

The body of John Garfield being placed in undertaker's hearse outside the apartment where he died.

Once again New York witnessed a mob scene as thousands of people gathered to view his body, to mill in the street, or just be a part of John Garfield's last scene. After a service at Riverside Memorial Chapel, John Garfield was buried in the Westchester Hills Cemetery in Mt. Hope, New York.

TOP: Outside of the Riverside Memorial Chapel in New York City, struggling women fans, some of them in tears, are held back by police.

MIDDLE: Over 500 fans came to view the body of John Garfield. 1952

BOTTOM: Last trip for John Garfield, as hearse is readied to carry his body from Riverside Memorial Chapel, NYC, to interment in Westchester Hills Cemetery, 1952.

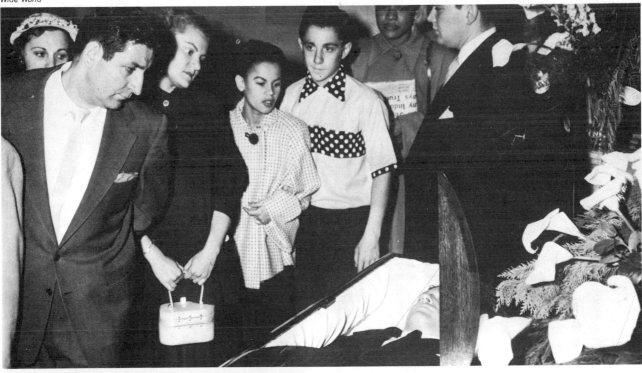

Julie Garfinkle, street kid, may have or may not have been aware of his political leanings and affiliations. John Garfield, grown-up, died according to author Larry Swindell*: "unaware that he had been the prophet of the new actor in America, onstage and in pictures. Prototype and archtype, he was the first of the rebels: John Garfield, the antihero in revolt against a world he never made." As this rebel died another one arrived in New York the same year . . . James Dean.

JOHN GARFIELD
Died: May 21, 1952
New York, New York

* Body and Soul: The Story of John Garfield, William Morrow & Co., Inc. New York.

JOHN GARFIELD
BROADWAY PLAYS

1932 LOST BOY, with Elisha Cook, Jr.

1932 COUNSELLOR AT LAW, with Paul Muni, John Qualen

1934 PEACE ON EARTH, with Julie Colin, Robert Keith, Clyde Franklin

1934 GOLD EAGLE GUY, with Clifford Odets, Elia Kazan, Morris Carnovsky

1935 WAITING FOR LEFTY, with Luther Adler, Ruth Nelson, Paula Miller

1935 AWAKE AND SING!, with Luther Adler, Stella Adler, Phoebe Brand, J. Edward Bromberg, Morris Carnovsky

1935 WEEP FOR THE VIRGINS, with Evelyn Varden, Phoebe Brand, Ruth Nelson, J. Edward Bromberg

1936 THE CASE OF CLYDE GRIFFITHS, with Morris Carnovsky, Phoebe Brand, Art Smith, Ruth Nelson, Paula Miller, Alexander Kirkland

1936 JOHNNY JOHNSON, with Russell Collins, Lee J. Cobb, Elia Kazan, Albert Dekker, Morris Carnovsky, Luther Adler, Robert Lewis

1937 HAVING WONDERFUL TIME, with Katherine Locke, Herbert Ratner

1937 GOLDEN BOY, with Luther Adler, Frances Farmer, Phoebe Brand, Morris Carnovsky, Lee J. Cobb, Elia Kazan

1940 HEAVENLY EXPRESS, with Aline Mac-Mahon, Art Smith, Philip Loeb, Russell Collins, Curt Conway

1948 *SKIPPER NEXT TO GOD — with Joseph Anthony, Simon Oakland
*See Award

1949 THE BIG KNIFE, with Nancy Kelly, J. Edward Bromberg

1951 PEER GYNT, with Mildred Dunnock, Karl Malden

1952 GOLDEN BOY (revival), with Bette Grayson, Art Smith, Lee J. Cobb, Jack Warden, Arthur O'Connell, Jack Klugman, Joseph Wiseman

AWARD

1948 Garfield won an Antionette Perry ("Tony") Award for his performance in SKIPPER NEXT TO GOD

FILMS

1938 *FOUR DAUGHTERS — Warner Bros.
with Claude Rains, Rosemary Lane, Priscilla Lane, Lola Lane
*Garfield was nominated for an Academy Award as Best Actor, and the film was nominated as Best Picture.

1939 THEY MADE ME A CRIMINAL — Warner Bros.
with Claude Rains, Gloria Dickson, Billy Halop, Ann Sheridan

1939 BLACKWELL'S ISLAND — Warner Bros.
with Rosemary Lane, Dick Purcell, Victor Jory

1939 JUAREZ — Warner Bros.
with Paul Muni, Bette Davis, Brian Aherne, Claude Rains

1939 DAUGHTERS COURAGEOUS — Warner Bros.
with Priscilla Lane, Claude Rains, Rosemary Lane, Lola Lane

1939 DUST BE MY DESTINY — Warner Bros.
with Priscilla Lane, Alan Hale, Frank McHugh, Billy Halop

1940 THE CASTLE ON THE HUDSON — Warner Bros.
with Ann Sheridan, Pat O'Brien, Burgess Meredith

1940 SATURDAY'S CHILDREN — Warner Bros.
with Anne Shirley, Claude Rains, Roscoe Karns

1940 FLOWING GOLD — Warner Bros.
with Frances Farmer, Pat O'Brien, Raymond Walburn

1940 EAST OF THE RIVER — Warner Bros.
with Brenda Marshall, Marjorie Rambeau, William Lundigan

1941 THE SEA WOLF — Warner Bros.
with Edward G. Robinson, Ida Lupino, Alexander Knox

1942 OUT OF THE FOG — Warner Bros.
with Ida Lupino, Thomas Mitchell, Eddie Albert

1942 DANGEROUSLY THEY LIVE — Warner Bros.
with Nancy Coleman, Raymond Massey, Moroni Olsen

1942 TORTILLA FLAT — MGM
with Spencer Tracy, Hedy Lamarr, Frank Morgan

1943 AIR FORCE — Warner Bros.
with Gig Young, Harry Carey, Arthur Kennedy

1943 FALLEN SPARROW — RKO Radio
with Maureen O'Hara, Walter Slezak, Patricia Morison

1943 THANK YOUR LUCKY STARS — Warner Bros.
with Dennis Morgan, Joan Leslie, Eddie Cantor

1943 DESTINATION TOKYO — Warner Bros.
with Cary Grant, Alan Hale, Dane Clark

1944 BETWEEN TWO WORLDS — Warner Bros.
with Paul Henreid, Eleanor Parker, Sydney Greenstreet

1944 HOLLYWOOD CANTEEN — Warner Bros.
with Dane Clark, Janis Paige, Robert Hutton, Bette Davis

1945 PRIDE OF THE MARINES — Warner Bros.
with Eleanor Parker, Dane Clark, John Ridgeley

1946 THE POSTMAN ALWAYS RINGS TWICE — MGM
with Lana Turner, Cecil Kellaway, Hume Cronyn

1946 NOBODY LIVES FOREVER — Warner Bros.
with Geraldine Fitzgerald, Walter Brennan, Faye Emerson

1946 HUMORESQUE — Warner Bros.
with Joan Crawford, Oscar Levant, J. Carroll Naish

1947 BODY AND SOUL — Enterprise-United Artists
with Lilli Palmer, Hazel Brooks, Anne Revere

1947 GENTLEMEN'S AGREEMENT — 20th Century-Fox
with Gregory Peck, Dorothy McGuire, Celeste Holm

1948 FORCE OF EVIL — Enterprise-MGM
with Beatrice Parsons, Thomas Gomez, Roy Roberts

1949 WE WERE STRANGERS — Horizon-Columbia
with Jennifer Jones, Pedro Armendariz, Gilbert Roland

1950 UNDER MY SKIN — 20th Century-Fox
with Micheline Presle, Luther Adler, Orley Lindgren

1950 THE BREAKING POINT — Warner Bros.
with Patricia Neal, Phyllis Thaxter, Juano Hernandez

1951 HE RAN ALL THE WAY — United Artists
with Shelley Winters, Wallace Ford, Selena Royle

Hank Williams—dressed as a cowboy, but wrote and sang as a country boy . . . a legendary figure was he. Circa 1952.

Ĥank Williams

Born: September 17, 1923, Mt. Olive, Alabama.

Hiram "Hank" Williams was born "po" on a tenant farm. He was a native son of the south and remained one, even though he called himself a cowboy. His songs always reflected his own life and his first-hand knowledge of what life was all about. Being a cowboy wasn't what he knew. Except for his theme song and his attire, everything else belied a cowboy.

At age 5 the family moved to Georgiana, Alabama and later to Montgomery . . . the place he called home. But he was just as poor in Montgomery as he had been in Mt. Olive and Georgiana. His mother was the organist at the Baptist church, where she taught him hymns and gospel songs. By the time he was 6 he could accompany her and by age 8, he was playing the guitar. He was a street kid who shined shoes, sold peanuts, worked at anything he could to bring home pennies. One of his street pals, an old black singer named Tee-Tot, taught him how to play the guitar. The Williams family repaid Tee-Tot by feeding him. Although poor, Williams had one very important thing going for him . . . his parents, especially his mother, who always encouraged him. He might have had to fend off hunger, but never the will of his parents. By the time he was twelve, he knew what he wanted to do and set about to do it.

His first attempt was a contest at the Empire Theatre in Montgomery, where singing his own tune *The WPA *Blues*, he romped home with the first prize . . . $15.00. This song, along with all of Hank Williams songs, depicted life as he saw it. His famous *Jambalaya*, about the gumbo stew he adored as a child, is another example. Everything he felt, went into his songs. Encouraged by his win, he set out to play music. At age 13 he had christened himself "The Drifting Cowboy" and was featured on radio WSFA, in Montgomery. By age 14 he had formed his own band, "Hank Williams and The Drifting Cowboys" playing local affairs, such as hoedowns and fairs. But work was hard to come by, so he began to drift. He went from town to town passing the hat, working in saloons, just one honkytonk place after another. "An itinerant minstrel" as he was later tagged.

In 1940, age 17, he married Audrey Shepherd, a singer whom he met in Banks, Alabama. Soon they had a son, three mouths to feed, and not enough money. Desperately poor and in desperation, Williams quit the road and returned to Mobile where he took a job in a shipyard. He never dreamed that in only a few years he would take a star journey on *Louisiana Hayride*, and then rip *Grand Ole Opry* apart: only his mother believed. In a little over three weeks he had quit the shipyard and was filling bookings in Montgomery, secured by his mother. From that time on it was the music business. It was the building of Hank Williams, not ships.

* WPA: Work Projects Administration established by President Franklin D. Roosevelt in 1935, was designed to increase the purchasing power of persons on relief, by employing them on useful projects such as construction of bridges and buildings, improving roads etc. . . . Later it was renamed the Works Progress Administration.

An older Mrs. Audrey Williams, first wife of Hank, shown in front of a life-sized cardboard likeness of her husband. She said that "the royalties from his hits 'Your Cheatin' Heart' and 'I'm So Lonesome I Could Die' grow larger every year," November 1974. Mrs. Williams died in 1975.

In 1946 he recorded with the Willis Brothers on the small Sterling label. With the Willises backing him, he sang his own compositions, but none became instant hits. The Nashville based music publishing company, Acuff-Rose, became his next target and he sent another of his compositions, *Move It Over,* to the firm. According to writer, Melvin Shestack,* there is an apocryphal story which involves Williams and Rose: "Rose, an executive and songwriter in his own right, was nobody's fool and said to Williams, 'I like your song, but

* The Songs of Hank Williams, Acuff-Rose International, Inc. NYC.

how do I know you wrote it'?" The story then goes on to say that Rose gave Williams a hypothetical situation and told him to go into another room and write a song about it. The result, about thirty minutes later, was *Mansion On The Hill.*

1947 found him on *Louisiana Hayride,* where he remained for two years. In 1948 he was signed by M-G-M Records, but 1949 was the stellar year. He broke it up on his first appearance at *Grand Ole Opry.* Big name stars like Minnie Pearl and Roy Acuff were on the bill, but it was Hank who received a standing ovation and was called back time after time. From that moment on he never had to look back. The days of the tanktowns were far behind and the only "passing the hat" was as one new hat after another passed along the closet shelf. He was rich, he was famous, he had his own mansion, he was published . . . but as the song he sang that memorable night on *Opry* said *I Got A Feelin' Called the Blues,* his life became the blues. He went from a local star in 1947 to a national star in 1949, but Hank Williams took his early beginnings and hard life with him. He poured out his heart and his problems via his songs to his audiences and they loved him for it. Billie Holiday did the same thing. Her songs, just as Williams' songs, told the listener exactly what was going on in her life and she shared the experience, good or bad. Both drank, both missed performances, both were forgiven by their audiences, who looked the other way and who overlooked their weaknesses. Holiday eventually lost her right to work in New York clubs, while Williams was finally fired by *Grand Ole Opry* in August of 1952.

Williams was a drug user which started when he was 17. He fell from a horse and used the drugs originally to combat the pain from a spinal injury. He was known to be moody and uncommunicative and the firing from *Opry* was stated as "for perpetual drunkeness." He was divorced by Audrey, but soon after married again. This time, the daughter of a Louisiana police chief, Billie Jean Jones.

Rev. L. R. Shelton married Hank Williams and Billie Jones in
New Orleans, La. on the stage of the municipal auditorium
during the Hank Williams Jamboree. October 1952.

Hank Williams plants a
kiss on the lips of the new
Mrs. Williams. 1952

En route to a gig in Canton, Ohio he deplaned because of bad weather in Tennessee, then hired a car and driver to take him through the snowstorm. When the driver, Charles Carr tried to awaken him at Oak Hill, Virginia he was unable to rouse the sleeping singer. Although there was an inquest into his death, it was ruled as "a heart attack from excessive drinking."

20,000 people turned out for the funeral services in Montgomery, Alabama. There isn't a singer in the world who doesn't at one time or another include a Hank Williams song in his or her repertoire, or who doesn't feel the lasting influence of his country music. George Hamilton played Williams in the film about his life, *Your Cheatin' Heart*. His son, Hank Williams, Jr.* contributed the music for the film and in his own right has continued the work and music of his father.

Wide World

Mrs. Hank Williams shown testifying to a legislative committee in Oklahoma City after the death of her husband. March 1953.

Hank Williams, Jr. carries on in his famous father's footsteps. Seen here campaigning for Alabama's former Congressman Carl Elliott, who was running for governor. April 1966

Wide World

* Hank Williams, Jr. born Shreveport, Louisiana May 26, 1949.

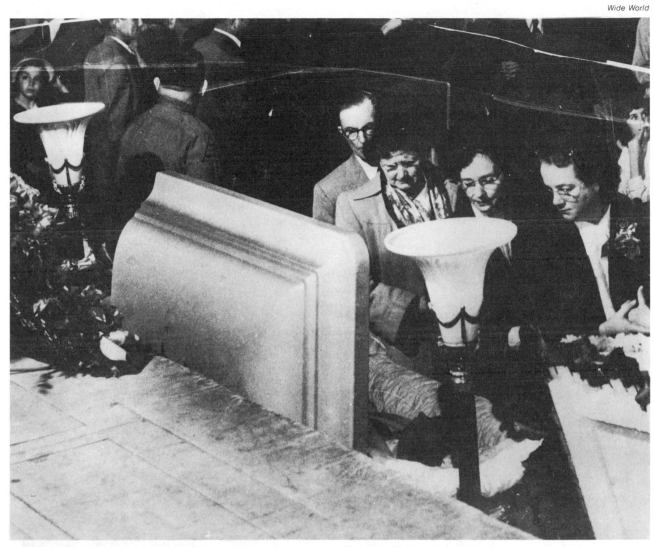

Firechief R. L. Lampley of Montgomery, Alabama reported that an estimated 20,000 people filed past the open casket of Hank Williams. 1953

Mrs. Hank Williams visited Hollywood during the filming of her husband's life story, "Your Cheatin' Heart." She is shown here with actress Ann Blyth, circa 1955.

But the final accolade came from fellow artists, who in 1961, elected him to Country Music's Hall of Fame. The small plaque in his honor reads:

"The simple, beautiful melodies and straightforward plaintive stories in his lyrics of life as he knew it, will never die."

Hank Williams' career and life were over by the time he was thirty, but his music is as strong today as it was then.

HANK WILLIAMS
Died: January 1, 1953 Kentucky

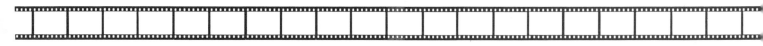

HANK WILLIAMS

1961 Elected to the COUNTRY MUSIC HALL OF FAME

GOLD RECORD AWARDS

(The Recording Industry Association of America began giving official Gold Record Awards in 1958, some years after Hank Williams' death. The following are for albums of reissues.)

1969 HANK WILLIAMS'S GREATEST HITS (MGM)
1969 YOUR CHEATIN' HEART (MGM)
1977 24 GREATEST HITS (Polydor/MGM)

HIT SONGS AND RECORDINGS

(Williams wrote over 100 songs, many of which were recorded by other country music artists in addition to himself, and several of which pioneered the cross-over of country songs into the pop and rhythm-and-blues fields. All of the following were recorded by Hank Williams and were then turned into hits in other fields by Jo Stafford, Frankie Laine, Tony Bennett, Joni James, Linda Ronstadt, Ray Charles, Teresa Brewer, and B. J. Thomas.)

HONKY TONKIN'
I'M SO LONESOME I COULD CRY
THERE'LL BE NO TEARDROPS TONIGHT
WHY DON'T YOU LOVE ME
RAMBLIN' MAN
COLD, COLD HEART
HEY, GOOD LOOKIN'
I CAN'T HELP IT (IF I'M STILL IN LOVE WITH YOU)
JAMBALAYA
YOUR CHEATIN' HEART

FILM BIOGRAPHY

1964 YOUR CHEATIN' HEART (MGM) with George Hamilton, Susan Oliver, Red Buttons, Arthur O'Connell

James Byron Dean, "Few knew him well, none knew him for long." He went from fame to death in less than three years and became the hero of his generation.

James Dean

Born: February 8, 1931, Marion, Indiana.

At birth James Byron weighed eight pounds, ten ounces but he didn't grow physically into the size one might have expected from such a weighty beginning. Some list him as five feet-six inches, while others record him at five feet-ten inches, but all agree that he had pale eyes, a small nose, a slight frame, and walked with hunched shoulders. His Quaker father, Winton Dean, was a dental technician who believed a person should bear children according to the number he could support. Jimmy was an only child. His Methodist mother, Mildred Wilson Dean, wrote poetry and spent most of her time with him. In 1936, the Veterans Administration transferred Winton to Los Angeles and it was there that Mildred devised a game which became Jimmy's favorite: Jimmy would write a wish on a slip of paper, place it under his pillow, and while he slept his mother would remove the paper. The next day she would try to fulfill his wish. She spoiled him beyond their means. Her premature death from cancer when Jimmy was nine years old evoked this later remark . . . "My mother died on me when I was nine. What does she expect me to do? Do it all by myself?" His resentment was very deep-seated and many who knew him said "it [his resentment] could sum him up." After his mother's death, it was his grandmother who suggested that Jimmy be raised by his aunt, Ortense Dean Winslow, and her husband, Marcus, back in Fairmount, Indiana. The Winslows had always wanted a son, so Jimmy was a welcome addition to their family as well as a younger brother and playmate for their daughter Joan, a lovely fourteen year old.

UPI

The home of his aunt and uncle, Marcus and Ortense Winslow, near Fairmount, Indiana, where Jimmy spent his boyhood.

Jimmy stayed ten years in Fairmount before rejoining his father and his new wife, Ethel, in Los Angeles. During high school, in Indiana, he played baseball, basketball, led the track team, and in his senior year, won a medal for best all-around athlete. He was a poor student but excelled in dramatics. Adeline Nall, his dramatic teacher, encouraged him to enter a state-wide public speaking contest, which he did, and won with his reading of an excerpt from *The Madman* by Dickens. Next, he entered a national contest in Colorado and despite the warning from his teacher about enlarging the work, he insisted on doing it and lost. For this he never forgave her. In Los Angeles, at his father's suggestion, he enrolled in Santa Monica City College to study law, but after a short time switched to UCLA. He lived alone for a while, later shared a room with William Bast, an aspiring young actor. It was Bast who got Jimmy his first job as an extra in a TV commercial. Up until that time, Jimmy had been making twenty-five dollars a week as a projectionist, but when the director of the commercial noticed his engaging smile, he elevated him to a "vendor" instead of just another extra riding the merry-go-round. This upped his salary to twenty-five dollars for a thirty second commercial spot. Bast later became a TV writer and wrote the still unreleased *James Dean Story*. History repeated itself when *Rebel Without A Cause* was shot in Griffith Park, the scene of Jimmy's commercial debut.

At nineteen, Jimmy knew he wanted to be an actor. "Why?" he was asked by James Whitmore and Jimmy didn't know. So Whitmore told him to find out. "Go to New York and learn something about the stage" was his advice. Although Jimmy had worked in Los Angeles as an usher, parking attendant, projectionist, extra, and in TV commercials, he felt he was stagnating, so in the fall of 1951 he headed by bus for New York City . . . to start all over again at the bottom. Of Whitmore he said: "I owe him a lot. He saved me when I got all mixed up."

If Jimmy had been tagged a lone wolf in Los Angeles, he became an even lonelier wolf in New York. He had no friends, girls, or money but what he did have was the ability to recognize a chance and grab it. He talked himself into a crewman's job on a yacht and when he discovered that the skipper had a friend casting for N. Richard Nash's play, *See the Jaguar*, Jimmy Dean got his first job . . . himself. Playing the part of a boy, who had been locked away in an ice house all his life, won him recognition from the critics as "a new talent worth watching." The play closed after five performances but James Byron Dean was on his way. The rave notices landed him TV jobs and a fair-sized part in Billy Rose's production of Andre Gide's *The Immoralist*. Perhaps his "gay" image started there, as he portrayed a blackmailing homosexual Arab. Off stage he was a beautiful boy who was now besieged with gifts and invitations. His other image had started also. He had a reputation for not taking direction well and his agent, Jane Deacy, had trouble getting casting directors to see him. This he substantiated by getting into a dispute with the director and then quitting *The Immoralist* after a week. But again, not before his performance had won him the David Blum award as "The Most Promising Newcomer of the Year." Jimmy studied people and Jimmy studied direction at Elia Kazan's Actors Studio and it was Elia Kazan who signed him to play Cal in *East of Eden*.

In May of 1954 he returned to Los Angeles, to live over a drug store, opposite Warner Brothers Studio; rental, fifty dollars a month; salary, one thousand dollars a week. He wasn't sure his luck would hold out. Word spread quickly about Kazan's new discovery, "another Brando", so during the shooting Kazan kept a closed set. Asked about his choice Kazan said, "He [Dean] was Cal Trask. He had a grudge against all fathers. He was vengeful; he had a sense of aloneness and of being persecuted. And he was suspicious. In addition, he was tremendously talented."

Jimmy met Pier Angeli while he was doing *Eden*, and as far as anyone knows, she was the only girl he ever loved. No one really knows why she broke their engagement and married singer Vic Damone. After the split-up Jimmy dated many starlets, always taking them to movies, movies, movies . . . any kind, any language, anywhere. He bought himself a camera and took pictures of himself when he was depressed or melancholy. "Acting," he said, "is the most logical way for people's neuroses to express themselves." He began to collect guns, to play chess, and to learn about music (bongos, recorder, piano). Leonard Roseman, who scored *Eden,* said: "Jimmy knew a little about everything but was always trying to fill in the gaps. Actually he knew very little about music but by testing my knowledge, and by asking me questions, and by talking about music by the hour, he was able to build up a good musical background." When the picture was finished, co-star, Julie Harris, found Jimmy "crying like a baby" in his dressing room. He loved to work, he lived his parts, and felt let down when it was over. He was always anxious to get on. Jimmy said that Harris had helped him a lot; help he was later to give to co-star Natalie Wood.

Co-star Julie Harris as she appeared in "East of Eden."

James Dean and Natalie Wood in "Rebel Without A Cause" (1955) Natalie Wood said: "He taught me to relax before playing tense. (A tense role) I had never thought of acting that way before."

95

Jimmy drank only coffee or beer and he rarely went to parties but would attend "cultural soirees." At one such soiree in the home of Nicholas Ray, Jimmy met photographer, Dennis Stock, and invited him to accompany him on a return trip to his native Indiana and to a sneak preview of *Eden*. Stock knew that Jimmy was going to be a big star, so he accepted both invitations. By doing this he was able to do research on Dean and to stockpile photographs. By the time they returned from Fairmount, the script for *Rebel Without A Cause*, was ready and the director . . . Nicholas "Nick" Ray: "My feelings," said Ray, "were that he (Dean) could have surpassed any actor alive." This opinion Ray maintained until later when he saw Laurence Olivier in *Coriolanus*. Stewart Stern who wrote the screenplay for *Rebel* had this to say about Dean: "I say I didn't know him. I think I sensed him." and "I think there was a metal-hard core, submerged, which allowed him to operate very consciously and never be the victim."

Simultaneously, what was emerging in the United States was the inarticulate no-cause teen-age rebellion and it had victims: well-meaning parents who had been denied as children were now lavishing their gains on their children. The first decade of teen-age affluence was upon us. The rebellion and Jimmy Dean were hitting their peaks, both with an underlying motive of self-pity. What had started as a middle class rebellion, carried over to all classes and was shaped in their music, their clothes, and most of all in their heroes. Jimmy Dean was one such hero and the fifties—sometimes called the Age of Dean.

Sal Mineo (left) playing Plato, who worshipped Jim Stark (Dean) in "Rebel Without A Cause," 1955. **Mineo**: "The very last time I saw him I had a feeling—I was sad and yet vibrant. I mean, those are the feelings I can understand, but I just knew that I was feeling something that I didn't feel with anything or anybody else."

UPI

Dean on himself: "I am terribly gauche and so tense I don't see how people stay in the same room with me. I know I wouldn't tolerate myself."

Elizabeth Taylor and Dean in "Giant," directed by George Stevens. **Stevens:** "Dean is to the atomic age what F. Scott Fitzgerald was to the 20's. He is what the young people believe themselves to be."

Giant, directed by George Stevens, co-starring Elizabeth Taylor was Jimmy's last film. He was dead four weeks when *Rebel* was released, followed by the release of *Giant*. Driving his silver Porsche Spyder at 86 mph, he collided with another car at the intersection of routes 466 and 41 near Paso Robles, California. His passenger Rolf Weutherich, a Porsche factory mechanic, suffered injuries to his head and jaw plus a broken leg. Dean's head was almost severed from his body. The driver of the other car, Donald Turnupseed, was only slightly injured. According to the patrolman, O. O. Hunter, he had issued a warning "to slow down" and a speeding ticket to Dean only two hours and fifteen minutes before the fatal crash.

The Eagles Rock Group sang about him: *You were too fast to live, too young to die.*

Dean water skiing along the Potomac River with Washington Monument in background and TV camera crew overhead. He was a good athlete, a daredevil, a loner.

UPI

Wreckage of Dean's car being towed from scene of accident.

Wide World

Audiences voted him Best Actor of the Year while four million fans became paying members of his posthumous fan club. (The count includes just the United States.) At Princeton University, in the Laurence Hutton Collection, there is a life mask of him next to Beethoven, Keats, Thackeray, and other immortals.

Writer Mark Dayton summed him up this way: "A spooky, oddball, nonconformist, sullen and withdrawn, a member of the dirty shirt school of acting, a crazy mixed up kid, a working eccentric and yes—a fourteen karat, ball-bearing genius."

Kenneth Kendall, painter and sculptor, at work on the face mask of Jimmy Dean.

JAMES BYRON DEAN
Died: September 30, 1955, Paso Robles, California

Jimmy Dean was buried October 8, 1955 in Fairmount, Indiana. His mother had named him after Lord Byron, who wrote in an entry in memoranda, on the success of Childe Harold, "I awoke one morning and found myself famous."

JAMES DEAN
PLAYS

1952 WOMEN OF TRACHIS — (Off-Broadway)
1952 THE METAMORPHOSIS — (Off-Broadway; dramatic reading)
1952 SEE THE JAGUAR
with Constance Ford, Arthur Kennedy, Cameron Prud'Homme
1954 THE IMMORALIST
with Geraldine Page, Louis Jourdan

FILMS

1951 FIXED BAYONETS — 20th Century-Fox
with Richard Basehart, Gene Evans
1952 HAS ANYBODY SEEN MY GAL — Universal-International
with Charles Coburn, Piper Laurie, Lynn Bari, Rock Hudson
1954 *EAST OF EDEN — Warner Bros.
with Julie Harris, Raymond Massey, Jo Van Fleet, Burl Ives
*Dean was nominated for an Academy Award as Best Actor
1955 REBEL WITHOUT A CAUSE — Warner Bros.
with Natalie Wood, Sal Mineo
*GIANT — George Stevens-Warner Bros.
with Elizabeth Taylor, Rock Hudson, Sal Mineo, Carroll Baker
*Dean was nominated for an Academy Award as Best Actor
1956 THE JAMES DEAN STORY — Warner Bros. Documentary

TELEVISION APPEARANCES

YEAR SHOW
1950 Father Peyton's TV Theatre. "Hill Number One"
1952 U.S. Steel Hour: "Prologue to Glory"
1953 Kate Smith Hour: "Hound of Heaven"
Treasury Men in Action: "The Case of the Watchful Dog"
Danger: "No Room"
Treasury Men in Action: "The Case of the Sawed-Off Shotgun"
Campbell Sound Stage: "Something for an Empty Briefcase"
Studio One Summer Theatre: "Sentence of Death"
Danger: "Death Is My Neighbor"
"The Big Story"
"Omnibus" (film clips of legit shows)
Kraft TV Theatre: "Keep Our Honor Bright"
Campbell Sound Stage: "A Long Time Till Dawn"
Armstrong Circle Theatre: "The Bells of Cockaigne"
Johnson's Wax Program: "Robert Montgomery Presents Harvest"
1954 Danger: "Padlocks"
General Electric Theatre: "The Dark, Dark Hours"
General Electric Theatre: "I Am a Fool"

1955 U.S. Steel Hour: "The Thief"
Lever Brothers' Lux Video Theatre: "The Life of Emile Zola", followed by an interview with James Dean
Schlitz Playhouse: "The Unlighted Road"
1954 Philco TV Playhouse: "Run Like a Thief"

POSTHUMOUS

1956 THE JAMES DEAN STORY — Warner Bros.
Motion picture "documentary"
1956 Steve Allen Show
Tribute
1957 A Tribute to James Dean — CBS-TV
Documentary

1964 Hollywood and the Stars — David Wolper Production
Telecast of teen-age idols
1974 James Dean: Memories of a Gentle Rebel — ABC Wide World Special

AWARDS

1954 *Theatre World* Award as "Most Promising Newcomer" for his performance in THE IMMORALIST
1955 PHOTOPLAY GOLD MEDAL AWARD given posthumously for his "outstanding dramatic appearances"
1955 Award presented by MODERN SCREEN magazine, in honor of its 25th anniversary. Presented on Colgate Variety Hour

Empty bookshelves and a quote from the man himself: "Educate me and we'll both be out of work," Mike Todd.

Mike Todd

Born: June 22, 1909, Minneapolis, Minnesota

Avrom Hirsch Goldbogen was the first child to be born in America of Chaim and Sophia (Hellerman) Goldbogen. The Goldbogens had nine children, eight survived, but not one survived in the way that Avrumele, as he was called by his family, survived. From the moment he hit the streets as a youngster, until his death, he was a promoter, hustler, and entrepreneur of the first ilk. Although he changed his name to Mike Todd, and lived as Mike Todd, there was a portion of him that always remained loyal to Avrom.

His parents were born and married in Poland. Chaim, the son of a rabbi, had wanted to live a life devoted to the Talmud but the lure of the new land, America, reached him and once in the United States he went from job to job in an effort to support his large family. He never lost sight of his ambition and never let the family lose sight of the religious customs and the meaning of being Jewish. He accepted his role in life, not too unlike Tevya. He was dearly loved by his family and especially by Avrom. Sophia played the mother role, seemingly a bit masochistic at times, as Mike pointed out. When he could afford to put her up at the finest hotels, he felt that she preferred dreaming about or talking about staying there, instead of being there.

The young Avrom was impatient with his parents' reminiscences of the old life. He was always anxious to get on to something new . . . the old ways bored him. And when the family moved to Bloomington, he did not despair, but thought up new ways to conquer the new city. He was only eight years old at the time. He attended school but it was more of an afterthought. He loved one thing about school and that was its annual play, *The Mikado.* It was a love that remained with him until he finally brought about his own production of it.

The young hustler learned quickly about the world. He would write away for items to be sold. The company that advertised promised to send valuable prizes to the seller, after the money was returned. Avrom sold the goods, sent the money, only to discover that the prizes were defective. He stopped sending the money and simply told the company that he lost their goods. He did indeed learn quickly. When he had his tonsils removed, he charged his friends "a nickel a look," and he ran a crap game at school taking his percentage from each pot. His only expense was paying a young friend, Fat Libitsky as the lookout. Fat went on to become more than a lookout . . . today he is known as Jack E. Leonard. Avrom was always a busy young man. World War I ended and the family moved to Chicago. Chaim's dream was fulfilled there when he became president of the Hasidic Northwest Synagogue. Mike quit high school after one year and commenced his unusual career.

Mike Todd, age five, at left with his brother Frank, sister Edith, and mother Sophia Goldbogen outside of their house in Bloomington, Minnesota.

Wide World

Mike Todd, at age 12, with a friend at Chicago's Municipal Pier.

First wife, Bertha Freshman, who died later in Los Angeles. They were married in 1927. Circa 1946.

He started a school for bricklayers with a token investment, just for sand and bricks. Most of his students were comprised of Chicago's large Polish community and these people, anxious to earn a better living, flocked to his school. As promised, they received diplomas, but the fly in the ointment was—the Union of Bricklayers didn't recognize Avrom's school. Operating just this side of the law, enabled the young promoter to walk off with about a $3,000 profit. By the time he was eighteen, he was operating a $2,000,000 building business and at age nineteen he was broke. Although he had gone financially bankrupt, emotionally he had filled his bank with a lovely wife, Bertha Freshman. They were married on Valentine's Day, 1927, by a Justice of the Peace at Crown Point, Indiana. Later they were remarried by a rabbi, with the love and blessing from his family, as he had married "a nice Jewish girl."

After the building business debacle, the couple moved to California where Avrom went into the business of building sound stages. With the advent of *The Jazz Singer*, the old Hollywood stages would soon be obsolete and someone had to build new ones . . . soundproof new ones. At twenty, Avrom was the most successful builder in Hollywood, only to be broke again when the depression hit. Again no funds—but again, another personal fund—his son Michael. Avrom's father died in September '31 at age 55 and the fact that his young Michael would never know his grandfather was a great sadness for Avrom. It was an era of his life which had gone and with its passing, so went Avrom. He decided to be a Michael, too, and took the name of Todd, a derivative of his nickname as a child, "Toat." His name was legalized in 1932.

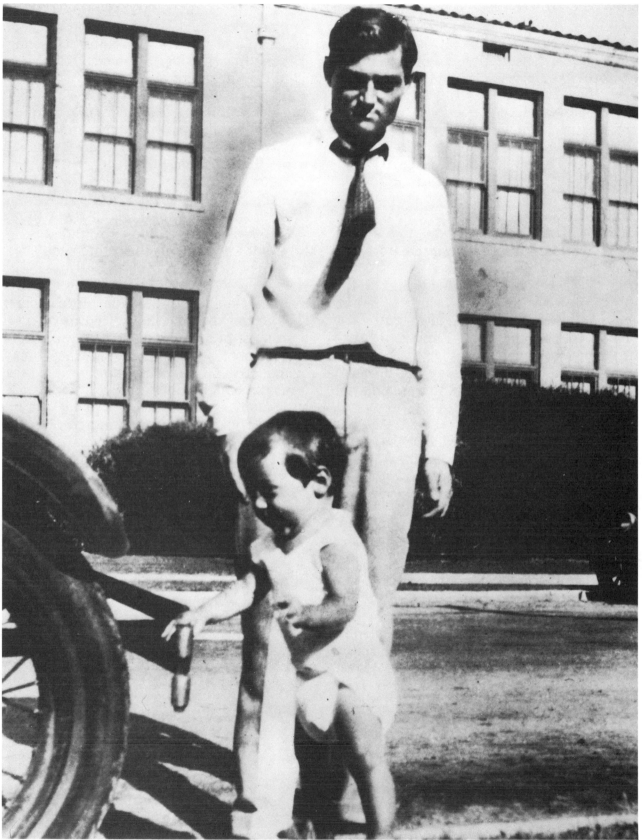

The two Michael Todds, Junior and Senior, in Los Angeles 1931.

There were fourteen million unemployed people in the United States and the new Michael Todd was one of them. Back in Chicago, Bertha's family had offered him a job for $35.00 a week, but Michael Senior said, "no." He had his eye on bigger things. Depression sufferers needed—wanted—escapes from their own dismal lives and show business was the answer. Movies flourished and so did the Chicago's *World* Fair. Mike Todd put together his first show, *Casino de Paris* for the Fair. Later with one of its main attractions as its nucleus, he put together *Bring On The Girls*, which toured successfully for fourteen months. But Mike grew bored. He loved show business, he now had his eye on Broadway, and his arrows pointed right at the heart of Florenz Ziegfeld's seat. He managed to pull off a deal involving the Lone Ranger, it backfired, but not before he pocketed several thousand dollars. This money was his stake for his first Broadway production, *Call Me Ziggy*, 1937.

It was not an overwhelming success, but Yiddish star Joseph Buloff held it together with his fine reviews. Todd's next show, *This Man From Cairo*, opened in April '38 and folded after twenty-two performances. Along with the play's disintegration, Mike's marriage was disintegrating just as rapidly. Bertha remained in Chicago where she raised Mike, Jr., just the way Mike, Sr. wanted, but Bertha had married Avrom, *not* Broadway producer Mike Todd. He could never again be the man she wanted.

By March of 1939 producer Mike Todd had learned many lessons about his trade. He was going to profit from the severest ones and would never spare any expense to give the public what he thought they wanted. He wanted *The Mikado* and gave the public a new view of it, *The Hot Mikado*, starring Bill Robinson. There's a showbiz story connected with the opening of this show. Lee Shubert, of the famous Shubert Theatre family, supposedly offered to pay the whole cost of the production for half of the rights . . . before the show opened. In other words, Todd's investment of a quarter of a million dollars was guaranteed, plus he would still reap one half of the profit. Todd flipped a coin to make his decision and kept the whole show. He also kept a lifelong friendship with Lee Shubert. *Hot* had a good run and then a road company. Star Bill Robinson was never any happier, especially when everyone in "the business" came to call. But Robinson's epic line about this is: "Ah cain't understand why them boys what wrote the show ain't even stopped by."

Todd's next stop was the New York World's Fair and a crack at crack showman Billy Rose. By the time the Fair was in its second season, Todd had surrounded Billy Rose with five shows, including such stars as Gypsy Rose Lee, Abbott and Costello, Harry James, Les Brown, Doris Day, Gordon MacRae, Gene Krupa . . . plus fourteen bars. He was the Midway Midas. He was smarter than most of his cronies and he was smart enough not to let on. He could sell anything to anybody. He had complete confidence in himself, which rubbed off on his friends and business associates. All of his life he needed backing, more and more funds . . . and he always got it. His financial ups and downs made Coney Island's roller coaster look like it moved in slow motion.

UPI

Todd's competition in the New York World's Fair. (l-r) Eleanor Holm about to break bottle of champagne to dedicate swimming pool, New York's Grover Whalen, and showman Billy Rose. 1939

TOP: Todd had to step to outshine Billy Rose's Aquacade at New York's World Fair, shown here in 1939. It is still regarded as one of the finest exhibits ever presented anywhere.

BOTTOM: Father and son, watching a rehearsal of "Star and Garter" in 1942.

At one point in his life he almost lost all of his friends and reputation when he backed Gerald L.K. Smith. The Smith who talked about "Franklin D. Rosenfeld and the kike capitalists who put him in the White House." But Avrom Goldbogen helped the FBI put Smith where he belonged, as Mike Todd's friends learned where he belonged, to what, and to whom. Todd had a brush with Chicago's big wheeler — dealer Frank Nitti, an Al Capone spawned product. This time Todd didn't flip a coin. He always wanted to be his own boss and any affiliation with Chicago's powerful underworld, he felt, eventually would mean relinquishing his autonomy. This decision was a little Avrom and a little Mike and probably a lot of what he wanted Michael, Junior, to think of him. He was a devoted father . . . Mike, Junior, was the most important thing in his life.

Star and Garter, his next Broadway production, starring Gypsy Rose Lee ran over 600 performances. He turned down *Oklahoma!* and opted for *Something For the Boys*, starring Ethel Merman. When he wasn't working he was playing gin rummy or shooting crap. He was a non-drinking heavy gambler. He also fell in love again. This time with actress Joan Blondell, wife of actor Dick Powell. He put her in one of his broadway shows, *The Naked Genius* '43 and courted her until her seven year marriage to Powell ended in January '44.

Meanwhile another war, World War II, had started and Todd, now 34, was turned down by the Navy because of colitis. But the ever-willing army accepted him, bestowing on him one star. Before the "general" departed for foreign shores he managed a herculean task by producing three more Broadway shows: *Mexican Hayride* starring Bobby Clark and June Havoc with music by Cole Porter; *Pick-Up Girl* with Pamela Rivers and William Harrigan; *Catherine Was Great* starring Mae West.

Mike Todd did the best job he could do for the army, but the red tape, protocol, and waiting—Army Hazards—had nothing to do with "Move Mountains Mike." He was always mystified by its seeming inertia, while the army misunderstood his miraculous movement. Fortunately for both, the war ended and Todd returned to his own arena . . . Broadway. But what do you do when you've had one success after another? If you're Mike Todd you look to other goals to conquer and follow the advice of Horace Greeley, "Go West Young Man." He was estranged from Bertha, had agreed to her divorce terms of a half a million dollars, madly in love with Joan, and earning about $20,000 a week. Not bad for a little boy who once had to run a block to use the outhouse. He accepted an offer from Universal-International Pictures to be an executive producer on salary plus a percentage of whatever he produced. Bertha, who was supposed to be en route to South America, took a rather unexpected turn and ended up in California. The western turn for Todd ended up in one disaster after another. He went deeper into debt than ever before, his gambling was out of control, he could not "Todderize" Hollywood, as he had done New York, and his production bombed at the Hollywood Bowl. Then quite suddenly Bertha died on the operating table from minor surgery. But not before an ugly story appeared in the papers accusing the couple of a knockdown, knife-hurling, fight. But Bertha's death was caused by "the collapse of the left lung and circulatory failure while under anesthesia." Mike was vindicated.

On July 5, 1947, Mike and Joan were finally married in Las Vegas. He was her third husband and she was his second wife. She was going to change everything . . . no more gambling (except he backed Truman for President at 20 to 1 odds!) and they moved back to New York, not the city, but upstate along the Hudson River. Michael, Jr. was entering college in the fall and had mildly fallen for the girl next door, Sarah Jane Weaver. The domesticity bubble was short-lived. Mike had a flop show and then had to borrow a lot of money for another show—a big portion of it from Joan. Then he had a hit show: hit and miss; up and down; rich and poor. Mike Todd loved the excitement and challenge of it all.

Mike Todd and his second bride, actress Joan Blondell, at their wedding supper in Las Vegas, Nevada, July 1947.

TOP: Todd and his wife, Joan Blondell, in the Cub Room of Sherman Billingsley's famous Stork Club, N.Y.C. in 1948. The two children, Norman Powell and Ellen Powell, are from her previous marriage to actor Dick Powell.

LEFT: Photo of the Todds before they decided to call it quits. Joan Blondell had been married, first to cameraman George Barnes, and then to actor Dick Powell, who died in 1963.

By the summer of '49, Mike, Jr. went off on a freighter to the Far East to find himself, Joan went back on the stage to re-find herself, and Mike was broke again. When their divorce became final, in June of 1950, he had produced his last show for Broadway, *The Live Wire* and had filed a bankruptcy suit: an almost unbelievable action. From 1937, Todd's sixteen shows had grossed about $18,000,000. A lot of people didn't

room displayed a spacious screen with pictures and the effect was exciting. The background to this screen started in 1939, when Fred Waller was experimenting with peripheral vision. He perfected the process and called it Vitarama. Later he was joined by Hazzard Reeves who added sterophonic sound and the new joint venture became known as Cinerama. Mike Todd knew immediately what this process could produce.

Wide World

Mike Todd, Junior and his wife Sarah Jane with Mike, Senior at the opening of "A Night in Venice" at Jones Beach, Long Island 1953.

buy the bankruptcy suit and a lot of people thought it was quite possible . . . it, the money, could have all gone on gambling. Mike, Sr. was concerned with what Mike, Jr. thought but Mike, Jr. believed him, not the gossip. Mike, Sr. believed his lawyer and took his advice. He withdrew the bankruptcy suit, acknowledged his debts, and agreed to settle. Back to the square root of one . . . one Mike Todd.

Todd-AO, a process for wide-screen filming, began for Mike Todd in Madison Square Garden where he attended a lecture and film by Lowell Thomas, Jr. The amount of people in the Garden and the size of the screen did not jive. Todd then found himself on Long Island in a projection room which was formerly a tennis court. The

The idea of seeing on a screen what the human eye could see was almost incomprehensible to the brain: three cameras filtered into one slot and presto an image. Todd went into the project with his usual enthusiasm, a film was made, and shown in New York in 1952. Everyone was thrilled with *This Is Cinerama*, except Todd. He was a showman and he knew that he couldn't show travelogues forever. And something else bothered him: the three separate cameras left seams on the screen . . . why not one camera to do the work? "Unheard of" screamed his friends and backers. Todd found Dr. Brian O'Brien in Rochester, New York . . . the dean of optics. Todd found the president of the American Optical Company, Walter A. Stewart. Todd then found backing, about twenty million dollars, and the biggest venture of his life began. The new camera would have "to perfect an entirely new geometric process for photographing and projecting film*." It involved a new lens, or lenses, special 65mm. film, special sound tracks for the stereophonic sound, and then all of it had to be reduced for 35mm., the standard size used in theatres. The official company Todd-AO (*A*merican *O*ptical) was created in June '54, and *Oklahoma!* was his choice for the first film. In dealing with Messrs. Hammerstein and Rodgers, Todd could not foresee the problems. They were interested in their show while Todd was interested in his process. He eventually lost artistic control over the film but not before an offer was made to buy him out . . . for over $7,000,000. It was déjà vu from Shubert's 1939 offer.

Mike, Jr. married Sarah Jane Weaver and Mike Todd, Sr. married twenty-four year old Elizabeth Taylor, February 2, 1957 in Acapulco, Mexico. Having lost control of *Oklahoma!*, then, Todd bought *Around The World in 80 Days*. This gigantic endeavor was filmed in 13 countries, used 11 studios,

Mrs. Francis Taylor (left) watches, as husband Francis Taylor and daughter Elizabeth Taylor sign marriage papers. Mike Todd leans over to say something to his son, Mike, Jr. Acapulco, Mexico 1957.   *Wide World*

Wide World

The newlyweds smile happily after the ceremony. (l-r) Parents Mr. and Mrs. Francis Taylor, Mr. and Mrs. Mike Todd, and Mr. and Mrs. Howard Taylor (brother of the bride) and Mike Todd, Jr. February 1957.

Elizabeth Taylor Todd is placed on a stretcher at Idlewild (now Kennedy) Airport, in New York, assisted by husband, Mike. She suffered a back injury as their plane flew into Mexico City from Acapulco. She was taken to Harkness Pavilion Hospital, where she underwent a back operation before her marriage. February 1957.

* The Nine Lives of Michael Todd; Art Cohn, Random House, New York.

Wide World

75,000 costumes, 680,000 feet of film, and a cast of 68,000—many of whom flew with Mike and his staff over 14 million air-passenger miles. The final cost was somewhere over $6,000,000.

Avrom, Avrumele, Mike had outshone Ziegfeld on Broadway, garnered all the roses away from Billy Rose, and finally had out-distanced Hollywood and its moguls, as *80 Days* would survive long enough to gross one hundred million. At forty-nine, Michael was the proud grandfather of Cyrus, the son of Michael and Sarah, and he had married the most glamorous girl in the world. He had it *all*. Including a daughter Liza.

RIGHT: Mike Todd holds Oscar he won for producer of "Around The World In 80 Days," named Best Picture of the Year, as a beaming Mrs. Todd gets ready to be kissed. March 1957.

BOTTOM: Mike Todd, Junior, shown here at age 28, says goodbye to Mike, Senior who was departing for Europe. April 1957.

Unidentified lady referee weighs the evidence as each Todd accuses the other Todd for missing their plane.

Mike tells driver to "step on it" as he charters plane to make up for one they missed.

Safely in Cannes "on time" for the film festival, Mike looks for approval from his wife, as General Secretary of the Festival, Favre Le Bret (left) looks on. Now who would have thought they missed their plane? 1957.

Mike and Elizabeth Todd prepare to board the "Liberte" at Southhampton, England after they attended the premiere of "Around The World In 80 Days," in London. Christopher Wilding is being held by Mike, and Michael Wilding walks alongside his pregnant mother. The boys are from her previous marriage to Michael Wilding. June 1957

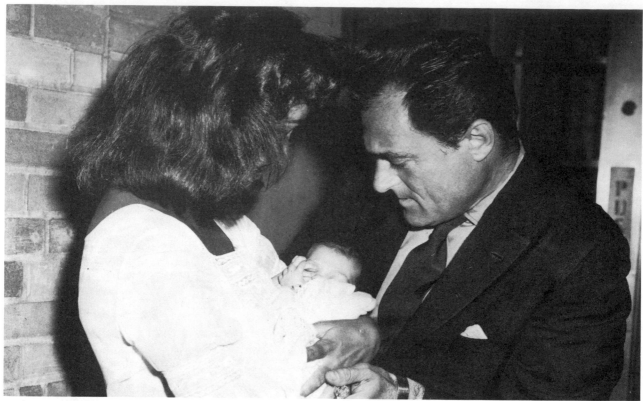

Liza Todd, daughter of Mike and Elizabeth, was born prematurely August 6, 1957. Shown here September 3, 1957 as the proud parents prepare to take her home.

One of the last pictures taken of Mike Todd shown here with daughter Liza, 6 1/2 months, and stepsons Michael, 4, and Christopher, 3, Wilding. March 1958.

One Friday night in March, he asked writer Art Cohn to accompany him to New York City where he was to receive the "Showman of the Year" award from the Friars Club. Mr. Cohn had already written Joe E. Lewis' biography, *The Joker is Wild* and was at that time working on Todd's biography. Elizabeth was ill with bronchitis and could not go with him. Todd, Cohn, the pilot and co-pilot boarded the "Lucky Liz" in California and somewhere about thirty-five miles southwest of Grants, New Mexico about 2:00 a.m. the plane crashed. There were no survivors.

This is the twin-engine Lockheed Lodestar private plane, owned by Mike Todd, which he named the "Lucky Liz."

Arrow locates place, approximately 20 to 35 miles southwest of Grants, New Mexico, where Mike Todd's plane crashed, killing all four on board.

COLORADO

UTAH

Durango

Aztec

Santa Fe

GRANTS

Albuquerque

ARIZ.

N. MEXICO

Tucson

El Paso

AP

0   100
STATUTE MILES

MEXICO

TOP: A blanket of snow shrouds desolate remnants of Todd's light plane.

LEFT: Two rescuers wrap remains of one of the victim's body, as a third rescuer looks away, at scene of plane crash.

BOTTOM: An ambulance prepares to load the remains of Mike Todd and the three passengers for the trip to Albuquerque, New Mexico.

Reporters clustered outside of the Todd home in West Los Angeles. Elizabeth Taylor Todd was inside the house under a doctor's care, March 1958

General view of the crowd that gathered at the Waldheim Cemetery in Forest Park, Illinois for the funeral of Mike Todd. 1958

RIGHT: Elizabeth Taylor Todd, as she leaves the grave site of her husband. She is being assisted by (l) her personal physician Dr. Rex Kennamer and (r) her brother, Harold Taylor. 1958.

BOTTOM: Brother David Goldbogen, shown at the family plot where his brother, Avrom (Michael Todd), was buried. 1958.

Of all the words written about him during his lifetime Todd's favorite* was a quote from Associated Press writer Mark Barron: "Mike Todd's show (80 Days) makes this a better world." Indeed it did.

Headstone for the grave of Mike Todd, Sr. 1958.

UPI

MIKE TODD
Died: March 22, 1958, SW Grants, New Mexico

* Source: The Nine Lives of Mike Todd; Art Cohn, Random House, New York.

MICHAEL TODD
BROADWAY SHOWS PRODUCED

1937 CALL ME ZIGGY, with Joseph Buloff

1938 THE MAN FROM CAIRO, with Joseph Buloff, Helen Chandler

1939 THE HOT MIKADO, with Bill Robinson, Eddie Green, Rosetta LeNoire

1942 STAR AND GARTER, with Gypsy Rose Lee, Bobby Clark

1943 SOMETHING FOR THE BOYS, with Ethel Merman

1943 THE NAKED GENIUS, with Joan Blondell

1944 MEXICAN HAYRIDE, with Bobby Clark, June Havoc, Wilbur Evans

1944 PICK-UP GIRL, with Pamela Rivers, William Harrigan, Edmond Nolley

1944 CATHERINE WAS GREAT, with Mae West

1945 UP IN CENTRAL PARK, with Wilbur Evans, Maureen Cannon, Noah Beery, Sr.

1945 HAMLET, with Maurice Evans

1946 THE WOULD-BE GENTLEMAN, with Bobby Clark

1946 JANUARY THAW, with Norma Lehn, Robert Keith, Lorna Lynn, Lulu Mae Hubbard

1948 AS THE GIRLS GO, with Bobby Clark, Irene Rich

1950 MICHAEL TODD'S PEEP SHOW, with Lina Romay, Corinne, & Tito Valdez, June Allen

1950 THE LIVE WIRE, with Peter Turgeon, Sheila Bond, Jack Gilford, Murvyn Vye

In 1952 Todd opened the Marine Theatre at Jones Beach with an extravaganza, NIGHT IN VENICE, which was enthusiastically received and ran for two summers.

FILM WORK

1952 THIS IS CINERAMA, co-produced and shot by Todd

1955 Todd was responsible for the development by Dr. Brian O'Brien, of American Optical, for the wide-screen filming process called Todd-AO.
OKLAHOMA!, Arthur Hornblow, Jr. — the first film done in Todd-AO
with Shirley Jones, Gordon MacRae, Rod Steiger, Charlotte Greenwood

1956 *AROUND THE WORLD IN 80 DAYS, Michael Todd
with David Niven, Cantinflas, Shirley MacLaine, Robert Newton
*see Awards, below

AWARDS

1956 Academy Award, Best Picture: AROUND THE WORLD IN 80 DAYS

1956 New York Film Critics' Circle, Best Picture: AROUND THE WORLD IN 80 DAYS

Buddy Holly, circa 1958. His recording of "Peggy Sue" became a classic.

Buddy Holly

Born: September 7, 1936, Lubbock, Texas.

The town in Texas where Charles Hardin Holly was born was settled by the Quakers in 1879 and is known as the trade center for the cotton and grain-growing Great Plains region of Texas and East New Mexico. It's a long way from New York, Memphis, or Nashville and not known for music. So young Charles Hardin Holly had to cut his teeth on hillbilly, black, or Mexican music via his radio. At age five, he entered his first talent show singing *Down The River of Memories*, taught to him by his mother. At age eight, he began studying the piano and violin, then switched to the guitar. With his friend Bob Montgomery, he became part of a local duo known for Western Bop. Later with drummer Jerry Allison, playing guitar and drum duos, they formed a most unusual combination for their Country and Western music. In 1956 at a rock show in Lubbock, featuring Bill Haley and the Comets, they were heard by a Decca Records' scout, who signed them to cut some singles in Nashville. They did two records, which were not particularly successful, but did produce two classics, *Midnight Shift* and *Rock Around With Ollie Vee*. The giant of early rock was beginning to grow. Rock of those days was fun, music was fun. It had not yet become an "art form" or turned into animal-sexual type performances.

In February 1957, in Clovis, New Mexico, they wandered into Norman Petty's studio and with bassist Larry Welborn recorded *That'll Be The Day* and *I'm Looking For Someone To Love*. Holly and the Crickets, as they were known, soared to the number 3 spot in the U.S. with their rendition of *That'll Be The Day*, written by Jerry Allison, and to the number 1 spot in Great Britain. Whatever the reason for his sidetracking from country music, it was a good decision for him, and for the growing audiences. Perhaps the success of Elvis and others in the rock field accounted for it but the kids danced to and bought his records as he became a big hitmaker.

Courtesy of MCA Records

Buddy Holly and The Crickets, circa 1958.

Holly began to work as a solo artist for Coral Records in 1957 and in August 1958 his personal life became a duet when he married Maria Elena Santiago, a New Yorker. They were married in Lubbock, his hometown, decided to go to New York, but went alone as the Crickets did not want to move. In early 1959, Buddy Holly's career was at the crossroads. Where he was going and what he would have done will always remain unsolved. Holly said: "We owe it all to Elvis." For indeed, Elvis Presley was a pioneer who opened up new frontiers of music and self-expression. But the stars of the sixties owe a lot to Holly. For it was he who pioneered the two guitar, bass, and drum lineup and double tracking, which future stars capitalized on. Certainly Holly and Chuck Berry were two of the great songwriter-singer-musician talents of the pop fifties.

Wide World

UPI

LEFT: Time has in no way diminished the influence of Buddy Holly and his music. Circa 1956.

RIGHT: The body of Richie Valens, one of the singers on board the fatal crash, lies in the snow. Behind is the wreckage of the chartered plane. 1959.

Buddy Holly remained on the charts until the mid-Sixties. After his death, the rights to his music were purchased by Beatle Paul McCartney. In 1978, Columbia Pictures filmed his life story, starring Gary Busey, entitled "The Buddy Holly Story." Two final tributes to a quickly rising star, remembered twenty years after his death: a death that claimed him when he was only twenty-two years old.

UPI

In January 1959, as a solo artist, Holly was on tour for GAC with Ritchie Valens, The Big Bopper, and Dion and the Belmonts. They were traveling by bus when Holly decided to charter a plane . . . to save time. The plane crashed on take-off from Mason City, Iowa. Valens and Bopper were also on board and all died.

RIGHT: Actor Gary Busey as Buddy Holly in "The Buddy Holly Story," Columbia Pictures 1978. Said Busey about his performance: "I wasn't doing an impression of anybody. It's all Gary Busey up there, within the perimeter of Buddy Holly's life." Robert Gittler, who was the screenwriter for the film, committed suicide on the day of the film's world premiere in Texas.

Courtesy of MCA Records

LEFT: When you know who you are, and where you are going, it never crosses your mind not to wear your glasses onstage. Buddy Holly was probably the first performer, rock 'n roll, who had the confidence to do just that. Holly, circa 1958.

BUDDY HOLLY
Died: February 3, 1959, NW of Mason City, Iowa

BUDDY HOLLY
RIAA GOLD RECORD AWARDS

1969 THE BUDDY HOLLY STORY (Album)
(Decca)
1060 THAT'LL BE THE DAY (Single) (Coral)

Billie Holiday, age 32, five feet-eight inches . . . all soul.

Billie Holiday
Born: April 7, 1915, Baltimore, Maryland

Eleanora was her Christian name, Billie came from screen star, Billie Dove. Her father, Clarence Holiday, played banjo and guitar in Fletcher Henderson's band in the early '30's. Billie with her mother, Grace, moved to 145th Street in Harlem in 1929. It didn't take long for Billie to start singing in Harlem clubs such as the Yeah Man, Log Cabin, and regularly at the Hot Cha Club on 139th Street. She was discovered by John Hammond and in November of 1933, she made her record debut with The King of Swing, Benny Goodman. Until she branched out as a solo artist in 1940, she sang with the bands of Teddy Wilson, Count Basie, and Artie Shaw. In January of 1936, while performing in a revue, *Stars Over Broadway,* she was taken ill and replaced by her idol, Bessie Smith.

Her solo work made her a regular at famous New York spots such as Cafe Society and Kelly's Stables. Her only film, *New Orleans,* was made in 1946, as well as her first solo concert in Town Hall, New York City February 16, 1946. Her first European appearance was in 1954 with Leonard Feather's *Jazz Club U.S.A.*

Milt Gabler, vice-president Decca Records said: "In 1936 I never dreamed that in two years I would start my own company, Commodore Records. Billie cut four sides for me, April 1939: *Strange Fruit, Yesterdays, I Got A Right To Sing The Blues,* and her big hit, *Fine And Mellow.* These recordings were her first 'pop hits' and her

RIGHT: Billie with Lionel Hampton, at Esquire's fourth annual All-American Jazz Concert, held at the Metropolitan Opera House in January 1944.

1944 Esquire's All-American Jazz Concert in New York City. Billie Holiday and drummer Sid Catlett.

Jazz history in the making in 1944. (L to R) Roy Eldridge, Oscar Pettiford, Billie Holiday, and Art Tatum.

career zoomed from that point on. Her later sides for Decca were agony. Billie was in trouble and getting in deeper all the time. The legal restriction (no cabaret card) imposed on her kept her from working in New York City clubs the last 12 years of her life."

Although she was financially successful, she was not successful in overcoming her drug addiction. In Philadelphia, May 1947, she was arrested for violation of United States Narcotic Laws and in June of the same year she was sentenced to one year and one day, which she served at the Federal Reformatory in Alderson, West Virginia. Upon her release she did a concert in March 1948 at Carnegie Hall. Her life was always further complicated by personal disasters. However, she took the disasters

Billie in Philadelphia, Pa. 1947 where she was arrested on charges of illegally possessing heroin. (L-R) Her road manager, James Asendio, and her pianist, Robert N. Tucker. *UPI*

Billie awaits hearing in Philadelphia for drug charges, 1947. *UPI*

and put the feelings into her art.

Singer Sylvia Syms said: "Billie was the most articulate as well as an intelligent singer even though she had no schooling or education. Her education was her search for the truth within herself. She used all of the things that happened in her life and made them work for her in her music."

One of the highest compliments an artist could receive was the recognition she was given by fellow artist/actor, Charles Laughton. He commenced each acting class he taught by playing Billie Holiday records. For as Laughton said: "She is the best teacher when it comes to defining the English language. When Billie Holiday says "easy" you know what "easy" is, or when she says "hard" you know what is meant by "hard."

Arthur Herzog, Jr. wrote the words to two of Holiday's most famous songs, *God Bless The Child* and *Don't Explain*. Herzog: "Billie learned songs by rote. When she recorded *Don't Explain* she mixed the lyrics of the first and second version. So

when the sheet music came out, happily we had already altered it to conform to the record."

According to pianist Jimmie Rowles, Holiday's long time accompanist: "It was Lester Young who named her 'Lady Day.' Anyone who knew Young knew that he spoke his own language so no one ever asked him why ... everyone, including Billie, just accepted it. As her name was an original so was she. Her uniqueness lay in her interpretation of a lyric. She told the story and that's what music is all about." The influence of "Lady Day" on

LEFT: Happier times for Billie, in 1948, at the Club Ebony with dancer Bill Robinson. The occasion . . . his 70th birthday. Mr. "Bojangles" Robinson was born in 1878 and died in 1949.

BOTTOM: Billie packing to go on the road for concert tours in early 50's.

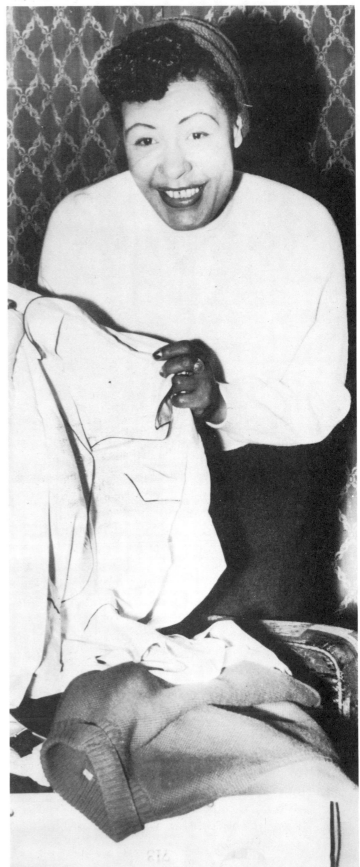

UPI

UPI

TOP: "Lady Day" as she looked circa 1950.

BOTTOM: Billie in recording studio. Circa 1960

TOP: Billie, and her pet dog, leaving Philadelphia court where she was released on bail for narcotic charges in 1956.

music and especially singers will never cease.

A few days after her last appearance at a benefit concert in Manhattan's Phoenix Theatre she was taken to Metropolitan Hospital. She was arrested on her death-bed. In those days under U.S. law narcotic addiction was a crime—not an illness.

BILLIE HOLIDAY
Died: July 7, 1959, New York, New York

Billie's casket being carried into New York church for a solemn requiem mass. Fifth from left standing is pianist, Teddy Wilson and fourth from right standing is Benny Goodman. Juanita Hall of "South Pacific" fame is at the right at the bottom of the steps.

BILLIE HOLIDAY

AWARDS

1944 *Esquire* Magazine Poll of Experts: Gold Award

1945 *Esquire* Magazine Poll of Experts: Silver Award
Metronome Magazine Readers' Poll: Best Female Singer

1946 *Esquire* Magazine Poll of Experts: Silver Award
Metronome Magazine Readers' Poll: Best Female Singer

1947 *Esquire* Magazine Poll of Experts: Gold Award

GRAMMY AWARD (Posthumous)

1977 Hall of Fame Award — "Strange Fruit" (released 1939) (Commodore)

FILM

1947 NEW ORLEANS — United Artists with Dorothy Patrick, Irene Rich, Louis Armstrong, Woody Harman

BROADWAY PLAY

1936 STARS OVER BROADWAY (revue)

Alvarado Street, one of the oldest in downtown Los Angeles, 1965.

"The Sixties and The Seventies"

Boundless fame. Blinding wealth. Bewildered identity.

Orange groves became freeways. Avocado pits became household plants.

Car hops were replaced by hop heads. Barbituate beauties and cocaine Charlies cavorted. Clandestine cuties came out of the closet.

Studio gates banged shut as they fell prey to television. Record companies mushroomed as hopefuls made track; double track, quadruple track, multiple track. Backtrack: Some made it, some didn't. Some could handle it, some copped out.

Cult figures cut deep into the countryside. Groupies joined the ranks along with the fans. America's new royalty was born.

The Harbor Freeway now cuts through downtown Los Angeles, 1974.

UPI

Young, beautiful, and smiling Marilyn Monroe. She was proudest of her flawless teeth. Circa 1950

Marilyn Monroe

Born: June 1, 1926, Los Angeles, California

Norma Jean Mortensen later Norma Jeane Baker acquired her names through her mother's past. Gladys Monroe Baker Mortensen was first married to Baker, had two children, whom Baker took with him when he divorced Gladys. Mortensen, an itinerant Danish bread-baker with a penchant for motorcycles, had been one of Gladys' bedmates—apparently she had a succession of them while working as a negative film cutter at RKO—and it was his name she put on Marilyn's birth certificate. Six months later her mother, Della, Marilyn's grandmother, had her baptized Norma Jeane Baker. The family had a long history of mental illness. Both grandparents had undergone treatment, an uncle committed suicide, and Gladys, shortly after Norma Jeane's birth, was sent to an institution. And so the story of Marilyn's tragic upbringing begins.

She became a ward of the court and for years was farmed out by the County Welfare Agencies. Foster parents received $20.00 per month per child and in one home Marilyn saw thirteen foster brothers and sisters come and go. In another home she was molested by an elderly man, who gave her a nickel "not to tell." When she did tell, she was severely punished for "making up a story about such a fine man." Her mother was released for a short time, took Marilyn back to live with her, but was recommitted. Again Marilyn was sent to an orphanage, where she earned nickels and dimes by washing dishes and toilets. At age eleven she was rescued by a close friend of her mother's, Grace Mc Kee Goddard. She sent the little girl to live with an aunt, Ana Lower, in Sawtelle, a Los Angeles slum. Again, Mrs. Goddard rescued her, and took her to live in her home, where Marilyn stayed for five years. This was the only time she had any security, but the die had been cast: Her life had no real structure, she was beset with hostility, anxiety, insecurity, and moral confusion. Throughout her life she searched for answers within herself and through others. The answer to her fears and her pain she found through pills and alcohol.

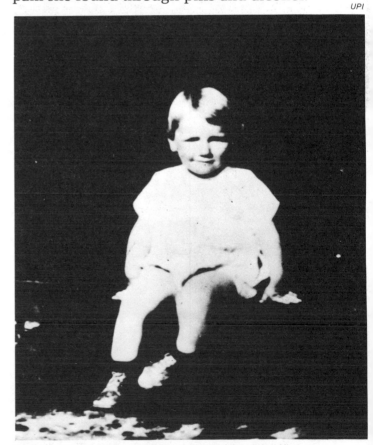

Born Norma Jeane Mortensen Baker the world watched the . . .

137

mutation of Marilyn Monroe.

She left high school in her junior year, because the Goddards were moving to West Virginia without her. In an attempt to save Marilyn from another orphanage Mrs. Goddard arranged a marriage with a neighbor's boy, James Dougherty. They were married in 1942. He went overseas in the Merchant Marine and she went to work at the Radio Plane Corporation's defense plant. David Conover, a photographer for *Yank*, spotted Marilyn and chose her as one of his subjects. She loved to pose, photographed like a dream, began to spend all of Jim's money on clothes and cosmetics, and left the plant when she found a job at The Blue Book Model Agency. Now her life began to turn around. Within a few years she had divorced Jim, had made a name for herself as a model, had appeared on the cover of every major magazine in the United States, and had posed for the famous calendar "nude" shot. In 1949, Tom Kelly, in need of one more picture to fill an assignment, remembered his poor neighbor, Marilyn, who agreed to pose. The original calendar was auctioned off in 1975 at Sotheby Parke Bernet for an estimated price of $200.00 listed under "Important 19th and 20th Century Photographs." Marilyn received $50.00 for posing and Kelly $400.00 for the total assignment.

Marilyn loved to pose and was a photographer's dream. 1951

Famous calendar nude shot of Marilyn for which she received a fee of fifty dollars. 1949

Tom Kelly

Her film appearances had been only minor ones and by 1948 Marilyn had gone from a minor contract with Fox to what she hoped would be a major one with Columbia. She had also gone from a failed romance with vocal coach, Fred Karger, to her first suicide attempt. Her lead in a B picture, *Ladies of the Chorus,* shot in just eleven days, made the studio sit up and take notice. Arthur Hornblow, Jr. cast her in *Asphalt Jungle,* her first big break. Hornblow: "She arrived on the set scared to death and dressed as a cheap tart." Marilyn had the quality that "touched the heart, evoked tenderness, made the blood race, and stirred the senses. This can only be found in a juvenile delinquent." She had it all. From *Asphalt Jungle* until her death, the world witnessed the mutation of Norma Jeane Mortensen Baker Dougherty to Marilyn Monroe.

Marilyn and Jane Russell appeared together in "Gentlemen Prefer Blondes." Shown here, Russell displays another talent as she sketches Monroe. 1952

Marilyn and Jane Russell put their footprints, and signatures, side-by-side in cement outside of Grauman's Chinese Theatre in Hollywood. Despite what columnists tried to say, both blondes said they enjoyed working together and felt no animosity. Shown here, two fans examine Monroe's hand prints. 1962

She met Joe Di Maggio on a blind date while filming *Monkey Business.* The Yankee Clipper was thirty-eight, divorced, and had a twelve year old son. They were married in San Francisco in January '54. Their life was complicated first, by geography, Joe had business in San Francisco, and second, by her fame as the Sex Goddess of the World. Part of her wanted to settle down, but the other part, that wanted fame and acceptance, won out. *Seven Year Itch* not only blew her skirt sky high (the famous shot of Marilyn wearing a backless white dress standing over a sidewalk grating, while a portable blower blasted away) it blew her marriage away, too. She turned to the study of acting, maybe at first as therapy, later it became an obsession with her . . . she was determined to be a real professional, a good actress. She joined the Actors Studio under the leadership of Lee Strasberg and his wife, Paula . . . both of whom remained her closest friends and teachers throughout her life. Although she had grossed $25,000,000 for Fox by 1953, she left and formed her own company with

friend and photographer, Milton Greene,
Marilyn Monroe Productions. Marilyn
Monroe had become an actress. Later
when she made *Some Like It Hot*, it became a classic. Without her that film
would have been just another picture.

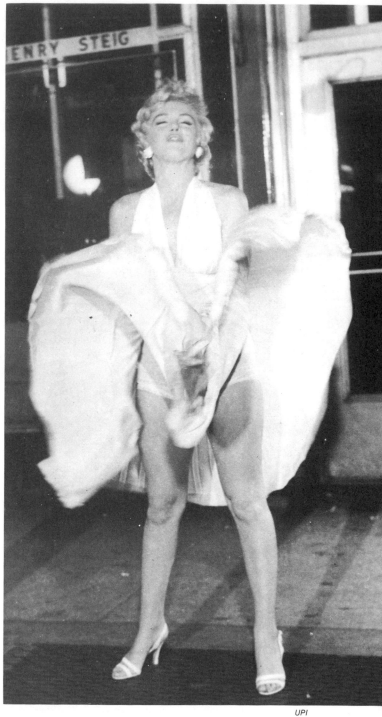

UPI

Marilyn's skirt blows in a scene from "The Seven Year
Itch" and her marriage to Joe Di Maggio blew
away at the same time. 1954

UPI

Marilyn weds second husband Joe Di Maggio in San
Francisco. 1954

An emotional Marilyn after plans for divorce from DiMaggio were announced. 1954

Marilyn back at work after divorce from DiMaggio. Shown here with news commentator, Edward R. Murrow, prior to taping for his famous TV show "PERSON TO PERSON." 1955

She worked hard in New York with the Strasbergs. She gave sensitive performances that knocked the other students out. She knew she would no longer be "that shallow movie star with the great body." She met and married playwright, Arthur Miller, in June 1956. Fresh from her huge success in *Bus Stop*, she and Miller went to London, where she started work on *The Prince and The Showgirl* with Sir Laurence Olivier. But several things began to happen. Miller was quickly getting caught up in the hectic, complicated, frenzied and very public life of his wife. She fell prey to Olivier's hate of "Method" acting. She began to lose confidence, her schedule had to fit her absorption of pills, she relied heavily on Paula Strasberg, she yearned for children and a home life, and yet she kept on working. Their life was one of confusion, appearances, drugs, photographs, drinking, more drugs, and finally divorce in January 1961.

(L to R) Marilyn with film stars Lauren Bacall and Betty Grable in "How To Marry a Millionaire" released in 1953. Betty Grable died in 1973.

Courtesy of Doug McClelland

Back to work Marilyn sings "After You Get What You Want, You Don't Want It," written for her by Irving Berlin for film, "There's No Business Like Show Business," released 1954.

UPI

144

A distraught Marilyn suffering from too many drugs and too much alcohol. Despite her self-assured air, she could come apart in seconds.

Top: Marilyn and photographer/friend Milton Greene formed the Marilyn Monroe Productions Company. Greene was named Vice-President. After a 14-month absence Marilyn returned to Hollywood . . . all smiles. 1956

Bottom: Marilyn chats with producer/writer/director Billy Wilder during a break while filming "Some Like It Hot." In one scene where Tony Curtis was eating chicken legs, rumors ran rampant about 42 takes because Marilyn flubbed her lines This adds up to 42 chicken legs for Curtis. 1958

Marilyn and third husband playwright Arthur Miller. Said Miller: "— —marriage to Monroe would be theatrically equal to five new works by Tennessee Williams."

Marilyn and husband Arthur Miller with his parents, Mr. and Mrs. Isidore Miller. 1956

Marilyn had a huge success in "Bus Stop." Shown here with co-star Arthur O'Connell.

Marilyn and Sir Laurence Olivier kiss on screen for "The Prince and The Showgirl" but off screen Marilyn and Sir Laurence didn't hit it off . . . he had no use for Method acting, as taught by the Strasbergs, at Actors Studio. 1956

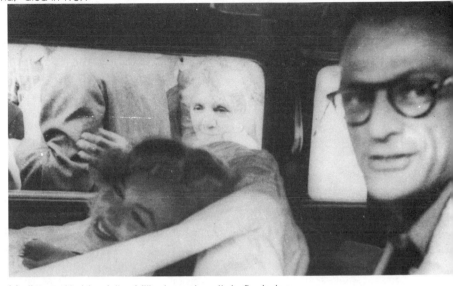

Marilyn with husband Arthur Miller in foreground and Sir Laurence Olivier and wife, Vivien Leigh. Miss Leigh, who won an "Oscar" for her performance in 1939 as Scarlett O'Hara in "Gone With the Wind," died in 1967.

Courtesy of Doug McClelland

Marilyn and hubby Arthur Miller leave hospital after losing their baby through a miscarriage in 1957.

While co-starring with Yves Montand in *Let's Make Love*, that's what they did . . . a brief love affair. When it aborted she went to work on *The Misfits* with Clark Gable written by Arthur Miller. This was her last completed film. She started work on *Something's Gotta Give* with co-star Dean Martin, but was fired. Dean Martin had the right to approve his co-star and his choice was Marilyn. He had nothing against replacement Lee Remick, but he had signed to do a picture with Monroe and when she was fired, he quit. The film cost the studio an untold amount of money, it was shelved eventually, and the firing of Monroe cost her more rejection and more insecurity, neither one could she handle. Even in one scene of the picture, her insecurity reared its head when playing a mother, who had not seen her children for years, and was not welcomed by them when she returned, Marilyn wanted the script rewritten: She wanted the children to be enchanted by her before they even knew she was their mother.

Monroe and Gable in their last picture, "The Misfits." Clark Gable died in November of 1960, at the age of 59, having been a top box office drawing card for more than two decades. 1960

Marilyn and co-star Yves Montand, "Let's Make Love," her next to last film. They were rumored to have had a romance, but Montand went back to his wife, actress Simone Signoret. 1960

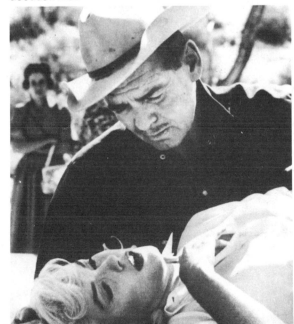

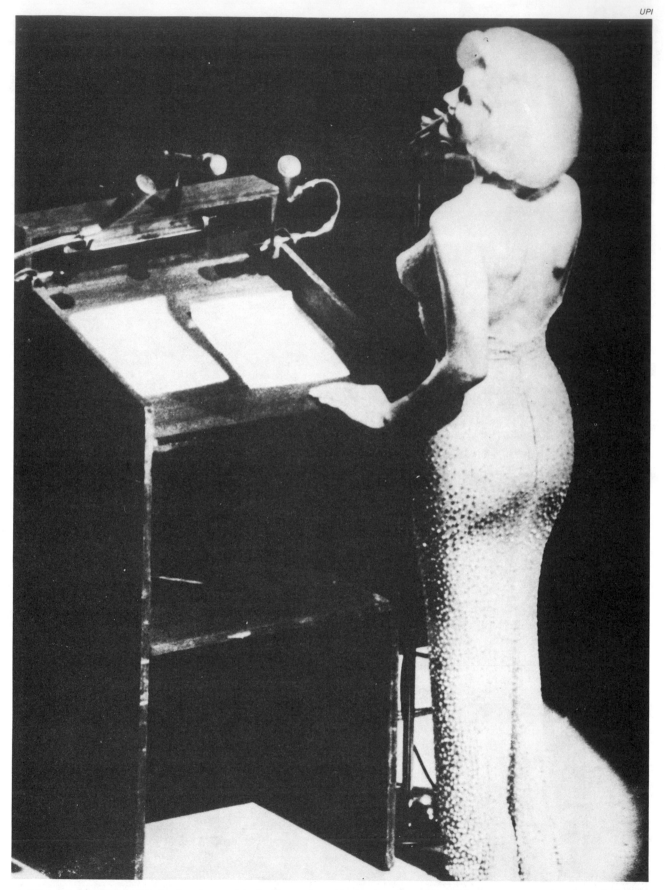

Just three months before her death, a happy Marilyn flew to New York to sing Happy Birthday to President Kennedy, at Madison Square Garden. After hearing her rendition the President said: "I can now retire from politics after having Happy Birthday sung to me by Miss Monroe." The President's brother-in-law, Peter Lawford, was supposed to have thought up the idea of having Marilyn sing. 1962

One of the last pictures taken of Marilyn as she appeared in public holding hands with Mexican writer, Jose Bolanos, at a Hollywood party. 1962

A lot of mystery surrounded her death. Did she try to call for help, did she deliberately take her own life, were the rumors about her involvement with the Kennedys true? What was true was: her involvement with Joe Di Maggio. They remained good friends and it was he who took over her funeral arrangements. Her friend and doctor, Ralph R. Greenson, made the definitive statement: "Marilyn Monroe died of an accidental overdose of barbiturates." Her dear friend, Lee Strasberg, delivered the eulogy. Her estate paid to keep her mother in a private sanitarium. Twice a week, six red roses are delivered to her crypt ordered by Joe Di Maggio. Carl Sandburg's statement: "She was more sinned against than sinning."

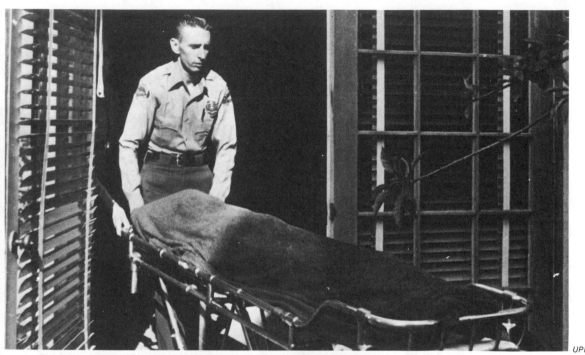

UPI

The body of Marilyn Monroe is removed to the morgue in Hollywood, Calif., after the actress was found dead in her home.

UPI

Marilyn Monroe's little dog, Moff, being led out of her house after she was found dead in her bedroom.

Joe DiMaggio and Joe DiMaggio, Jr. (in Marine uniform) walk across cemetery behind the hearse carrying the body of Marilyn Monroe. Joe, Sr. made all of the funeral arrangements. She came into the world tragically and she left the same way.

But the greatest truth probably came from Marilyn herself: "I always felt insecure and in the way—but most of all I felt scared. I guess I wanted love more than anything else in the world."

MARILYN MONROE
Died: August 5, 1962,
Los Angeles, California

MARILYN MONROE

1926 - 1962

Joe DiMaggio ordered six roses, twice a week, to be placed in the vase on his former wife's crypt . . . to be placed there forever.

MARILYN MONROE FILMS

1948 SCUDDA HOO! SCUDDA HAY! — 20th Century-Fox
with Lon McCallister

1948 DANGEROUS YEARS — 20th Century-Fox
with William Halop, Ann E. Todd, Jerome Cowan, Daryl Hickman

1948 LADIES OF THE CHORUS — Columbia
with Adele Jergens

1950 A TICKET TO TOMAHAWK — 20th Century-Fox
with Dan Dailey, Ann Baxter, Rory Calhoun

1950 THE FIREBALL — 20th Century-Fox
with Mickey Rooney, Pat O'Brien

1950 RIGHT CROSS — MGM
with Ricardo Montalban, Lionel Barrymore, June Allyson, Dick Powell

1950 LOVE HAPPY — United Artists-Mary Pickford
with The Marx Brothers, Ilona Massey, Raymond Burr

1950 THE ASPHALT JUNGLE — MGM
with Louis Calhern

1950 ALL ABOUT EVE — MGM
with Bette Davis, Ann Baxter, George Sanders, Gary Merrill

3951 HOME TOWN STORY — MGM
with Marjorie Reynolds, Jeffrey Lynn

1951 LOVE NEST — 20th Century-Fox
with William Lundigan, June Haver, Jack Paar

1951 AS YOUNG AS YOU FEEL — 20th Century-Fox
with Monty Woolley

1951 LET'S MAKE IT LEGAL — 20th Century-Fox
with Claudette Colbert, MacDonald Carey, Zachary Scott

1952 CLASH BY NIGHT — RKO
with Barbara Stanwyck, Paul Douglas, Robert Ryan, Keith Andes

1952 WE'RE NOT MARRIED — 20th Century-Fox
with David Wayne

1952 DON'T BOTHER TO KNOCK — 20th Century-Fox
with Richard Widmark, Anne Bancroft

1952 MONKEY BUSINESS — 20th Century-Fox
with Cary Grant, Ginger Rogers, Charles Coburn

1952 O. HENRY'S FULL HOUSE (The Cop and the Anthem) — 20th Century-Fox
with Charles Laughton

1953 NIAGARA — 20th Century-Fox
with Joseph Cotten, Richard Allan

1953 GENTLEMEN PREFER BLONDES — 20th Century-Fox
with Jane Russell

1953 HOW TO MARRY A MILLIONAIRE — 20th Century-Fox
with Betty Grable, Lauren Bacall, David Wayne, Rory Calhoun

1954 RIVER OF NO RETURN — 20th Century-Fox
with Robert Mitchum, Rory Calhoun

1954 THERE'S NO BUSINESS LIKE SHOW BUSINESS — 20th Century-Fox
with Ethel Merman, Dan Dailey, Donald O'Connor, Mitzi Gaynor

1955 THE SEVEN YEAR ITCH — 20th Century-Fox
with Tom Ewell

1956 BUS STOP — 20th Century-Fox
with Don Murray

1957 THE PRINCE AND THE SHOWGIRL — Warner Bros.-Marilyn Monroe-L.O.P. Productions
with Laurence Olivier, Sybil Thorndike

1959 SOME LIKE IT HOT — United Artists-Mirisch-Ashton
with Tony Curtis, Jack Lemmon, George Raft, Joe E. Brown

1960 LET'S MAKE LOVE — 20th Century-Fox
with Yves Montand

1961 THE MISFITS — United Artists Seven Arts-John Huston
with Clark Gable, Montgomery Clift, Eli Wallach

POSTHUMOUS

1963 MARILYN — biography

SAM: Sexy and Soulful COOKE: Contained and Contagious 1964.

Sam Cooke

Born: January 22, 1935, Chicago, Illinois.

His father, Charles Cooke, was a Baptist minister and it was in his church that Sam Cooke became a gospel singer. He attended Wendell Phillips High in Chicago, and there he sang in a group called The Highway Q.C. Sam was one of eight children, one brother also sang in the Highway group.

At age 20 he replaced R. H. Harris as lead singer for the Soul Stirrers . . . one of the most popular gospel groups. Cooke stayed with the group for six years, travelling back and forth across the country. Later he became the lead singer with another group, the Pilgrim Travellers, who spawned and boasted of another fine singer, Lou Rawls. Unlike many gospel-oriented singers, Cooke always retained complete vocal control, he did not get carried away. But he did get carried away from the limitations of the stirring of the soul audiences to the swimming in the stream of the boundless pop music industry.

Under the name of Dale Cooke, with a guitar under his arm, he recorded *Lovable* for the Specialty Label. Specialty had recorded the Soul Stirrers, so Cooke was no stranger to Art Rupe, head of Specialty. But Cooke's new image was a stranger, and Rupe rejected what he heard, calling it "bleached." Rupe missed the boat, for when the single release, *You Send Me*, came out in 1957 it sold over a million copies. Sam's brother, L. C. Cooke, was the composer, Keen, a new label, was the recipient, Bumps Blackwell was the producer, and friend, J. W. Alexander, was the brain behind the Cooke experiment. Alexander had witnessed Cooke's mesmerizing of the black groups, secluded as they were, and asked himself: "Why not

the white pop public?" He was right . . . Cooke took the purity of his church music, the purpose of his being, his personality and good looks, snapped his fingers while he tapped his feet and popped into "pop."

RCA Records

Cooke paved the way for the explosion of soul singers in the sixties.

In 1960, he became the first major black singer to sign with RCA Records. Calypso singer, Harry Belafonte, was there, but it was a gamble for both Cooke and RCA to see if they could permeate the pop market. His second release for RCA, *Chain Gang*, in October '57 hit the top 40, and by October '58 Cooke had won worldwide acclaim. He remained at the top until his death, although the purity of soul music had to wait for Otis Redding, and Aretha Franklin, to be put on the charts. Cooke never forsook his gospel/blues training, he just explored his soul and then exploited it. For example, the first time he appeared in New York City no one had heard of him, so the next time he made certain the whole city would know he was there. Working at the Copacabana (June '64) he announced it, by having a reproduction of his head hoisted in Times Square, at a cost of $10,000 a month, which read: "Sam, The Biggest Cooke In Town." During a performance at the Copa, Sam quipped to a customer: "I don't mind if you eat (during the show) but chew in my direction." Once Sam found his direction, it was straight ahead.

Wide World

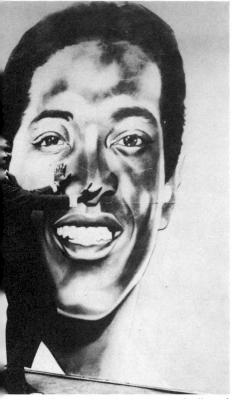

Cooke checking out reproduction of his head which was raised in Times Square . . . 1964.

Cooke as he looked in his appearance in New York's famous Copacabana . . . 1964.

Other black artists might have dreamed about starting their companies, but Sam Cooke did it. He founded his publishing company, Kags Music and his own record company, Sar/Derby. Among his discoveries, along with discovering that he was becoming a black capitalist, were the Womack Brothers, Billy Preston, Johnnie Taylor, and the aforementioned great, Lou Rawls.

RCA took a chance and it paid off. Cooke became world famous and one of the first black capitalists in his field. Cooke shown here during recording session. Circa 1962.

He married his high school sweetheart, Barbara Campell, in 1959, in Los Angeles. They had three children, one of whom drowned in their swimming pool, at the age of four years, in June of 1964.

His death was mysterious, unsavory, and never fully explained. He picked up a girl, Elisa Boyer, at a party and offered her a lift home. Instead he took her to a Los Angeles motel, registered as Mr. and Mrs. Cooke, forced her to the room and then tore off her clothes. Supposedly, while Cooke was in the bathroom, Miss Boyer grabbed his clothes and ran out to call the police. The motel manager, Bertha Franklin, reported that Cooke (dressed only in a jacket and shoes) banged on her apartment door demanding to know the whereabouts of Miss Boyer and when Mrs. Franklin did not open the door, Cooke knocked it down. She reported that he assaulted her and then she shot him three times. Apparently the shots only wounded him, then Mrs. Franklin testified that when he came at her again, she clubbed him with a stick-like weapon. He was dead when the police arrived.

LEFT: First she shot him 3 times and then clubbed him to death. Bertha Lee Franklin, manager of the Los Angeles motel, was not held in the fatal shooting of Cooke.

BOTTOM: (l) Wearing sunglasses Bertha Franklin, motel manager, who shot Cooke. Death was ruled 'Justifiable' at coroner's inquest. (2nd row right) Barbara Cooke, widow of the singer.

Wide World

Wide World

Cooke's body was returned to Chicago for burial. Hundreds filled both chapels at the Leak Funeral Home, while thousands pushed and shoved outside, to get a last look at their hero . . . to the black population he *had* become their hero: A graduate of the gospel circuit, with a Ph.D. in pop, and summa cum laude for lifestyle.

SAM COOKE
Died: December 11, 1964, Los Angeles, California

SAM COOKE

R & B (Rhythm & Blues) records at the time Cooke was recording seldom crossed over into the pop field, where million-sellers were made; nevertheless, at least 28 of his singles hit the *Billboard* Pop Music Chart, including:

YEAR OF RELEASE	TITLE (and Label)	POSITION ON CHARTS	
		R & B	POP
1957	YOU SEND ME (Keen)	1	1
1959	EVERYBODY LIKES TO CHA CHA CHA (Keen)	2	31
1960	WONDERFUL WORLD (Keen)	2	12
1960	CHAIN GANG (RCA Victor)	2	2
1962	TWISTIN' THE NIGHT AWAY (RCA Victor)	1	9
1962	BRING IT ON HOME TO ME/HAVIN' A PARTY (RCA Victor)	2	13
1962	NOTHING CAN CHANGE THIS LOVE/SOMEBODY HAVE MERCY (RCA Victor)	2	12
1963	SEND ME SOME LOVIN' (RCA Victor)	2	13
1963	ANOTHER SATURDAY NIGHT (RCA Victor)	1	10
1965	SHAKE/A CHANGE IS GONNA COME (RCA Victor)	2	7

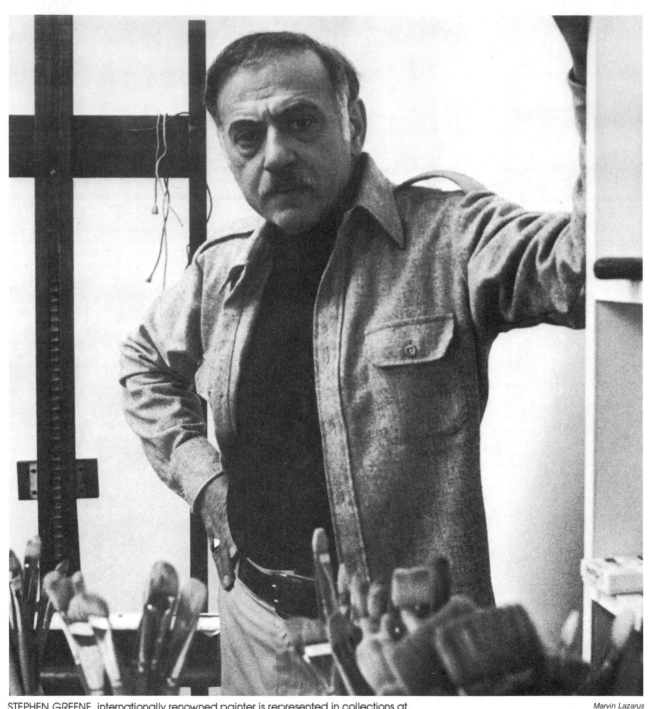

STEPHEN GREENE, internationally renowned painter is represented in collections at the Metropolitan Museum, Guggenheim Museum, Museum of Modern Art, Whitney Museum, all in NYC and the Tate Gallery, London. He currently exhibits at the Marilyn Pearl Gallery in NYC.

Marvin Lazarus

by
Stephen Greene

Of the many artists who used Marilyn Monroe as a central figure in particular works, the one of Marilyn Monroe in the collection of the Museum of Modern Art, N.Y.C., is the most revealing. It is by Andy Warhol. What Warhol does is emblazon vulgarity to the idea of the icon. He takes what is the grotesqueness of our myths,

160

Continued on page 169

Color photography did not come into its own until after World War II. George Eastman introduced "kodachrome" in 1935, but it wasn't until 1942 that "kodacolor" appeared. Photographs in color prior to that time had been hand-tinted. Although George Gershwin appears in the color section, it will be noted that the color portrayal is a reproduction of a painting, not a photograph, as Mr. Gershwin died in 1937.

Marilyn Monroe is depicted by a reproduction of artist Andy Warhol, although many color photographs of the star are available. Her attraction to leading artists of the time remains unique. Never before in the history of radio, stage, screen, or television has a star been immortalized by so many great artists and sculptors.

Andy Warhol's "Marilyn Monroe Diptych" detail done in 1962.

Courtesy of Leo Castelli Gallery
From the collection of Mr. and Mrs. Burton Tremaine

George Gershwin, an artist himself, seated at his easel with a collage of his Broadway shows behind him.

Courtesy of Hancock Life Insurance Co. via UPI.
Painting by Carroll Jones

Judy Garland: "Part waif, part woman, all heart."

Montgomery Clift and friend, Elizabeth Taylor, who said: "He was my brother — he was my dearest friend."

Jimi Hendrix during a ``live'' performance in Los Angeles in the mid-sixties.   *John R. Adler*

Jack Cassidy and his wife of eighteen years, Shirley Jones.

Wide World

particularly in the case of Marilyn Monroe as "star" and returns this item of worship to us as a distasteful glory, glamorized and packaged in advertising techniques. The cheap and the tawdry are returned enshrined.

The painting is composed at first glance like an Albers, rectangle within a rectangle, and the difference comes with the large surrounding space being gold color and the small rectangle center top is of Marilyn Monroe, silk screened, in glaring florescent like colors. Again, this is the movie star as an icon, a manner relating to the use of popular subject matter, a form of Americana so prevalent in American Art of the Sixties. Movie stars are often referred to as American royalty . . . and in this case the "royalty" is given an aura of vulgarity as in de Kooning's *Marilyn Monroe*.

Willem de Kooning's *Marilyn Monroe* was so titled well after the original image was conceived but it still remains as the source of an attitude taken up by Pop artists, that of a gargantuan breasted woman painted in a seemingly Dionysian frenzy that established the Bosch-like hell of certain cultural aspects of American society.

I went with Frank Stella to the opening of *The Misfits* at the Capitol Theatre, even though I had seen the film earlier at a private screening. The producer, Frank Taylor, was a friend. Like many painters, I was curious about Marilyn Monroe. I even had Frank Taylor promise to introduce me to her, which he was to do at an intended party for her after the opening. The party did not occur, apparently she was deeply upset about the breakup of her marriage to Arthur Miller. The more important thing for me was actually seeing her at the theatre. She came down the aisle on the arm of Montgomery Clift and it was an incredible apparition. One, she seemed lit up, an aura surrounding her as if she were a statue of a madonna being brought down a church aisle during a special religious holiday in a country other than ours. Two, the tight black dress, scalloped neckline, the somewhat pouting lips, and obvious

sexual desirability of this woman added a strong dash of possible cheapness . . . and with all that the look of a child, absolutely innocent. What a spectacular combination! Success and the forlorn cheap failure. Could this be in any way American? Vulgarity and getting aheadness? Ernest Hemingway committed suicide. F. Scott Fitzgerald did it in his way by drink and such. Later, in our time, Mark Rothko cuts his wrists, Jackson Pollock had his suicidal drunken accident and there are unproven questions about David Smith's accidental death. Frank Stella and I sat two rows behind Marilyn Monroe and I was drawn to watching her more than the movie, which is a pretentious bit of heavy thinking: The killing of horses for the manufacture of dog food does not make an exciting or valid symbol of man's inhumanity as handled by Arthur Miller. By the end of the movie Marilyn was in some sort of state of distress. She left with Clift, her head on his shoulder, and almost carried out to a side exit as if she were in mourning or as a sick child.

So then, like many painters/artists, we do very much want that bitch success and perhaps Marilyn Monroe, for a while, epitomized that need in all its vulnerability and questionable outcome. Possibly we do not sufficiently value success in work as a value in itself and unfortunately expect it to pay off well in our lives . . . and it didn't in Marilyn Monroe's case. The latter, too, may be part of cheap myths.

I find it difficult to think of the self-inflicted wounds or deaths of stars without recalling Judy Garland. Later Garland, like Marilyn Monroe, epitomized an engratiating vulnerability and a myth-like ability to overcome endless odds, at least, for quite a while. Garland made endless comebacks, rising phoenix-like to reconquer her world but finally it was a myth, destroyed by the reality that life forces cannot endlessly be rejuvenated within one individual and that flirtation with failure may also eventually bring with it the final embrace of failure.

Young Montgomery Clift, age 30—1954.

Montgomery Clift

Born: October 17, 1920, Omaha, Nebraska

Edward Montgomery Clift was born at home after the arrival of his twin sister, Roberta. There was an older brother, Brooks, who had preceded them by eighteen months. "Monty," as he was known to friends and family, was not only the baby of the family but the beauty of the family: A combination that was to work for and against him all of his life. For it was Monty who was pampered, sheltered, and adored by his mother, Ethel "Sunny" Fogg Clift.

Sunny was born out of wedlock in Philadelphia, Pennsylvania in 1888. The doctor who delivered her, Edward Montgomery, was responsible for placing her in a foster home when she was a year old. But the doctor was acquainted with the true facts of her past and before she entered Cornell University, at the age of eighteen, he revealed all he knew: she had been born of two parents with a long lineage in the south; the father's family name was Blair; the mother's family name was Anderson. Sunny spent her entire life, in vain, trying to gain acceptance by both families, and what energy was left over was spent raising her children as if they were born of royalty. Tutors were hired instead of regular schooling and the children were much more at home in a rented villa in Europe than they were in a two room Greenwich Village walkup; a condition forced on the Clifts during the depression. Their lives consisted of luxury usually way beyond the means of their father and of a delusive social position way beyond the family's position; the latter a product of Sunny's desires.

Sunny was aided and abetted in her *raison d'être* by her husband William Clift, whom she met at Cornell, and later mar-

ried in 1914. She confided in him the secret about her past, gained his support as she searched for her own family, and was allowed to spend his money on the rather absurd upbringing of the children. By 1924 the family had moved to Chicago from Omaha, where William Clift, in the banking business, finally made a lot of money; money that was to enable Sunny Clift to travel and raise her family as aristocrats. Except for the stock market crash in the thirties, the Clift family managed to find a way to further Sunny's wishes. Thus began the strange saga of filmdom's even stranger star, Montgomery Clift.

Monty gave his first performance at the age of eight, in a villa, before an audience that was comprised of his mother, tutor, and nurse. By the time he was twelve he had developed his love of acting, and in his thirteenth year, he arrived on Broadway, via summer stock, in a play, *Fly Away Home*. Even at such a tender age Monty had no fear of the stage and none when performing in front of people. He began at an early age to be involved with and fascinated by the intracacies of acting and remained so throughout his career. Almost everything he did or every character he portrayed was researched thoroughly. He tried to walk in the character's shoes, not just the writer's head. He grew up in and around the New York theatre, which allowed him exposure to the finest artists of that time, many of whom became lifelong friends. The actors and actresses with whom he appeared on the stage comprise a list of Who's Who in the Theatre: Frederic March, Florence Eldridge, Tallulah Bankhead, Sydney Greenstreet, Thomas Mitchell, Kevin McCarthy and Jessie

Royce Landis, plus many others.

He dropped his formal education to study acting, music, or anything else related to his craft. He read a lot, kept a journal, kept pretty much to himself . . . lonely perhaps, confused for certain. He had been raised in a cocoon complete with silk spun by his mother and as he emerged he followed the silkworm's habit of feeding off of others; not in the parasitic sense, but more like a barnacle. He would cling to what or to whom he thought to be his. His attachments, as well as his strong transferences, to people are well documented in Patricia Bosworth's biography.* Alfred Lunt and his wife Lynn Fontanne, whom he regarded as surrogate parents, are but one example. Despite this, he learned a lot about his craft from them, which became apparent when he appeared in *There Shall Be No Night* on Broadway in April of 1940. For a long time it was thought that he emulated Lunt in his performances and style of acting. But Clift did emerge very much himself on the stage and in films. Although many offers from Hollywood were forthcoming, Clift stayed with the theatre through fourteen shows, a total of slightly more than ten years, before he was finally lured to the west coast. At the time he made his first film, he was a thoroughly groomed and an accomplished actor.

Wide World

Clift, Dennis King and Cornelia Otis Skinner in a scene from Lillian Hellman's play "The Searching Wind," which opened on Broadway April 12, 1944.

Wide World

Clift boards plane for London with pals actress Betsy Blair and dancer/actor Gene Kelly. Circa 1948

*Montgomery Clift: A biography, Harcourt Brace Jovanovich, Inc. New York City

172

His private life had been shaped by then, also. He was known to have men friends, lovers, and although he was constantly in the company of women, beautiful, talented, wealthy women, he had abandoned his AC-DC role for the homosexual route. His women friends, like his theatre friends, were another sort of "Who's Who" list: Most notable was his lifelong friendship with Elizabeth Taylor. He persisted in keeping his friends apart as a child will hide its best toys from a playmate. He had strong attachments to women like Libby Holman, Nancy Walker, Myrna Loy, his secretaries, his coach; many of whom seem to be mother figures. The ambivalence of breaking from Sunny, and yet always replacing her, was a strong motivating force behind Clift's behavior. His adult life role was as complex and varied as his early childhood and the battle against breaking with his mother had to contribute to his homosexuality, a role that seems to have plagued him and the one that he played out for as long as he lived. He tried many times to break with her, to get out from under her influence, but even when he finally moved into his own quarters, she was a constant presence with whom he had to reckon. His father, on the other hand, did not approve of his youngest son's actions or deeds and eventually they had a big contretemps when as a wealthy actor Monty never deferred to his father for advice in money matters; an area in which his father was well qualified.

Clift's first film was *Red River* with star John Wayne, released in 1948, and then immediately he went into *The Search* for director Fred Zinneman. *The Search* was a big success for Monty and "put his map on the map" so to speak. From then on it was one film after another and one huge salary increase after another. He had received about $60,000 for *Red River* but by the time he signed for *The Heiress,* which was released the following year with co-star, Olivia de Havilland, his salary was $100,000.

Never more beautiful than the way he looked as Morris Townsend in "The Heiress," released in October 1949.

Clift in "The Heiress" which co-starred Olivia de Havilland, and gave her a second Academy Award, 1949. At right actor Ralph Richardson.

Clift in "The Big Lift" 1950, filmed in West Berlin and Frankfort.

He was rejected by the army during World War II for chronic diarrhea and spent a couple of months in a hospital, trying to find a cure. His health continued to disintegrate, despite his efforts to maintain his good physical body, and by 1950 he had added allergies and colitis to his other chronic illnesses. He had by now a problem with pills and an even more severe drinking problem. He continued to make fine films, grew more dependent on alcohol, which resulted in some unfortunate scenes during filming and away from it. Eventually in 1954 he returned to Broadway in *The Seagull*. He had by then acquired a west coast surrogate family, Jeanne and Fred Greene, a coach Mira Rostova, dozens of new close friends and a second psychiatrist, Dr. William V. Silverberg, who treated him for about fourteen years. He had a big career, a lot of money, people who cared deeply for him, and yet he was tortured and persecuted by himself.

174

TOP: Shelly Winters and Clift in "A Place In The Sun," 1951. Charlie Chaplin said: "This is the greatest movie ever made about America." The film was adapted from Dreiser's book, "An American Tragedy."

Author's Collection

Wide World

MIDDLE: Clift receiving Italy's "Oscar" known as the "Silver Ribbon" for best actor of the year. Anna Magnani won the "Silver Ribbon" as best actress, but was not present. At left: Adriano Baracco, President of the Italian National Syndicate of Movie Newspapermen shown handing Clift the award. Rome, Italy November 1952.

BOTTOM: Co-stars Anne Baxter and Clift of "I Confess" greet Carmen Gingras (l) age 13 and Renee Hudon age 10, two French Canadian girls as they arrived in Hollywood to play acting roles in the film. The young girls were discovered in Quebec by director Alfred Hitchcock. Photo taken 1952, film opened in 1953.

Wide World

(l-r) Clift, Burt Lancaster, and Frank Sinatra in "From Here To Eternity." 1953. Joan Crawford quit and was replaced by Deborah Kerr. Sinatra was married to actress Ava Gardner at the time. Clift lost the "Oscar" to William Holden ("Stalag 17") but Sinatra won for Best Supporting Actor.

Courtesy of Doug McClelland

Clift met Elizabeth Taylor when he was twenty-nine and she a mere seventeen. He escorted her to the premiere of *The Heiress* as arranged by their studio, a commonplace promotion stunt for Hollywood. They were to co-star shortly afterward in *A Place In The Sun*, and for the time being certainly would star as the most beautiful couple in the world. But of all the roles Elizabeth Taylor played in Monty's life, her biggest part came the night of his almost fatal automobile accident, May of 1956. He wrapped his car around a tree shortly after leaving her home, where he had attended a small dinner party. His jaw had been completely shattered, his nose broken, and the rest of his face a bloody mass. He was also choking to death from two teeth lodged in his throat. It was Taylor who reached down and extracted them, allowing him to breathe normally. She did indeed save his life.

Wide World

TOP RIGHT: Seventeen-year-old Elizabeth Taylor adjusts the bow tie of her escort, Clift, as they arrive for the Hollywood première of "The Heiress." Taylor had just broken her engagement to William Paley, Jr., and before that, she was the girlfriend of All American football player Glenn Davis. October 1949.
BOTTOM: Puppy love or love of a puppy? Elizabeth Taylor and Clift, November 1949.

Wide World

Wide World

The wreckage of rented car that Clift drove into a power pole. Police officers question close friend Kevin McCarthy (right), about the West Los Angeles accident which occurred shortly after leaving the home of Elizabeth Taylor. May 1956.

Elizabeth Taylor and Clift in "A Place In The Sun," 1951. Film critic Andrew Sarris said: "Clift and Taylor were the most beautiful couple in the history of cinema."

Author's Collection

A meeting at Idlewild Airport, now known as Kennedy Airport. Elizabeth Taylor, her brother Howard, and Clift. Taylor and Clift denied any romantic attachment at the time. Circa 1951

Clift escorts Elizabeth Taylor to the Palace Theatre to see Judy Garland. New York City 1951.

But in the long run it was up to Clift to save his own life. He fought his way back to work and through work. He ultimately finished *Raintree County*, (the film was half-way through production when the accident occurred) and he went on to make eight more films before he died, some of which were his best. Whatever Montgomery Clift was in his personal life, professionally . . . he was a pro. He had to grapple with his new face, he had to face the camera, and then face "that new face" on film, and he did it. For he was at heart an actor, maybe a beautiful-faced-actor but he came into the world with the face, a fact he could not change. But the man became the actor.

Clift with Agnes Moorehead in "Raintree County," 1957. Miss Moorehead died in 1974 at the age of sixty-eight.

Wide World

TOP LEFT: Elizabeth Taylor and her husband, Mike Todd, arriving for the première of "Raintree County" in which she co-starred with Clift. Louisville, Kentucky, October 1957.

TOP RIGHT: Myrna Loy and Clift as they appeared in "Lonelyhearts" released March 1959. Rumors persisted about their love affair and some even hinted at marriage.

BOTTOM: Judy Garland and Clift as they appeared in "Judgment At Nuremberg" 1961.

Wide World

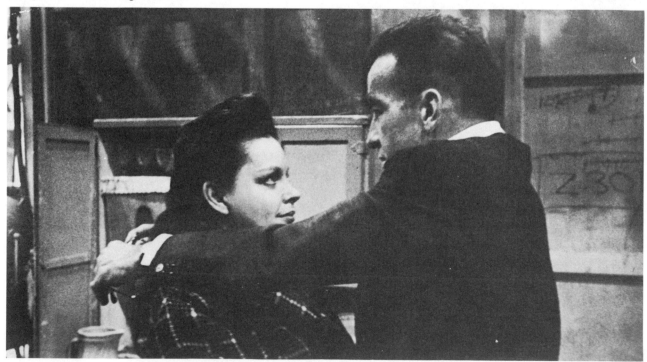

Author's Collection

He never overcame his alcoholism. He never beat his addiction to pills, nor his apparent guilt for homosexuality. After the accident he battled intense physical and emotional pain daily. He also battled Hollywood about his screen image and won. He always knew the kind of roles he was capable of playing; not the handsome slick leading man type they would have preferred. He knew what he wanted, fought for what he wanted, and won. As a human being, he shortchanged himself— but he never sold out in his profession.

Marilyn Monroe and Clift dining in San Francisco during the filming of "The Misfits" 1960. The film was released in 1961.

Wide World

Monroe's emotional and physical problems shut down production. Clift's drinking didn't help. Gable drank but for different reasons. Somehow the picture was finished . . . very overdue and a lot over the budget. "The Misfits" . . . released 1961.

As for the rest of his family his twin sister had married and lived in Texas. His brother Brooks married three times, which equalled the number of Academy Award nominations Monty had amassed. His father died in 1964, but not before a reconciliation after Monty's accident. Elizabeth Taylor went from one marriage to another, always returning to her brother-friend Monty for solace. Monty went from one drinking escapade to another. His mode of behavior was a constant source of sorrow and displeasure to those who loved him. Friends tried to look the other way, co-workers scorned him, he held up shooting on several films, and finally a law suit was brought against him for his behavior on the set of *Freud*. His tolerance for liquor was diminishing and with it, sullenness and depression were taking over. He had a disastrous relationship with a young Frenchman named Giles and when Giles was finally banished from the Clift abode, it was decided that Clift needed a keeper . . . someone to watch over him and take care of him. The job was competently filled by companion Lorenzo James, a college graduate with theatrical ambitions, who had not made the grade; to augment his income, James took care of ill persons. He managed very slowly to get Monty to be civil to his mother and he managed to get old friends to drop by. They began to fix up Monty's brownstone in New York, and Elizabeth Taylor finally convinced the studio to take a chance on Monty in her next film, *Reflections in a Golden Eye*. But time had run out for Montgomery Clift.

One morning in the early a.m., James found Clift lying on top of his bed, nude and dead. An autopsy report stated: "Mr. Clift died of occlusive coronary artery disease." The funeral was private and small. He was buried in Brooklyn in a Quaker cemetery. Elizabeth Taylor was not there but his mother, Sunny, and his sister Roberta were . . . as they had been at the beginning.

TOP: Pallbearers carry the casket bearing Monty Clift from the St. James Church in New York City. Only 150 people attended the private service as invitations were limited. July 1966.

BOTTOM LEFT: Mrs. Ethel "Sunny" Clift, mother and Brooks Clift, brother, of Monty Clift shown leaving the St. James Church after the service. New York July 1966.

MONTGOMERY CLIFT
Died: July 23, 1966, New York, New York

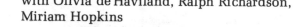

MONTGOMERY CLIFT
BROADWAY PLAYS

1935 FLY AWAY HOME, with Thomas Mitchell
1935 JUBILEE, with Melville Cooper, Mary Boland; Score: Cole Porter
1938 YOUR OBEDIENT HUSBAND, with Dame May Whitty, Fredric March
1938 EYE ON THE SPARROW, with Barry Sullivan, Katherine Deane
1938 THE WIND AND THE RAIN, with Celeste Holm
1938 DAME NATURE, with Jessie Royce Landis, Onslow Stevens
1939 THE MOTHER, with Alla Nazimova, Reginald Bach
1940 THERE SHALL BE NO NIGHT, with Alfred Lunt, Lynn Fontanne
1942 MEXICAN MURAL, with Libby Holman, Mira Rostova, David Opatoshu
1942 THE SKIN OF OUR TEETH, with Tallulah Bankhead, E. G. Marshall
1944 OUR TOWN, with Marc Connelly, Martha Scott, Evelyn Varden
1944 THE SEARCHING WIND, with Dudley Digges, Cornelia Otis Skinner
1945 FOXHOLE IN THE PARLOR, with Reginald Beane, Ann Lincoln
1945 YOU TOUCHED ME!, with Norah Howard, Edmund Gwenn
1954 THE SEAGULL, with Judith Evelyn, Kevin McCarthy, Mira Rostova

FILMS

1948 *THE SEARCH — MGM
with Aline McMahon, Wendell Corey
*Clift was nominated for an Academy Award
1948 RED RIVER — Howard Hawks-United Artists
with John Wayne, Joanne Dru, Walter Brennan
1949 THE HEIRESS — Paramount
with Olivia de Haviland, Ralph Richardson, Miriam Hopkins

1950 THE BIG LIFT — 20th Century-Fox
with Paul Douglas, Cornell Borchers
1951 *A PLACE IN THE SUN — Paramount
with Elizabeth Taylor, Shelley Winters
*Clift was nominated for an Academy Award
1953 I CONFESS — Warner Bros.
with Anne Baxter, Karl Malden, Brian Aherne

1953 *FROM HERE TO ETERNITY, Columbia
with Burt Lancaster, Donna Reed, Frank Sinatra, Deborah Kerr
*Clift was nominated for an Academy Award
1954 INDISCRETION OF AN AMERICAN WIFE — Vittorio De Sica-Columbia
with Jennifer Jones
1957 RAINTREE COUNTY — MGM
with Elizabeth Taylor, Eva Marie Saint
1958 THE YOUNG LIONS — 20th Century-Fox
with Marlon Brando, Dean Martin, Hope Lange
1959 LONELYHEARTS — Dore Schary-United Artists
with Robert Ryan, Myrna Loy, Maureen Stapleton
1959 SUDDENLY LAST SUMMER — Columbia
with Elizabeth Taylor, Katherine Hepburn
1960 WILD RIVER — Elia Kazan-20 Century-Fox
with Lee Remick, Jo Van Fleet
1961 THE MISFITS — Frank E. Taylor-United Artists
with Clark Gable, Marilyn Monroe, Eli Wallach
1961 *JUDGMENT AT NUREMBERG — Stanley Kramer-Roxlon-United Artists
with Spencer Tracy, Judy Garland, Burt Lancaster
*Clift was nominated for an Academy Award
1962 FREUD — Universal
with Susannah York, Larry Parks, Susan Kohner
1966 THE DEFECTOR — Raoul Levy-Seven Arts
with Hardy Kruger, Roddy McDowell, David Opatoshu

Clift's first three Academy Award nominations were for Best Performance by a leading man. The fourth was for Best Supporting Actor.

Lenny Bruce doing what his autobiography says, "How To Talk Dirty And Influence People," Circa 1963.

Wide World

Lenny Bruce

Born: October 13, 1925, Mineola, New York

Kenneth Tynan in his foreword to Lenny Bruce's biography* said: "Constant, abrasive irritation produces the pearl: it is a disease of the oyster. Similarly—according to the Gustave Flaubert—the artist is a disease of society. By the same token, Lenny Bruce is a disease of America." The Bruce pearl had a chronic disease, never a malignant one.

The outspoken, misunderstood conscience of our time was born Leonard Alfred Schneider. His parents were divorced by the time he was five, and for most of his life he lived with his mother and his Aunt Mema. According to Bruce, Aunt Mema was primarily concerned with sexual folklore and sexual fantasy and could, in conversation, reduce both aspects down to the bottom line. If Bruce were alive today he would no doubt have a more sound interpretation of "bottom line," but in this case, accept the accepted meaning. His mother, Sally Kitchenberger, lived Aunt Mema's fantasies, but again, according to Bruce, he never saw his mother in bed with anyone . . . in fact he never even saw her kiss anyone. She just had a lot of male callers. Sally was a young, attractive woman, who perforce had to rely on welfare checks along with her occasional jobs as a waitress or as a housemaid. As Sally Marr she had tried to break into show business but failed. She used to take Lenny on her rounds to the various agents but after a day's worth of "sorry, don't call us, we'll call you," mother and son would have something to eat and take in a show. She had a good sense of humor and was fun to be with. She also was a mimic and as Bruce's talent developed he

*Lenny Bruce, *How To Talk Dirty and Influence People,* Playboy Press, Chicago, Illinois

would mimic her mimics. The discipline of the young Lenny was left to the times his father would come to visit. Myron "Mickey" Schneider was a decent, serious man from an upstanding middle class Jewish family; a family that had suffered financial reverses. Although most of his life he sold shoes, he did attend night school and did make attempts to improve his lot in life. But as far as his son was concerned his main duty was to punish him and that he did by giving him a week's worth of piled up whippings. Something Sally could never bring herself to do — maybe because most of Lenny's "bads" had to do with what he did behind the bathroom door . . . as any normal boy his age would do. Beside the discovery of how to please himself physically, he found another pleasure from listening to the radio. Money was very seldom available for movies or candy or any of the other tiny luxuries most boys could take for granted. They lived in primarily non-Jewish neighborhoods and it was not until Lenny began to hang out with show biz types, that his knowledge of Yiddish developed. And so the stage was set: Lenny living vicariously through the lives of his radio friends and occasionally through the lives of his movie heroes and heroines; alone most of the time but observing all that went on around him. The curtain went up on his first act when he dropped out of school and ran away.

At age 16 [1941] he found employment on a Long Island farm for $40.00 a month, plus room and board. He lived with a Swedish-German family, the Denglers, whom he adopted as surrogate parents but the feeling was not reciprocal. To the Denglers he was a hired hand not a lost boy in search of Andy Hardy-type parents. He was further disillusioned when he discovered that the Denglers slept in separate bedrooms. Something "JUDGE HARDY" would have overruled. In 1942, age 17, he enlisted in the Navy and after basic training was shipped overseas where he saw action at Anzio, Salerno, Sicily, and southern France. He also saw plenty of action in the Italian bordellos which eventually would work in his favor. For when he decided he wanted out of the Navy he dreamed up the gag of dressing up as a WAVE. Nightly he would walk patrol in his girl garb until finally he was reported, court-martialed, analyzed, and given an undesirable discharge. But when his track record at the bordellos was attested to and confirmed, the record was set right ... honorable discharge. His introduction to drugs also came about in Italy and the diagnosis of his rare ailment, narcolepsy, was treated with the standard and accepted method of the time ... amphetamines.

He came home, now twenty years old, with no future, no real training but with an $80.00 a month standard pay from the Veterans Administration to ex-GI's. For a time he lived with his mother until he discovered the GI Education Bill. With the money alloted him for education, he enrolled in a dramatic workshop in Los Angeles. But when the Hollywood agents gave him the "don't call us" routine, he headed back to New York and Sally. In his absence Sally had started and closed a dancing school, but now had a new career as part of a dancing team. She was ekeing out a living on the local circuit. One night the emcee where Sally was working got into trouble with the law (pot in the trunk of his car) and Sally arranged for her son to do the spot. A nervous, diarrhea-stricken Lenny Marr ... no, his mother had another name ... Marsalle ... a nervous, diarrhea-stricken Lenny Marsalle walked on stage and got his first laugh. A heckler at the bar shouted, "Bring on the broads." The heckler had a couple of ladies with him and when he re-

peated his "Bring on the broads" Lenny replied: "I'd like to but then you wouldn't have any company at the bar." His second addiction started ... show biz.

Lenny then started hitting the amateur shows. He won a few, lost many, until his big break ... The Arthur Godfrey Show. With the Godfrey win came a certain amount of real bookings in real clubs. He did okay in New York, but the out-of-town audiences didn't "dig" his material or simply didn't understand what the young comic was trying to get across. He knew the work of his peers, some of which he accepted and some he couldn't stomach: Be funny/humorous in your work but tell the truth. Sally had always drilled "truth" into her son. And he knew that jokes from joke books or jokes from another comic's routine were not his thing. He also knew that poking fun at physical handicaps was not a true source of comedy. He talked about topical subjects, personal experiences, and private views. His routine had been tried in the "clubhouse for comics" in New York, known as Hanson's Drug Store. There all the comics would congregate; those who were trying to get started and those who had made it. Lenny had tried his material out on them. The "them" knew it all, had played every aspect of comedy, so he had to come up with something new and different. His "something" was part of his mind, part of his soul, and his attitude about life. The public, no matter how square it might appear, always recognizes sincerity. It, the public, recognizes truth, too, even if it can't accept it. But the out-of-town receptions discouraged him and off he went again ... this time, the Merchant Marine.

By the time he had finished with the Merchant Marine, which took him to several foreign countries and according to Bruce's own count, "over 200 broads," he realized that he was deeply in love with a stripper he had met prior to going abroad. He called her from Spain, told her how he felt, and upon his return they were married. His bride, born Harriet Lloyd, was then known as Honey Harlowe, a non-

Jewish beauty with red hair, two divorces, and one arrest. When they married she became Honey Michelle Bruce. Lenny adored her, loved her, worshipped her, and all of which led to the final demise of the marriage as he allowed and/or permitted, her to exploit him. Their life was not easy. Money was always lacking, jobs were hard to get, so Lenny who despised his wife's career as a stripper, decided to change Honey into a singer. But stripping brought in money—her singing did not. While working on the road she suffered a horrible auto accident and spent months flat on her back, not knowing if she would ever walk again. Fortunately, she did make a full recovery, was able to produce one girl child, Kitty, but unfortunately the bonds of her heroin habit were stronger than her bonds of matrimony. After seven years Lenny walked out and in the divorce settlement was given custody of their daughter. Eventually he bought a house in Hollywood, Sally moved there to be close to him and her grandchild and helped out by taking charge of Kitty when he was on tour.

Honey Harlow, whom Bruce described as: "A composite of the Virgin Mary and a $500.00-a-night whore."

Daughter Kitty Bruce, as she looked age 20. Circa 1976.

How much the hectic marriage and the divorce contributed to Lenny's new image cannot be estimated, but without Honey he could work full-time on his routines, his "bits," his career. Around 1958 big bookings began to come in. The clubs he called "toilets" were flushed out of his life along with the cheapie burlesque houses. One of the stops along the road to success was Ann's 440 Club in San Francisco, which was previously only for the "gay" crowd. Lenny was hired to work there when the manager decided the club was going "straight." Lenny, who had been playing it straight with the tough guys in the burlesque house audiences, quickly noted their reaction to his performance. His comedy didn't make them laugh but when he inserted four-letter words they laughed. So at Ann's 440 he had the opportunity to develop the act . . . four-letter words and all. In the hands of a master like Lenny Bruce (he changed it to Bruce back at Hanson's Drug Store) the four-letter words were not used for shock value, but were used as an attempt to shock people into reality. Another change in the act had to do with his "bits." These had been the core of his act but they began to diminish as his ad libs took on more importance. The short ad libs were extended into lengthier streams of consciousness. If he tired of the material, he would soon drop it and find other topics to weave into his tapestry of indignation. Writer Kenneth Tynan put it this way: "He has the heart of an unfrocked evangelist."

Hugh Hefner, founder of the Playboy empire, heard about Bruce and flew out from Chicago to catch his act. This resulted in record albums which put Bruce before the public: a public that would never get to see or hear him, as Bruce felt there were only three cities in the United States: New York, Los Angeles, and San Francisco; the rest he termed as "Biloxi." Hefner also arranged for Bruce to appear at his Chicago Playboy Club and this exposure led to Mister Kelly's, another very famous Chicago nightclub. It was there, in 1959, that the tag "foul-mouthed" comic was christened. Lenny suffered from the "below the belt blow," personal foul, but tightened his belt another way.

Lenny Bruce (left) shown here with his attorney, Seymour Lazer, leaving a California city jail after having posted bail for hitting back. This time he had taken a swing at a TV cameraman. 1962.

He began to develop a good business sense. What he lacked in formal education he compensated for by reading and by always studying what was going on around him. He had keen intuition and could sniff out where to work. For example, in New York in 1959, he sniffed out a club, Duane's, that was folding. He approached the owner with the proposition — if you can't afford to pay me $1,250.00 per week then pay me scale, $125.00, plus $1.25 for each customer who comes in. The first week he made over $1,000.00 so the club owner opted for a flat salary of $2000.00 per for the rest of the engagement . . . and the owner did not lose money. Bruce had a following. He was becoming a cult figure. He was also beginning to feel the pressure of success and the added pressure, slowly bearing down on him, about his performances and related material. His explanation of the material was: "The kind of material I do isn't going to change the world, but certain areas of society make me unhappy and satirizing them — aside from being lucrative — provides a release for me."

One of his first arrests for illegal possession of drugs was cleared as all of the drugs found in his possession had been issued by a physician. Bruce was suffering from the aforementioned narcolepsy, then hepatitis, and eventually pleurisy. He was hooked on amphetamines and he did inject himself with Methedrine, a liquid amphetamine. The next charge, and the one he was to fight until his death, was obscenity. Throughout the United States he was charged with obscenity, bookings were cancelled, and club owners were threatened with revocation of their licenses, if they permitted Bruce on stage. The more Bruce was threatened, the harder he fought. The most written about incident occurred in San Francisco's Jazz Workshop, a Greenwich Village type operation. It became common practice for police to attend his shows, issue complaints, (from unknown and unidentified callers) and then arrest him. Later the police taped his shows when their memories failed, along with their ineptness to repeat in context exactly what Bruce had said. But during the San Francisco melee columnist Ralph Gleason managed to record the offstage confrontation between Bruce and the arresting officer: Bruce: "Why am I being taken in?" Officer: "On a violation of Police Code 205, using obscene language in a public performance . . . I took exception . . . I took offense . . . I don't see how you can break down that word."
(The officer was referring to Bruce's analysis of the word "cocksucker" which Bruce felt was limited in its use.)
Bruce: "You can break it down by talking about it. How about a word like clap?"
Officer: "Well, clap is a better word than cocksucker."
Bruce: "Not if you get clap from a cocksucker."
In his book Bruce says: "They said it was a favorite homosexual practice. Now that I found strange. I don't relate that word to a homosexual practice. It relates to any contemporary chick I know, or would know, or would love, or would marry." Bruce's raison d'etre was to show that *attitude* is dirty, *not* words.

Early in his career he did appear on TV. Shown here with Steve Allen, circa 1960.

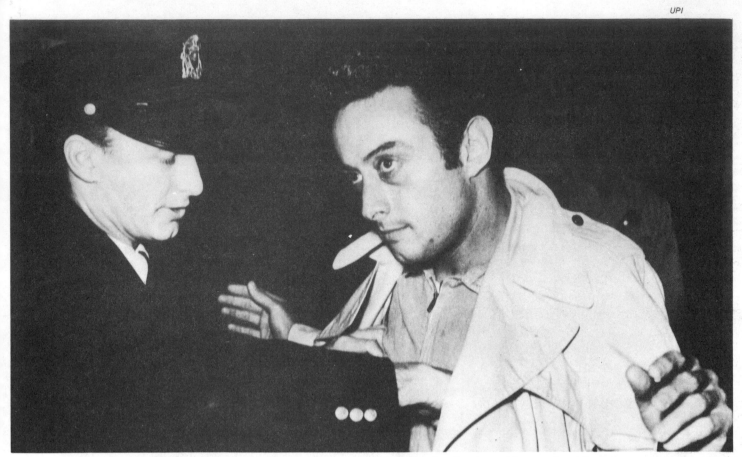

TOP: Bruce and his friends claimed he was never a junkie. Amphetamines, yes . . . Heroin, no. The arresting officer was no doubt borrowing a match.

BOTTOM: Outside a Los Angeles courtroom Bruce is probably explaining to his attorney, John Marshall, why a father should tell his child the truth: "These are not deflated white balloons, they are condoms." Inside Judge Landis who had sent Bruce to the psychiatric department for an examination, waits to sentence Bruce after the results of the report are revealed. Circa 1963

He was beginning to be banned from hotels as well as clubs. The Clift Hotel in San Francisco asked him to move out after the above arrest. But the Clift Hotel also did not permit Seeing Eye Dogs. Fortunately the famous and very grand hotel in San Francisco, the St. Francis, opened its doors to Bruce (and Seeing Eye Dogs) and he was back at work the same night he had been booked. It is, and was, at that time illegal anywhere in the United States to bar a dog used by the blind, but the Clift Hotel was never arrested for an obscenity far worse than the breakdown of the word cocksucker. And that was the point of Lenny Bruce's hammering away, and for that, he was constantly being arrested.

He caused a sensation in England on his first visit. Later the country barred him and even deported him. He did a one-man show at Carnegie Hall and played to an SRO audience that didn't budge even when the sound system broke down. He was cancelled in Vancouver, fired in Australia [only two performances], arrested in Los Angeles, once for illegal possession of drugs, and then for obscenity in two languages ... Yiddish and English. The words in question were — fress, schtup, schmuch, tits, ass, and jack-off. Today the show-stopper in a Broadway show, *A Chorus Line*, is the song, *Tits and Ass*. But in New York, April of 1964 he was arrested for obscenity and his trial, which became known as "the court of the absurd," was to consume him the rest of his life. He played one last engagement in Westbury, Long Island, July 1964, and that was his last appearance in the Empire State. The case was tried before three judges as the obscenity charge was a misdemeanor. According to New York law, misdemeanor calls for judges, not a jury. Lenny and his long list of supporters went to court to defend his right to say "fuck" in his act. Any salesclerk, taxi driver, housewife, clergyman, and bank president could say it, but from the stage it was verboten. In one testimony on

Bruce's behalf the witness launched into a discussion of linguistics and casually mentioned that the word in question was of common use in the armed forces. One of the judges, Judge Murtagh, interjected: "I was in the army for several years and never heard it." The other two judges, Kenneth Phipps and J. Randall Creel, blinked their eyes in disbelief. The courtroom kibitzers stifled laughs as Bruce's lawyer answered with: "Your experience surely was unique." But Lenny Bruce, who always had his hand, as well as his heart, on the pulse of any situation, came to the defense of Judge Murtagh. Said Bruce: "He's telling the truth. He probably was an officer and never heard the word, because he's not the kind of guy you say 'fuck' in front of." Bruce lost the case, two judges for conviction, one against. His appeal to the New York Circuit Court also ended in defeat. He never appealed to a higher court but jumped bail and left for California. Two months later in Florida, June 22, 1964, another obscenity case decision was reversed by the United States Supreme Court. Henry Miller's book, *Tropic of Cancer*, was ruled, "not obscene."

Wide World

In April 1962, Lenny Bruce was a smash in London. Shown here April 1963, in Kennedy Airport, on his return from England where he was refused entry. He was forced to leave London two hours after his plane arrived from the States.

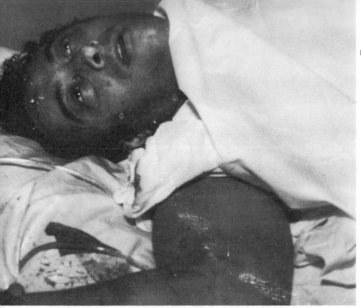

For the remainder of his life Bruce became obsessed with law in regard to himself and with the law, itself. He became grossly overweight for his size toppling the scale at over 200 pounds. He shut himself up, and worked three or four days at a stretch, finally collapsing from fatigue and ill health. In 1965, having earned only $2,000.00 for one year, he was forced to file suit as pauper. His last performance was June 25, 1966, in San Francisco's Fillmore Auditorium. Ironically he played opposite a group, Frank Zappa and the Mothers of Invention, who stepped carefully in the tracks made by Bruce. The youngsters of the time applauded the group's sick humor(?) and obscenity(?).

Lenny was talking to friends in a San Francisco Hotel and literally got carried away. He fell twenty five feet from a window sill and was heard to say (as he fell): "I'm SuperJew." Here he is shown entering the hospital. 1965.

The TV show, "That Was The Week That Was," recognized Lenny Bruce by bestowing upon him an honorary Doctor of Letters: "To the man who won fame using them four at a time." He was by then barred from the networks. Shown here—1964

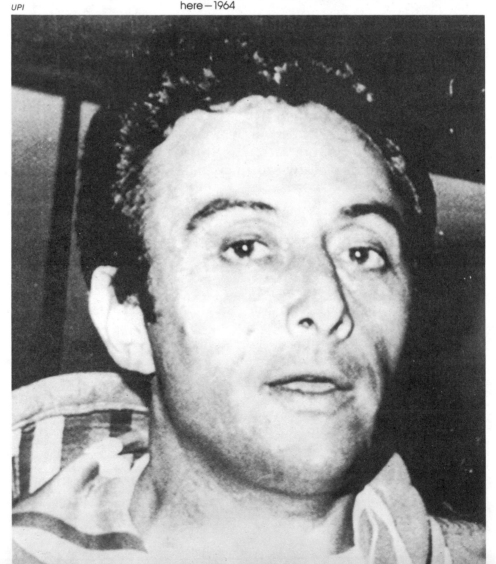

Bruce was alone when he died. Whether in need of a shot to keep going, or just an upper to lift his downed spirit, he injected himself and the result according to the coroner's two autopsies was called: "Accidental death from acute morphine poisoning." Just as Judy Garland, who died three years later, both were WORN OUT. The police did an unforgivable thing when they allowed reporters/press to photo-graph his body. Bruce had sat down on the toilet, tied a belt around his arm, took the shot, and then fell to the floor. This is how he was photographed. Bruce had been accused of bad taste all of his life. He was certainly the victim of it in his death. But had he been able to speak, he would have defended the right of the press to print what "it saw fit."

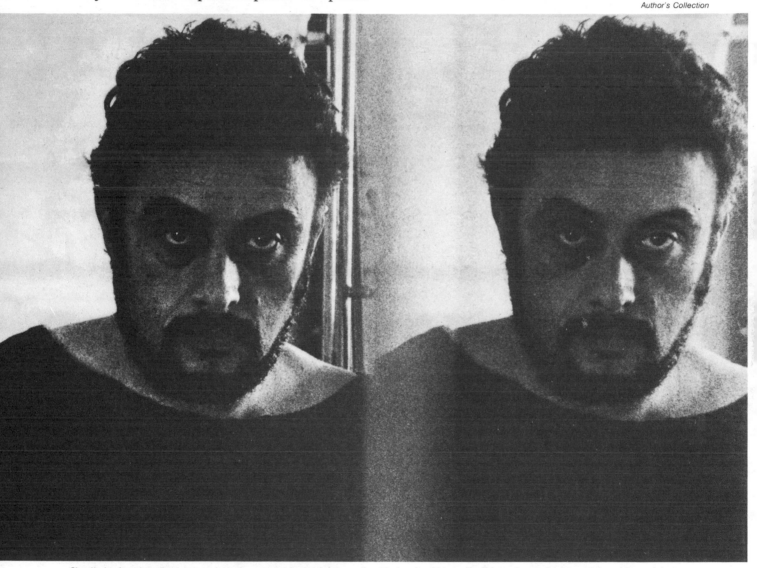

Shortly before he died, Lenny barely moved from his typewriter. He had cut himself off from the outside world, as his world was consumed with the law, and his trials. 1966

In California, Sally arranged an Orthodox funeral for her son. In New York, at the Judson Memorial Church, over a thousand friends and fans gathered for a memorial service. Both events would probably have been frowned on by him but he would have understood that the living must do what makes them comfortable. And if Allen Ginsburg felt comfortable singing a Hindu funeral chant, in a Protestant Church, to the memory of a Jew, then that's another four-letter word, OKAY.

Leonard Alfred Schneider (Lenny Bruce) learned and said: "When you're hungry, sing, when you're hurt, laugh," Dustin Hoffman, shown here as Bruce.

LENNY BRUCE
Died: August 3, 1966, Hollywood, California

LENNY BRUCE
FILM

1967 LENNY BRUCE — Film-Makers
Photographic record of a Lenny Bruce
night club routine

RECORDINGS AVAILABLE
as of 1978

Albums:
BERKELEY CONCERTS — (double) (Reprise)
BEST OF LENNY BRUCE — (Fantasy)
LENNY BRUCE — AMERICAN (Fantasy)
BRUCE AT CARNEGIE HALL — (triple)
(United Artists)
INTERVIEWS OF OUR TIME — (Fantasy)
LIVE AT THE CURRAN THEATRE — (triple) (Fantasy)
THE REAL LENNY BRUCE — (double)
(Fantasy)
THE SICK HUMOR OF LENNY BRUCE —
(Fantasy)
THANK YOU MASKED MAN — (Fantasy)
TOGETHERNESS — (Fantasy)
WHAT I WAS ARRESTED FOR — (Casablanca)
25 YEARS OF RECORDED COMEDY, with
other artists — (Warner Bros.)

FILMED AND STAGED BIOGRAPHIES
WITH MATERIAL BY BRUCE

1971 LENNY, a play based on the life and words
of Lenny Bruce, by Julian Barry
Cliff Gorman won an Antoinette Perry
(Tony) Award as Best Actor for his performance in the title role
1974 LENNY, a film based on the above play —
Marvin Worth, producer
with Dustin Hoffman, Valerie Perrine

Brian Epstein, manager of the Beatles, from Liverpool to London to the World in six years.

Brian Epstein

Born: September 19, 1934, Liverpool, England

The eldest son, of a Liverpool Jewish family, was born with a destiny to be one of the most famous entrepreneurs of all time. At twenty-five he showed no promise, but by the time he was twenty-nine he had not only become a millionaire but had made four others millionaires, also. His slow beginning wasn't due to laziness, in fact he was just the opposite, but until he found his niche he floundered. He attended seven schools before he quit Wrekin College in 1950, at the age of sixteen. Then a stint in the army, which he hated as much as school. He returned to Liverpool where he tried fashion designing, then selling furniture in the family business. Neither job was to his liking, so he switched to the Royal Academy of Dramatic Art in the hope of becoming an actor. Again, schooling was not his thing, so back to Liverpool, where he started a record department ... in a new store ... owned by his family. The department started with just Epstein and one assistant. It also started with a promise and policy to its customers: "They *could* and *would* supply any record requested." In October '61, a youth, Raymond Jones, sauntered in one day and asked for *My Bonnie*, a disc by the Beatles. A few days later some other customers made similar requests and Epstein, true to the store's policy, started his search for the record. He discovered, One-that the disc had been made in Germany and was not available in Great Britain. Two-that the group in question was working nearby in a converted warehouse, now a jazz club, the Cavern, for a measly 75 shillings per night-about nine dollars. Epstein was immediately attracted by the stage presence and personal magnetism of the

boys. Furthermore, confidence in his judgment had been reinforced by his ability to stock the store in advance with discs he personally thought would "make it." When customers would flock to his record department he was ready for them. The original department had grown to three floors and had a staff of thirty, as opposed to its original two, which proved Epstein knew what he was doing. He thought the four lads he had seen at The Cavern had something the public was ready for and followed through with his judgment by arranging an appointment with them the next day. He also knew they were in need of some polishing and refining. Their smoking, eating, and stage language would not be acceptable to important ballroom owners and certainly not what the BBC would tolerate. But he was smart enough never to tamper with their music, just their demeanor. They drew up their own contract and Epstein went to work. He started a systemized account of their earnings, meager the first year, astronomical in future years, and slowly, he began to organize everything about them. He beleaguered record companies, always predicting that his Beatles would one day surpass Elvis. But the record companies didn't bite until he went to EPI. George Martin said, "yes" and in October '62, their first record, *Love Me Do* was released, followed by *Please, Please Me*.

Their popularity did not hit at once, which led to some interesting data about their contractual agreements. Epstein was a stickler for honoring commitments. Inasmuch as bookings were made months in advance, the group found themselves working for £25 to £40 (pounds) a week, from previous contracts when they were now working for £100. By the time they had jumped to £1,000 per week they were still honoring the £100 weekly gigs. (The pound (£) was about $2.40 at that time) Epstein's commission ranged from ten to twenty-five percent of their earnings. However, he did not reach the twenty-five percent figure until the group was earning at least £800 weekly. Although he was extremely shrewd, his integrity was never questioned. In 1964, when an unbelievable offer came to him, to sell a portion of his Beatle contract, he put it on the line to the boys. By his own admission Epstein said that he was extremely tired. The constant telephone calls, pressure from social affairs, and the traveling, all had become a strain . . . but he would not sell until he consulted with the four mop-heads. George Harrison never looked up, when he said: "You're joking." Ringo Starr said: "Tell us again." John Lennon said: "Get stuffed." Paul McCartney said something less than polite, but then added: "Tell us and we'll pack up completely. We'll throw the whole lot up tomorrow." Epstein, a very sensitive man, was so overwhelmed by their loyalty that he replied: "I don't think all the money in the world would be enough (for the sale) . . ."

Author's Collection

Beatlemania hit Great Britain in the fall of '63 and in one year they became the best known group in the world. For the first time a foreign group surpassed anything America had to offer and they proved to London that the little guys from Liverpool could surpass what London had to offer. The teen-agers of the world, feeling like outsiders in a society they neither understood nor accepted, grabbed on to Beatle music and made it their own. Older people just nodded, knowing that this phase would pass, as rock 'n roll of the fifties had done. In the beginning, the Beatles sang no message music, no protests were in their lyrics, but after their first trip to the States, where they were exposed to Dylan and Baez, they did change. Using their own emotional structure and the messages they wanted to impart, they fell on the world with as much force as an atomic explosion. The rest is history.

UPI

TOP: Princess Margaret, and her (then) husband, Lord Snowdon (right) have the Beatles and manager, Epstein, (2nd right) presented to them at the premiere of their first film, "Hard Day's Night" 1964. Outside, in Piccadilly Circus, police cordons snapped, one after another, and people collapsed in the crush, when 20,000 adults and screaming teen-agers jammed the area.

TOP LEFT: There was a time when Epstein thought of quitting, but the Beatles wouldn't hear of it.

RIGHT: Epstein in 1963. The world was his oyster, and his oyster contained four pearls, John, Ringo, Paul and George.

The Epstein era started October 28, 1961. He founded his empire, called NEMS Enterprises, North End Music Stores, and ran the Beatle's earnings from ($9.00) nine dollars a night to ($840.00) eight hundred and forty dollars for just one minute during a half hour show. This was when they hit their peak in America in 1964. Fans had bought more than 200 million records in spite of Decca Records' Dick Rowe, who had turned them down in 1962: "Not to mince words, Mr. Epstein, we don't like your boys' sound. Groups of guitarists are on the way out." Epstein enlarged his empire by adding other performers to his stable: Cillia Black, the coatroom attendant from The Cavern became one of Great Britain's top female recording stars; The Dakotas, Billy J. Kramer, The Fourmost, all successful; Gerry and the Pacemakers, top stars. His personal assistant, Derek Taylor former journalist, ghosted his biography, and later came to the States to become part-owner of the Beach Boys: Epstein's stardust was sprinkled everywhere.

There was also another side of Epstein's life that did not come to light until after his death. In 1959, when he was setting up the record department, he met 24-year old Rita Harris, who was employed by the store, and assisted him. They began dating quietly as she was a Roman Catholic and he, Jewish. Epstein feared that his family would not approve and he was never certain how hers would react. However, their relationship was further complicated by the fact that Epstein, by his own admission to Rita, was a homosexual. In an interview in London's *Daily Express*, after Epstein's death, Rita said: "He admitted he was homosexual and talked about it frequently. It used to make him very depressed. He hated himself for it. He never remembered being any other way." Despite that, Rita did fall in love with him and realizing that there was no future in it, she fled in 1961 to Jersey, the largest of the Channel Islands, where she took a job as a waitress. There she met a man with whom she became seriously involved. She

and Epstein continued to be friends and carried on a lengthy correspondence. Epstein devised a code, which enabled him to write about his relationships with his male friends. He referred to them as New Releases: "New Releases make business brisk" or "New Releases—I could probably get into the Spanish Top Ten." As Epstein was open with her, so she was with him. She told him about her new love, Peter, and later introduced him to Epstein. But in 1963, Peter was killed in an automobile accident. Epstein tried to comfort Rita and did propose marriage to her. She fled back to Jersey saying: "I didn't want to hurt his feelings by refusing him." Epstein wrote to her: (in part) "You are the only girl who has ever had any impression on me. The only girl I have, or will, care about. The only girl I need. The terrible thing is, that I feel we both know that a decision must be made and clearly cut. Or can we compromise? I suppose there are only two alternatives. That you virtually leave me for a married life and forget (or try) everything that was between us. The other is that you see me . . . come back to me . . . and . . . and . . . but I've no right. I offer *nothing*." Rita married another man in Jersey and of course Epstein went on to great fame with the Beatles and became a millionaire.

Epstein, at a happier time in his life, said: "I believe in my friends, and in my close associates, and I believe in life, because it holds forth hope for the future." *Author's Collection*

Perhaps his biggest success was his understanding of the boys, John, Ringo, George, and Paul. The Beatles were his first real friends ... he was "Eppie" to them and in a showdown situation Eppie knew how to handle them. The boys might win an argument, but Eppie won the point. Once Paul was very late for an appointment and to assuage Eppie's annoyance, George said: "He's having a

UPI

bath." Eppie: "He'll be very late." George: "But very clean."

John put it this way: "You see, he's the only one we take things from. He's one above us. Everybody else packs it in when we start screaming at them, because they're frightened. We couldn't be run by anybody but him—not anybody, I tell you."

Epstein bought the Saville Theatre, maybe with the idea of someday returning to his dream of becoming an actor. He loved bull-fighting and Sibelius; he lived lavishly in his Belgravia London house, stocked with a fine wine cellar; he drove three cars, a red Rolls-Royce, a grey Bentley Continental, and a second hand mini; but except for his staff, he lived alone. Alone ... except for his highs on marijuana and binges on alcohol. He felt that: "Alcohol constitutes a much greater danger to society. I am not a habitual drug-taker, but I have found in the past

few years that drugs have helped to clear my mind." To also help clear his mind, he consulted several psychiatrists and to put his stamp of approval on his feelings about drugs he signed the advertisement by *The Times* (London), to legalize marijuana.

Epstein had been ill for about a year with jaundice, had been treated for bouts

TOP: Epstein (3rd from left), and Beatle Paul McCartney (front), and Ringo Starr (4th from left), attend world premiere of "Help," 1965.

LEFT: Princess Margaret presents the Carl-Alan Dance Award, for the "Most Outstanding Group," 1965, to Brian Epstein, who accepts for the Beatles. The group could not attend, as they were in the Bahamas.

of glandular fever, and had suffered severe depression after his father's sudden death, several weeks prior to his own. When his Spanish valet and housekeeper could not rouse him one afternoon, they summoned a doctor and the police. At first, his death appeared to be from natural causes, but an overabundance of pill bottles found in his quarters made an inquest necessary. The official record stated, after the inquest, that there was enough evidence of insomnia, anxiety, and depression to warrant their final statement: "Accidental death through sleeping tablets." Even so, the son of Harry and Queenie Epstein ended his life abruptly, shrouded in mystery, and with tragedy.

Elvis Presley sent a telegram to the Beatles: "Deepest regrets and condolences on the loss of a good friend to you and to all of us."

The fifth Beatle was gone.

Brian Epstein (left) and the Beatles taking off on holiday. 1966

BRIAN EPSTEIN
Died: August 27, 1967, London England

BRIAN EPSTEIN
FILM PRODUCED

1965 FERRY CROSS THE MERSEY (co-produced with Michael Holden) with Gerry and the Pacemakers

BEATLES FILMS (through 1967)

1964 *A HARD DAY'S NIGHT — United Artists with Victor Spinetti, Anna Quayle, Kenneth Haigh
*The Beatles' score was nominated for an Academy Award
1965 HELP! — United Artists with Leo McKern, Eleanor Bron, Victor Spinetti
1965 GO GO MANIA — Harry Field-American International with Matt Monro, The Animals, Herman's Hermits

BEATLES' GRAMMY AWARDS
(through 1967)

(Capitol)
1964 Best New Artist of 1964
1964 Best Performance by a Vocal Group: A HARD DAY'S NIGHT
1966 Song of the Year: MICHELLE (Lennon & McCartney)
1966 Best Contemporary Solo Vocal Performance, Male:
ELEANOR RIGBY (McCartney)
1967 Album of the Year: SERGEANT PEPPER'S LONELY HEARTS CLUB BAND
1967 Best Contemporary (Rock 'n Roll) Album: SERGEANT PEPPER'S LONELY HEARTS CLUB BAND

BEATLES' RIAA GOLD RECORD AWARDS
(through 1967)

(Capitol)
1964 I WANT TO HOLD YOUR HAND (single)
1964 CAN'T BUY ME LOVE (single)
1964 A HARD DAY'S NIGHT (single)
1964 MEET THE BEATLES (album)
1964 THE BEATLES SECOND ALBUM (album)
1964 SOMETHING NEW (album)
1964 THE BEATLES' STORY (album)
1964 BEATLES '65 (album)
1965 HELP! (album)
1965 EIGHT DAYS A WEEK (single)
1965 YESTERDAY (single)
1965 BEATLES VI (album)
1965 Help! (album)
1965 RUBBER SOUL (album)
1966 WE CAN WORK IT OUT (single)
1966 NO WHERE MAN (single)
1966 PAPERBACK WRITER (single)
1966 YELLOW SUBMARINE (single)
1966 YESTERDAY AND TODAY (album)
1966 REVOLVER (album)
1967 PENNY LANE (single)
1967 ALL YOU NEED IS LOVE (single)
1967 HELLO GOODBYE (single)
1967 SERGEANT PEPPER'S LONELY HEARTS CLUB BAND (album)
1967 MAGICAL MYSTERY TOUR (album)

Redding in the mid-sixties. Known as "Mr. Pitiful" and the "Champion of Soul."

Otis Redding

Born: September 9, 1941, Dawson, Georgia.

Although Redding moved to Macon, Georgia when he was a child, there he lived as he had lived in Dawson; the rural, low class life of a southern poor black. His musical influences, from his "neck of the woods," were far from poor . . . Little Richard and Ray Charles. His greatest influence and one that remained with him all of his life, was northern-born Sam Cooke. Later, Redding almost always included a Cooke song in his albums. His exposure to music was again, like the others of his ilk, limited to country and western, folk, blues, and gospel. He started singing in the church choir. He was, and remained, a soul singer . . . a folk artist.

In the early years he worked with Johnny Jenkins and the Pinetoppers, traveling the music circuit, working wherever they could. In 1962, Jenkins was given an audition in Memphis, for Atlantic Records, and although he did not plan to use Redding, he did ask him to drive the group there. After the Pinetoppers finished their taping, forty minutes worth of tape was left-over and Redding got permission to record one of his own tunes. His record, These Arms of Mine, launched him as a solo artist. Memphis always remained the place for Redding recordings and the musicians who played with him, remained with him, too. This says a lot about what kind of a man he was.

Another facet of the man was that he remained black. In doing the soul music that he loved, he stayed with what he believed and what he had developed as his style. As much as he wanted fame and fortune, which he eventually got, he remained true to himself and his art. "Mr. Pitiful," as he was known due to his soul ballads, with their sentimental lyrics (Pain In My Heart), came on the scene when the white people were still listening to Sinatra for their love songs and slow songs. His [Redding] popularity was mainly with the blacks. In the early '60s, Rhythm and Blues artists were starting to make inroads into the top 40, with James Brown leading the way as the King of R&B*. But it was not until 1965, when the Rolling Stones "acknowledged the importance of soul into the new rock," that Redding began to gain acceptance and catapulted into prominence. The Stones album, Out of Our Heads incorporated and put the stamp on the music of Redding and Brown. So when Redding's own composition, Respect hit the market it was a smash on the "soul" charts. But again it was not until Aretha Franklin's entrance in 1967, that Respect got the respect it deserved from white audiences and a place on the "pop" charts. Redding knew that he would have to add some uptempo music, and he did it with Satisfaction, a sort of "thank you" to the Stones. According to writer, Jon Landau in his article for The Rolling Stones Illustrated History of Rock & Roll: "If the white DJ's who control suburban radio had given [Satisfaction] more airplay, the record could have been a giant hit."

Redding toured Europe in '66 and '67 making a tremendous hit. Although Elvis had been the numero uno male vocalist for ten years in London, he was replaced by Redding in Melody Maker, a music publication.

*Soul is more blues oriented than R&B.

Redding upset the Presley applecart when he became the Number One male vocalist in England.

Back in the United States, Vice President Hubert Humphrey asked Redding to go to Viet Nam and Redding accepted. The Veep also requested a *Stay In School* album from Redding, which he recorded in Memphis on Stax-Volt. Redding loved his work, he was articulate, his emotion was deeply rooted in religion . . . it was a way of life to him. *Dictionary of Soul* states it.

Redding was on the verge of superstardom when he died. His relaxed, soft soul ballad *Dock of the Bay*, done two weeks before his death, stayed on the charts for almost a year, part of the time in the number one slot. It was issued in January 1968, thirteen months after his death, and Jerry Wexler of Atlantic Records said: "It's his epitaph and it proves that a singer can do his own thing and still be commercially successful. Otis is tremendously responsible for the fact that . . . the young white audience now digs soul, the way the black does."

Traveling to an engagement in the midwest, the plane on which he was flying, along with other group members, attempted an instrument landing. There was heavy fog and rain and the plane crashed into Lake Monona, only three miles from the airport. One person survived and despite the hours of search by the police, Redding and four others drowned. The plane belonged to Redding, which he had bought two months prior to the accident.

4,500 people jammed into the auditorium in Macon for the funeral service, while another 3,000 stood outside to pay their respects to "The Big O." In 1974, a former Alvin Ailey dancer, George Faison, staged a tribute to Otis at Hunter College in New York City. Using *Suite Otis* as the music for his dance, he also included *Reflections of a Lady*, as a tribute to the late Billie Holiday.

TOP: The battered wreckage of the airplane being pulled from Lake Monona.

RIGHT: The body of Otis Redding being lifted from the icy waters of Lake Monona.

BOTTOM: James Alexander (l) and Carl Simms (r) view, from atop the Madison Hotel, the lake in which the plane bearing Otis Redding crashed. Both boys missed being aboard due to lack of space. They were members of an R&B group called the Bar Kays.

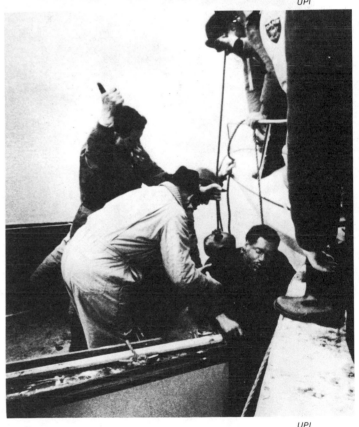

Many years ago Redding had performed in Boston and apparently the audience had sat through two hours of dullish performances while waiting for Redding. In an interview after Redding's death, Steve Cropper, guitarist and a friend of Redding's said: "Every singer prior to Redding had started with 'Let me see you clap your hands.' The first thing Redding said when he came on was 'Let me see you clap your hands.' I immediately forgot the preceding hours and clapped my hands. The audience knew instantly it was in the presence of an absolute master. The band had not played a single note, yet every person in the hall was standing."

The casket bearing the body of Otis Redding being brought into Macon City Auditorium for the funeral services.

Friends pay their final respects to Otis Redding, "Mr. Rock 'n Soul."

OTIS REDDING
Died: December 10, 1967, near Madison, Wisconsin

210

OTIS REDDING
GRAMMY AWARDS

1968 Best Rhythm & Blues Performance, Male:
     (SITTIN' ON) THE DOCK OF THE BAY
     (Volt)
     Best Rhythm & Blues Song:
     (SITTIN' ON) THE DOCK OF THE BAY
     (with Steve Cropper)

RIAA GOLD RECORD AWARDS

1968 (SITTIN' ON) THE DOCK OF THE BAY
     (single) (Volt)
1970 JIMI HENDRIX/OTIS REDDING AT MON-
     TEREY (album) (Reprise)

FILMS

1969 MONTEREY POP — Leacock-Pennebaker
     with Jimi Hendrix, Janis Joplin, The Mamas
     and The Papas
1969 POPCORN — Sherpix
     Documentary with Jimi Hendrix, The Roll-
     ing Stones, Joe Cocker
1972 SUPERSTARS IN FILM CONCERT — Na-
     tional Cinema
     with Jimi Hendrix, The Rolling Stones

Judy Garland in the early 40's

Judy Garland

Born: June 10, 1922, Grand Rapids, Minnesota.

Frances Ethel Gumm, to the delight of her piano-playing mother, sang the only song she knew at the time, *Jingle Bells.* She sang chorus, after chorus, after chorus, until her father, Frank, dragged her off of the stage. She was supposed to have been three years old when this happened. Probably what happened was the beginning of her love affair with audiences and the beginning of their love for her. She must have sensed their reaction . . . a reaction that would sustain her throughout her life. And that night probably revealed the reaction of her parents: Her father, whom she glorified, tried to remove her from the demanding audience while her mother, whom she denigrated, continued to play. If this seemingly unimportant event was the foundation of the performing Judy, another event could have been the foundation of the frightened Judy. Hospitalized as a child for a month, with a near fatal illness, she faced pain, desperately feared it, and then became terrified at being alone.

The family moved to Los Angeles in 1926 where the three Gumm daughters, Jimmie, Susie, and Frances embarked on a vaudeville career. Their parents worked professionally as Jack and Virginia Lee, also in vaudeville. As early as 1930, Judy had an audition as a "single" at Paramount Studios, but nothing came of it, so the sisters remained together until August 1935. A clip of their last performance can be seen in *That's Entertainment.* Shortly after Judy's twelfth birthday, with her working papers in order, she reported to MGM as a contract player for one hundred dollars a week. After signing, her first appearance was on KFI radio, The Shell Chateau Hour, hosted by Wallace

Beery. She sang *Broadway Rhythm,* and then returned three weeks later to sing *Zing Went The Strings of My Heart.* Air checks, still available, showed—she had it. She was quite happy in those days as she attended school on the studio lot with other future stars such as Mickey Rooney, Ann Rutherford, Lana Turner, and Ava Gardner. She had a sense of belonging . . . she was just another teen-ager, but *The Wizard of Oz* changed all that. She became

Wide World

Judy Garland at age 17 in her most famous role, Dorothy in "The Wizard of Oz." And one of her most famous lines: "Oh, Auntie Em, there's no place like home."

an important piece of property and that meant a tutor and aloneness. Her father had died from meningitis, one sister had married, and now Judy was separated from her pals. What she got in return was Louis B. Mayer, sovereign over the studio and over her. Biographers agree that Mayer ordered the MGM doctors to feed her pills: pills for her pudgy figure; pills to keep her awake, sometimes as long as seventy-two hours at a stretch; pills to put her to sleep, and the hardest pill to swallow—a mother who didn't care. If Judy's body hadn't been so hospitable to the pills, she might have given out sooner. Instead she sang, danced, and acted through twenty-nine films for MGM in fourteen years. Before she was twenty-one, she was not only living on pills, but was seeing a psychiatrist regularly. Mayer's word was absolute, so when he ordered her brief love affair with Tyrone Power to end—it ended. Later, when she was married to arranger-composer, David Rose, when her pregnancy was ordered to be aborted—it was. Judy, 19, and Rose, 31, eloped to Las Vegas in 1941 "to get away from Mama," said Judy, but she could not get away from Mayer. His disapproval of the union sent Judy on a lengthy USO tour. The marriage lasted almost four years. And a week after the final decree, she married thirty-two year old director, Vincent Minelli . . . with Mayer's blessing. During this three year marriage their only child, Liza, was born on March 12, 1946.

Judy and first husband, David Rose, shortly after their engagement had been announced. *UPI*

UPI

Judy and second husband, Vincent Minelli, who directed her in "Meet Me In St. Louis."
Liza Minelli and her famous mother. March 1946. *UPI*

UPI

Judy and her mother, Ethel Gumm Gilmore, at a Movie Stars' Mothers Party (!!) "According to my mother it was 'either go on stage and perform or get wrapped around a bedpost'," said Judy.

By the time Judy was twenty-eight, just eleven years from *Oz*, she had had two husbands, one child, had made over twenty films, attempted suicide, had a mother who, with her new husband, was squandering Judy's money, and a studio head who rose to the occasion by suspending her twice before kicking her out in 1950. Samuel Goldwyn said, at the time of Mayer's death: "So many people came to his funeral because they wanted to make sure the SOB was dead." If Judy had chosen Mayer as her father image, it was indeed a most unfortunate choice.

TOP LEFT: "A rose was a Rose was a Rose." Judy and singer, Martha Raye, both former wives of David Rose.
MIDDLE LEFT: (l-r) Judy, Hedy Lamarr and Lana Turner in "Ziegfeld Girl" in 1941.
MIDDLE RIGHT: Judy and Mickey Rooney in "Babes in Arms" in 1942.

Courtesy of Doug McClelland

Courtesy of Doug McClelland

Judy and Gene Kelly in "For Me and My Gal" in 1942.

Courtesy of Doug McClelland

Judy and Margaret O'Brien in "Meet Me in St. Louis" in 1944.

(l-r) Virginia O'Brien, Frances Langford, Judy, Dorothy Lamour, Ginny Simms, and Dinah Shore – circa 1944.

Judy and Fred Astaire in "Easter Parade" in 1948.

Judy in "The Harvey Girls" in 1946. (l-r) Edward Earle, Ben Carter, William Hall.

Now that Hollywood had written her off, she fled to New York where she met former test pilot, Sid Luft. He was a small time hustler, who was handling a few celebrities, Eleanor Powell for one, until he dreamed up concert tours for Judy. These tours have become legendary, along with the stories of her weight problem, drinking problem, and pill problem, but even so, she managed to break all attendance records at the Palace in '51, '56, '67, as

Judy and Van Johnson in "The Good Old Summertime" in 1949.

well as establishing new records at the Palace, Carnegie Hall, and London's Palladium. Her audiences knew her history of failures and cheered her on to her history of successes. The Luft marriage lasted until 1965, produced two children, Lorna and Joseph, then culminated in a series of custody suits, plus several more suicide attempts.

Judy and third husband, Sid Luft, cutting celebration cake upon completion of "A Star is Born." *UPI*

Judy with Lorna, 4, and Joseph, 2, both children from her third marriage to Sid Luft.

UPI

UPI

MGM buddies, Judy and Elizabeth Taylor, chat backstage at the old Met Opera House as Liz's new husband, Eddie Fisher, looks on.

UPI

Judy and Sid Luft, 1953, at funeral for her mother.

Judy at the Palace. "Audiences have kept me alive."

TOP: Judy backstage at the Palace with her children, Lorna and Joey Luft. The kids are part of the act—Lorna, 14, sings and Joey, 12, plays the drums.

BOTTOM: Judy, accompanied by a nurse, leaves hospital after another suicide attempt.

During this time, she returned to Hollywood to make *A Star is Born*, co-starring James Mason. Her *tour de force* performance won her an Oscar nomination but Hollywood didn't know what to do with her, so back she went to more concerts and back to relying on Luft, which unfortunately she continued to do even after the divorce. Two more calls came in from Hollywood, but she was fired from both films, *Annie Get Your Gun* and *The Barkleys of Broadway*. Later she was dropped from *Valley of the Dolls* and replaced by Susan Hayward. But in 1961, she turned a cameo part into another *tour de force* performance; the Jewish *hausfrau* in *Judgment at Nuremberg*. Only a professional like Judy could receive $50,000.00 for nine minutes on the screen. Director Stanley Kramer called her after her completed footage was shown in the booth where he sat with Spencer Tracy, Richard Widmark, and writer Abby Mann to tell her that all had burst into applause by her performance. Again she was nominated for an Oscar. Still Hollywood didn't know what to do with her.

TOP RIGHT: Jacqueline Susann, author of "Valley of the Dolls," chats with Judy, before she was dropped from film. "The set hasn't been built yet, and they have me walking off of it," said Judy.

BOTTOM RIGHT: Judy takes direction from Stanley Kramer in "Judgment at Nuremberg," in 1961.

Judy in a scene from "A Star is Born" in 1954. One of the great film performances of all time. She lost the Oscar to Grace Kelly, "The Country Girl."

Susan Hayward singing "I'll Plant My Own Tree" (dubbed by Margaret Whiting) in "Valley of the Dolls." The song was originally written for Judy Garland, by André and Dory Previn. Judy was dropped from the film.

Courtesy of Doug McClelland

Once again she took to the road and more concert tours. Suffering from a voice crackup, she was viciously booed from the stage by 7,000 fans (?) in Australia. She fled by boat and flew into her fourth marriage with actor, Mark Herron, fourteen years her junior, and by far, her most forgettable husband. The marriage lasted two brief years, 1965-67, and then she met

Mickey Deans. "Finally, finally I am loved," she said about her fifth husband. But she had been loved by millions, from the very first time she sang *Over The Rainbow*, to the last time she sang it, by her count 12,380 times. Spencer Tracy said: "A Garland audience doesn't just listen, they feel. They have their arms around her when she works." Columnist Earl Wilson put it another way: "Where else can you get two shows—Judy and The Audience? Audiences start by just applauding tunes in the overture, sometimes even the segues—then the audience stands up and begins to scream and she hasn't even put on her shoes."

Courtesy of Doug McClelland

Courtesy of Doug McClelland

Judy and pals on TV, (l) Dean Martin, (r) Frank Sinatra.

Courtesy of Doug McClelland

Judy and friends (l) Tony Bennett, (r) Duke Ellington.

BOTTOM LEFT: Judy and Burt Lancaster in "A Child is Waiting" in 1963.

BOTTOM RIGHT: Judy and fourth husband, Mark Herron. "He married me for business reasons," said she. UPI

Liza gets a big hug from Mama, for her success in the revival of "Best Foot Forward." It was Liza's off-Broadway debut.

Liza, 17, and Judy doing a tramp-clown dance for TV. *UPI*

Wide World

Judy and fifth husband, Mickey Deans. They were married only a few months before she died.

I Could Go On Singing (and she did) was her last film. She had been in the public's eye for thirty years. Eli Wallach said: "It's tragic. She is somehow the painful product of the worst part of Hollywood." The Hollywood of Judy's youth supposedly gave the public what it wanted . . . this so-called want was determined by its tasteless and tyrannical studio heads, who ran to the bank while its robot stars ran themselves into the ground.

Judy's last film "I Could Go On Singing" was made in London, with co-star Dirk Bogarde, shown here at the premiere in Piccadilly. *UPI*

Judy in a scene from "I Could Go On Singing," 1963, with Dirk Bogarde.

Courtesy of Doug McClelland

223

Unlike Marilyn Monroe, who perhaps died from choice, or James Dean who died daredeviling, Judy simply ... W-O-R-E O-U-T. Her daughter Liza said: "She lived eighty lives in one. And yet I thought she would outlive us all. She was a great star, and a great talent, and for the rest of my life I will be proud to be Judy Garland's daughter." Judy once said: "If I'm such a legend, then why am I so lonely?" It would be nice to think that she saw the 22,000 people who filed past her bier in New York City to say good-bye.

Mickey Deans, fifth husband of Judy Garland, arrives in New York, having accompanied the body of his wife from England.

UPI

(From left to right) ANDY HARDY (Mickey Rooney) and SCARECROW (Ray Bolger) came to the funeral in New York City. NORMAN MAINE (James Mason) delivered the eulogy.

UPI

JUDY GARLAND
Died: June 22, 1969, London, England

Judy in the 50's. The path of sorrow, and that path alone, leads to the land where sorrow is unknown.

——William Cowper

JUDY GARLAND FILMS

1930 THE MEGLIN KIDDIES (short) — Mayfair
with Virginia and Mary Jane (or Jackie and Susie) Gumm

1930 THE VITAPHONE KIDDIES (short) — Warner Bros.
with Virginia and Mary Jane (or Jackie and Susie) Gumm

1936 EVERY SUNDAY (short) — MGM
with Deanna Durbin

1936 PIGSKIN PARADE — 20th Century-Fox
with Patsy Kelly, Jack Haley, Stu Erwin, Betty Grable

1937 BROADWAY MELODY OF 1938 — MGM
with Robert Taylor, Eleanor Powell, George Murphy, Sophie Tucker

1937 THOROUGHBREDS DON'T CRY — MGM
with Mickey Rooney

1938 EVERYBODY SING — MGM
with Fannie Brice

1938 LOVE FINDS ANDY HARDY — MGM
with Mickey Rooney, Ann Rutherford, Lana Turner

1938 LISTEN, DARLING — MGM
with Freddie Batholomew, Mary Astor, Walter Pidgeon

1939 *THE WIZARD OF OZ — MGM
with Ray Bolger, Jack Haley, Bert Lahr, Margaret Hamilton
*see Awards

1939 BABES IN ARMS — MGM
with Mickey Rooney, Charles Winninger

1940 ANDY HARDY MEETS DEBUTANTE — MGM
with Mickey Rooney, Ann Rutherford

1940 STRIKE UP THE BAND — MGM
with Mickey Rooney

1940 LITTLE NELLY KELLY — MGM
with George Murphy

1941 ZIEGFELD GIRL — MGM
with Hedy Lamarr, Lana Turner, Jackie Cooper, James Stewart

1941 LIFE BEGINS FOR ANDY HARDY — MGM
with Mickey Rooney

1942 BABES ON BROADWAY — MGM
with Mickey Rooney

1942 WE MUST HAVE MUSIC (short) — MGM
A number cut from Ziegfeld Girl was used

1942 FOR ME AND MY GAL — MGM
with Gene Kelly, George Murphy

1943 PRESENTING LILY MARS — MGM
with Van Heflin

1943 GIRL CRAZY — MGM
with Mickey Rooney

1943 AS THOUSANDS CHEER — MGM
with Mickey Rooney, Gene Kelly

1944 MEET ME IN ST. LOUIS — MGM
with Margaret O'Brien, Mary Astor

1945 THE CLOCK — MGM
with Robert Walker

1946 THE HARVEY GIRLS — MGM
with Angela Lansbury, Cyd Charisse

1946 ZIEGFELD FOLLIES — MGM
with Fred Astaire, Gene Kelly, Fanny Brice, Red Skelton
1946 TILL THE CLOUDS ROLL BY — MGM
with Van Heflin, Lucille Bremer, June Allyson, Lena Horne
1948 THE PIRATE — MGM
with Gene Kelly
1948 EASTER PARADE — MGM
with Fred Astaire, Ann Miller
1948 WORDS AND MUSIC — MGM
with Mickey Rooney, Tom Drake
1949 IN THE GOOD OLD SUMMERTIME — MGM
with Van Johnson
1950 SUMMER STOCK — MGM
with Gene Kelly

1954 *A STAR IS BORN — Warner Bros.
with James Mason
*Garland was nominated for an Academy Award as Best Actress
1960 PEPE — Columbia
with Cantinflas
Garland sang on the sound track
1961 *JUDGMENT AT NUREMBERG — United Artists
with Spencer Tracy, Maximilian Schell
*Garland was nominated for an Academy Award as Best Supporting Actress
1962 GAY PURR-EE (cartoon feature) — Warner Bros.
Garland played the voice of the leading lady, a cat
1963 A CHILD IS WAITING — United Artists
with Burt Lancaster, Steven Hill
1963 I COULD GO ON SINGING — United Artists
with Dirk Bogarde

AWARDS
FILM

1939 Garland won a special Academy Award "for her outstanding performance as a screen juvenile during the past year" in THE WIZARD OF OZ

RECORDING
GRAMMY AWARDS

1961 Album of the Year: JUDY AT CARNEGIE HALL (Capitol)
1961 Best Solo Vocal Performance, Female: JUDY AT CARNEGIE HALL (Capitol)

RIAA GOLD RECORD AWARD

1962 JUDY AT CARNEGIE HALL (Capitol)

227

Brian Jones once after his first arrest for drug abuse: "It never did anything positive for me but brought me trouble and interrupted my career." Circa 1967

Brian Jones

Born: February 26, 1944, Cheltenham, England.

Early in life he was a junior architect in Cheltham, England, before going to London, where he founded the Rolling Stones. According to his own words: "I am The Stones." He lived the Stones twenty-four hours a day. His obsession in life was, the present and the future of the Stones. He dreamed that someday the Stones would surpass the Beatles: A thought that must have crossed the mind of Andrew Oldham, first London publicity officer for the Beatles. Oldham left the Beatles to manage a then unknown group, introduced to him by Beatle George Harrison, The Rolling Stones. It was Brian Jones who discovered the obscure black blues of Americans, Bo Diddley and Chuck Berry. It was Jones who imported their records and then, put their words into the language of the Stones. And it was finally, because of his love for this kind of music, that led to his leaving the Stones. He felt they had gone too far astray from the original concept. But Brian Jones, person, had also gone far astray.

He was born Lewis Brian Hopkins-Jones, was a self-taught musician, whose father hoped he would follow in his profession, aeronautical engineering. He quit school at fifteen and worked for a while at a bus company. He met Pat Andrews, a local girl, they began dating, and six months later she became pregnant. Their child, Julian Mark was born October 23, 1961. Miss Andrews said that they never considered marriage, but that Brian was good to her when she was in the nursing home having the baby. "He sold all of his LP's to buy me presents, but two months later he left for London." There he slept on the floor at the home of Alexis Korner, a blues guitarist. Miss Andrews followed him to London, where for five months they lived together in Kensington, while the baby was placed in a foster home. After a row, she returned to Cheltenham and the shelter of her parents' home with the baby. She returned to London one more time, but by then Jones was well into forming his own group, and she returned to Cheltenham to stay.

In London, Jones secured a job in a department store earning £10 a week. In the evening he would go to the Ealing Broadway Jazz Club to listen and sometimes to "sit in." It was there he met Mick Jagger and Keith Richards. The boys decided to form their own group, took an apartment together, and worked and practiced in a pub in Soho. Within a few months they were back at Ealing's playing to packed houses. In 1963, Bill Wyman and Charlie Watts joined them. By 1964, they were firmly established. But Brian was far from established in his personal life, which in the end spilled over into his life with the Stones.

In 1964, The Rolling Stones met "Big Bertha" and "Tiny Tina," who performed with the group on ABC-TV's Hollywood Palace. (L-R standing) Mick Jagger, Keith Richard, Charlie Watts. (lower) Bill Wyman and Brian Jones.

UPI

He suffered from asthma and must have suffered immeasurably with every performance, wondering if and when, he'd have an attack. He suffered from severe mental depression and was placed in a nursing home on several occasions. And he suffered from drug abuse. In 1967, he was arrested and sentenced to nine months in prison, when *cannabis* was found in his apartment. He pleaded guilty and confessed to allowing others to smoke hemp in his apartment. He spent 24 hours in jail, while outside teen-agers protested his arrest. He had become a martyr to them. He was released on bail and put on probation for three years. The sentence was changed to a stiff fine, when Jones' psychiatrists testified that "prison would destroy his mental health and that he could not stand the stigma of a prison sentence." Jones sent a telegram to his parents: "Please don't worry. Don't jump to hasty conclusions, and please don't judge me too harshly. All my love." Later that same year he was hospitalized for severe strain, and still later that year, he collapsed in his flat and was again hospitalized. A year later, he was once again arrested for the same offense. On tour in the United States, he overdosed and had to be hospitalized. Then after another incident, plus arrest, he was barred from the U.S. When he could not obtain a visa to perform in America, he was replaced by Mick Taylor.

Brian Jones arriving at court in London after his first arrest for possession of drugs. 1967

UPI

230

By now, 1969, his position with the Stones was gone. They simply didn't know what to do with him, and it was his decision to quit, "to play my own music." Meanwhile he had fathered another son, another Julian—born to ex-girl friend, Linda Lawrence, who lives in Hollywood. He, by his own admission, had fathered quite a few other children, and bragged about the number of girls he had given V.D. He was the "ecstacy" of the teenagers and the "agony" of the adults.

Perhaps he became bored with sex and turned to drugs. According to his chauffeur, Brian Palastanga: "Pot, opium, LSD—he tried them all." According to Jones: "I smoke hash, but no cocaine. That's not my scene." But that statement was made in 1967, and the chauffeur's, made after Jones' death. From reports of his strange behavior, it does seem as though a personality change had taken place, or had become more extravagant. Always recognizable, with his orange blond hair, he took to covering it with floppy Ascot-style hats, which made him look like a girl. Or "he would dress up in a parody of clergyman's robes—and buy incense from a shop near Westminster Cathedral, which specializes in church goods." Before he was barred from the United States, he was the first heterosexual male to wear jewelry, which he had purchased from New York's Saks Fifth Avenue. He was not the victim of a poor childhood, but quite the opposite. But he was the victim of breaking with the tradition of quiet Cheltenham, attaining world-wide fame, unlimited wealth, and with it all—no peace of mind.

He made his last album *Joujouka* in Morocco with a local folk group, called "The Pipes of Pan" and then retired to his estate to rest—and as all hoped—to get it together. He was living there with a new Swedish girl friend, Anna Vohlin, as he had just broken up a long romance with model, Suki Poitier. His estate, Cotchfield Farm, is a 16th-century showplace, which had once belonged to author, A.A. Milne (Winnie the Pooh). Jones had purchased it

in 1968, for $75,000.00. On a warm July evening, he went for a swim alone and drowned. His asthma inhaler was poolside and at first, the report was that he had over-used it following an attack. But the coroner's report stated: "He drowned while under the influence of drugs and alcohol."

His funeral took place in his native Cheltenham. Over 500,000 people gathered outside to mourn, while inside the 900 year old church, where Brian Jones had once been a choirboy, Rector Hugh Hopkins delivered the eulogy: "He [Jones] had little patience with authority, convention, and tradition. In this he was typical of many of his generation, who have come to see in The Rolling Stones, an expression of their whole attitude to life."

The casket of Brian Jones is carried through the churchyard for burial. His mother and father follow immediately behind the casket, as friends and fans look on. 1969

UPI

Only eight years had passed since Brian Jones had left Cheltenham. Only two years had passed since the Beatles lost their founder, Brian Epstein. And now the founder of the Stones was gone.

BRIAN JONES
Died: July 3, 1969, Cheltenham, England

A free concert in London's Hyde Park became a requiem for Brian Jones. 250,000 fans attended. July 1969.

BRIAN JONES
RIAA GOLD RECORD AWARDS

Albums unless designated as single: (London)

1965 (I CAN'T GET NO) SATISFACTION (single)
1965 OUT OF OUR HEADS
1966 BIG HITS (HIGH TIDE AND GREEN GRASS)
1966 AFTERMATH
1967 GOT LIVE IF YOU WANT IT
1967 BETWEEN THE BUTTONS
1967 RUBY TUESDAY (single)
1967 FLOWERS
1967 THEIR SATANIC MAJESTY'S REQUEST
1968 BEGGARS BANQUET
1969 HONKY TONK WOMEN (single)
1969 THROUGH THE PAST, DARKLY
1972 HOT ROCKS
1973 MORE HOT ROCKS (BIG HITS AND FAZED COOKIES)

FILMS

1969 POPCORN — Sherpix
Documentary with Otis Redding, Joe Cocker, The Beach Boys
1970 SYMPATHY FOR THE DEVIL (1+1) — Pearson & Quarrier, New Line Cinema
with Anne Wiazemski, Iain Quarrier

Jimi Hendrix . . . the first black sex symbol to "turn on" the middle-class white teen-agers. Circa 1965.

Jimi Hendrix

Born: November 27, 1942, Seattle, Washington

As audible and as unpredictable was the music of James Marshall Hendrix, inaudible and unpredictable describes his early life. He never talked too much about those early Seattle years and yet as a dependable person and an outstanding student, one day he quit high school in his junior year. His life became a series of chapters and verses.

His mother Lucille was only a teenager, 17, when she married. Almost immediately her husband went overseas leaving the young half-Cherokee bride not only alone, but pregnant. A story very familiar during World War II in the early forties. Lucille was a party-loving, pretty young thing who drank a little too much and died when Jimi was ten. She had one other child, Leon. When Jimi spoke of his mother it was always how much he "dug" her. What he didn't talk about was the feeling of loss and of abandonment that must influence a youngster. In his case one can only surmise that his aloneness, shyness, and introvertedness have their roots somewhere buried along with his mother. Later he was known for beating up his girls as well as destroying his guitars. What might have appeared then as showmanship certainly had its roots planted back there to the ten-year-old who didn't express rage.

His father, James Allen, "Al", was a landscape gardener whose occupation provided money for the family at least part of the year. The rest of the year it was hit and miss . . . mostly miss, they were not very rich. Al was a two-sided man: his head was on straight, his soul was religious, his demeanor was controlled, and his attitude toward his sons, stern. The other side was his love of music which he "let out" by tap dancing and by playing the saxaphone. It was Al who encouraged Jimi in the pursuit of music. After dabbling around on the violin and the harmonica, Jimi was given a guitar at the age of 12. He became a self-taught player overcoming the almost impossible feat of playing a right-handed guitar as a left-handed person. Had there been a teacher available or if funds had been available, chances are the teacher would have rejected him as a pupil. Most teachers will not go to the trouble of learning and of rearranging the fingering for a left-handed pupil. So Jimi learned the hard way. He developed his own fingering technique and learned music via the records of B.B. King, Muddy Waters, and Chuck Berry plus others.

He was raised in a predominantly white neighborhood and dated white girls. This led to his being expelled from school as the teacher couldn't handle his holding hands with a white girl friend. The school said: "For habitual tardiness and excessive numbers of illegal absences." Instead of joining another class he joined his father for a short time as his assistant. About 1963 he left Seattle and became a paratrooper in the army. This lasted about one year as he was injured on a jump. His unfortunate landing left him with enough damage to be discharged, but fortunately he was not seriously injured.

He did not return to Seattle but commenced his haul to fame and fortune. He played guitar with an assortment of R&B groups on the road for about $30.00 per week, one of whom was the Isley Brothers. He left them to join a package group forming in Nashville featuring among others B.B. King and Sam Cooke. This tour ended when Jimi missed the bus so he headed for Atlanta and hooked up with Little Richard, as a back-up guitarist. Jimi was already biting the guitar and plucking it with his teeth. As electrifying as it was, it is a wonder that he wasn't electrocuted. Little Richard admitted that Jimi was headed for stardom but not on his course . . . . Little Richard was the star and didn't want to be outshone by any of his sidemen. So in 1966 Jimi hit the road and ended up in Harlem . . . the mecca for the black artist. But not for Jimi's particular kind of artistry. For starters, his fellow blacks didn't like his outlandish garb, his strange hair, his music, and his lack of being completely black. They didn't know his white background but they sensed he wasn't exactly one of them. Jimi was not aware of an attitude that made him different . . . he wasn't color blind, he was only interested in making music—his way—white or black or blue. The music lines were drawn . . . R&B, Soul, Rock, Jazz, and Blues and Jimi wanted to do it all. The train that had "let him off uptown" now took him downtown to Greenwich Village. There, in the Village, he starved until he met guitarist, John Hammond, Jr. who gave him a job with his group, the Screaming Nighthawks. It was about the same time that Jimi discovered Bob Dylan. When he heard Dylan's voice or lack of voice he decided that he, too, could sing. He had wanted to sing but had been afraid of his sound. While he was playing with the Nighthawks in Village spots such as the Café Wha' and Café Au GoGo he met Linda Richards, wife of Keith Richards, (Rolling Stones) who introduced him to Chas Chandler, bassist with the Animals. Chandler wanted to be a manager, was taken with Jimi's musicality and interesting looks, so put together a group called Jimmy James and the Blue Flames (he had not changed his name). Before Jimi knew it he was back again at the Café Wha' and back to the paltry sum of $3.00 a night. Chandler agreed that he was going nowhere with the Village gigs so took Hendrix to England. In London, Chandler got Jimi together with drummer Mitch Mitchell and bassist Noel Redding . . . actually Redding had been a guitarist, but the new group wanted him, so it was his second instrument, the bass, that earned him the job. Then Chandler changed Jimmy Hendrix to Jimi and then he came up with the name of the group— "The Jimi Hendrix Experience." Jimi Hendrix lived up to the group's name . . . every show became an experience.

Some said he was "spooky." Others said, "spaced out." All agreed he was "a musician of extraordinary talent." He redefined the way to play the guitar. Circa 1964.

236

The first record Jimi made *Hey Joe,* was well received and well reviewed, for he was an outstanding musician, but Chandler knew in order to achieve big success he had to be seen. Bookings throughout Europe and England followed. Jimi on stage in his freaky clothes, wild look, great guitar playing, were all just background to the sex show. His work with the guitar in the recording studios is legendary and the sounds he got are in themselves legend. A lot of the sounds he produced were understood by his peers but could not be duplicated. His extraordinary use of the wah-wah pedal, which continues the sound long after his hands are removed from the instrument, is just one of many ways he implemented his music. He was concerned with volume and used it to deafening proportions. He was concerned with getting more and more out of his instrument, using ways that even today are not understood by engineers, artists, or anyone closely connected with him. Hendrix himself was never particularly impressed with his skills even though he saw others watching in amazement as they heard the sound of two guitars with only one person playing: Playing it upside down because of his left-handedness was quite enough. As other musicians have done on other instruments, Jimi Hendrix redefined how to play the guitar.

England, particularly London, loved him and hailed him as their own. But to Jimi the recognition had to come from the States, so in 1967 he came home. After his performance at the Monterey Pop Festival in June '67 no one really knew what had happened . . . just that something had. To open the show Brian Jones introduced him. To close the show Jimi let lighter fluid flow from his genitals, simulating urine, and then set fire to the guitar. When the ritual was over the fans flocked to the dressing room of their new shepherd.

His first album, *Are You Experienced,* was released in the United States in September of '67 shortly after the Monterey experience and his popularity exploded. Along with the explosion came another one for Jimi . . . the "mad chemist of San Francisco", Owsley, let loose with his own bomb . . . LSD . . . and along with uppers and downers, sniffing both cocaine and heroin, Jimi took LSD and marched into madness. He had always been involved or intrigued with space, from the first paperback issue he had read, to space films like *2001,* to his seclusion later on to produce what he called "sky church music." Even his clothes looked like they had swallowed LSD. The drug was big in England, having been introduced by the musicians through their lyrics. According to writer Gary Owen: "In England, one of the first musical expressions of the LSD experience was the Beatles' *Lucy in the Sky with Diamonds.* Lucy, Sky, Diamonds—dig those initial caps."

Jimi stopped off in Seattle to see his father, who by now had remarried an Oriental lady. He toured the U.S., making a shambles in Cleveland as the teen-agers trampled everything in sight just as they had done for the Beatles only a few years before. Jimi by now was tagged as Super Stud, Mr. Black Cat, any name you can think of to describe his sexual prowess . . . he was it all, plus a little more. He had many girls but none were ever considered serious. His real girl was his guitar which he called "Electric Lady." And he had come from making $3.00 a night to $2,500 a night and eventually a lot more. He lived in a high manner, spending money everywhere and on everything.

After the U.S. tour he returned to England and continued touring. In Sweden in 1968 he was arrested: Not for his sexual show but for drugs. It was the first arrest, but not the last. By 1969 Jimi Hendrix was tired and was in search of himself and a different approach to music. He was tired of the sexual image, tired of his side-show antics, tired of living up to the reputation he had created as the stud, he wanted out—so in '69 he took time off to search for what he wanted. He returned in 1970, but floundered with one short-lived group called "Band of Gypsies," with a new bassist and drummer. Then he tried to regroup with his original musicians, Redding and Mitchell. But none of it really worked. The sixties explosion was over—the seventies with its new group of teenagers could have possibly said, "Jimi who?" And he knew it.

Said Hendrix: "The everyday mad world we're living in today compared to the spiritual world is like a parasite compared to the ocean and the ocean is the biggest living thing you know about." He tried to turn himself around but the acid trips had burned too deeply. Circa 1969.

Warner Bros. Records

He made his last album in New York, *Cry of Love*, and then went to the Isle of Wight off the coast of England to do a concert opposite Joan Baez. The audience received him well, they were glad to have him back, and anxious to hear what he was going to do. But by now he was confused from drugs, some say he was going deaf from the years of the intense volume, he was unsure of his new role, and wondered about its acceptance . . . put it all together and you get a mediocre show. After the Isle of Wight Festival, the group went on tour to the Continent, but the tour was cancelled when bassist Cox suffered a breakdown. Jimi returned to London to work on his new act . . . his new self.

In London he was seeing a lot of German ice-skating teacher Monika Danneman on a regular basis, spending more time at her flat than in his own expensive quarters. It was she who found him in a pool of his own vomit and summoned help. He had taken at least nine sleeping pills, Vesperax, a German product which calls for, at most, only one tablet. A post-mortem examination explaining his death issued this statement: "The inhalation of vomit following barbituate intoxication." Result: Suffocation. The coroner couldn't spell it out but nine tablets instead of one hardly suggests that he wanted to live.

His body was flown home to Seattle where private services were held at the Dunlap Baptist Church and burial at the Greenwood Cemetery. He left a lot of songs, some finished, some half-written. He left a lot undone, his friends wondered if he could have ever gotten it together. He left poems, one of which was only partly disclosed, but those close to him felt it was a suicide note: "The story of love is hello and goodbye . . . until we meet again."

UPI

(Left) Leon Hendrix is embraced by girl friend as he grieves over the death of his brother Jimi. Funeral services were quiet although originally a massive rock funeral had been planned. October 1970.

Friends and relatives gather around the gravesite in Seattle at the funeral service for Jimi Hendrix, native son. October 1970.

JIMI HENDRIX
Died: September 18, 1970
London, England

JIMI HENDRIX
RIAA GOLD RECORD AWARDS

Albums:
1968 ARE YOU EXPERIENCED (Reprise)
1968 AXIS: BOLD AS LOVE (Reprise)
1968 ELECTRIC LADYLAND (Reprise)
1969 JIMI HENDRIX SMASH HITS (Reprise)
1970 BAND OF GYPSIES (Capitol)
1970 JIMI HENDRIX/OTIS REDDING AT MON-
     TEREY (Reprise)
1971 THE CRY OF LOVE (Reprise)
1971 RAINBOW BRIDGE (Reprise)
1972 HENDRIX IN THE WEST (Warner/Reprise)

FILMS

1969 MONTEREY POP — Leacock-Pennebaker
     with Otis Redding, Janis Joplin, The Mamas
     and The Papas
1969 POPCORN — Sherpix
     Documentary with Otis Redding, The Roll-
     ing Stones
1970 *WOODSTOCK — Warner Bros.
     with Joan Baez, Joe Cocker, Arlo Guthrie
     *Film won an Academy Award as Best Docu-
     mentary Feature
1972 SUPERSTARS IN FILM CONCERT — Na-
     tional Cinema
     with Otis Redding, The Rolling Stones
1973 FREE — Indie-Pix
     Documentary on Rock Festivals
1973 JIMI PLAYS BERKELEY — New Line
     Cinema
1973 JIMI HENDRIX — Warner Bros.
     Documentary
1973 KEEP ON ROCKIN' — Pennebaker

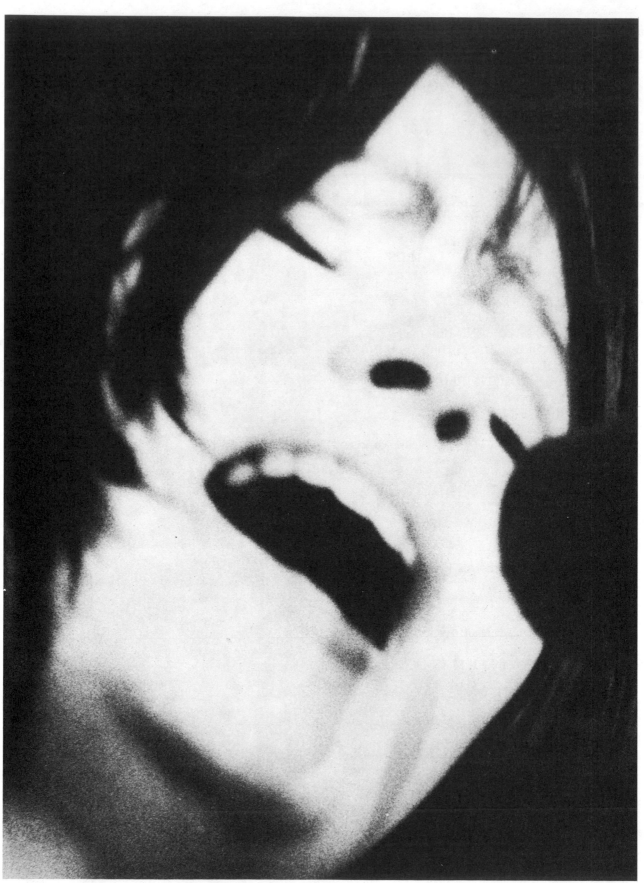

Janis Joplin . . . she played the game well, but in the end she lost. Circa 1965.

Janis Joplin

Born: January 19, 1943, Port Arthur, Texas

Into the tumultuous sixties tumbled Janis Lyn, oldest of three children; a sister Laura and a brother Michael. She was the oldest and the oddest; oldest works in a town such as Port Arthur, oddest does not. And by the time she was eighteen, she had made the first attempt to flee her home town where different would work; Janis was always different in dress, in mood, in likes and dislikes, and in what she wanted from life.

Her mother Dorothy had won a vocal scholarship but turned it down to work in the field of education. She was the Registrar at a local college and not as close to Janis as she was to Laura. Seth, Janis' father, was a college graduate with a degree in engineering, who worked for Texaco. Janis was close to her father and through him developed her love of books. He insisted on a library card and resisted any temptation to install television. Well-read and extremely sensitive were two other features that could make a young girl different in that smoke-filled town in Texas.

As a young child Janis was a lovely blonde but adolescence was unkind to her. The lovely blonde hair turned a mouse-color brown, her figure became pudgy, and her skin became a mass of pimples. The pain of unattractiveness turned her into a tough-swearing, beer-drinking tomboy . . . a facade she wore well and was accepted by the local hot-shot teen-age boys. Although she sang in the church choir, singing was her second love. Painting was her first choice, so when she graduated from high school in 1960, she enrolled in Lamarr College in Beaumont, Texas to study art. This is not to say that her love of music wasn't devel-

oped because she had already been fascinated by Bessie Smith and had already developed the desire to sing black music á la Smith and others. But she was shy about singing in front of friends and opted for art.

In 1961, she dropped out of school for a brief time to see about the world outside of Texas, but by 1962 she was back at school; this time it was the University of Texas in Austin. She began singing in public, and met Chet Helms, a resident of San Francisco, a poet, a crusader of the times, who was visiting Texas. He convinced her she could and should make the scene in California and together they set off. She left her beer-drinking days behind, started with wine, and ended with hard booze. She also added plenty of sex and plenty of pot-to the pot . . .the Sixties Sexual Baby was on her way. She was living out her own words: "Stay stoned and have a good time." 1963 found her in North Beach, California, the west coast's answer to Greenwich Village. She sang in coffeehouses, doing her blues and folk numbers, sometimes accompanying herself with her autoharp, but her appearances did not cause even a tremor. By 1964, she wasn't making it in the voice department but was making it in the speed and smack department. As she sank lower and lower she started shooting Methedrine, and was on strong 80 percent proof booze. She returned to Port Arthur and tried to kick everything through determination and therapy. Eventually, when Helms sent for her, she had had it and was easily lured away. Joplin said Helms sent an old beau, Travis Rivers, who wooed her away (she had given up sex along with booze and drugs) and kept it up until they reached San Francisco. Helms had, by this time, become a music promoter and it was he who put Big Brother and The Holding Company together with Janis.

The group, their wives, girlfriends, and Janis all lived together in a rented summer place, worked on their act, and started to perform. In no time Janis was back on booze, drugs, sex . . . bisexual by now. She donned her granny gowns, slipped her feet into handsewn sandals, and walked into the Haight-Ashbury scene, complete with her own set of music idols . . . Otis Redding and Tina Turner . . . and her own set of friends, the psychedelic pushovers, offsprings of LSD's chemist, Owsley, The Grateful Dead, and others. Her stage image began to develop as one of complete sexuality. Her lesbian liaisons and leanings did not permeate her onstage appearance. In real life she might have become the victim of her own sexuality and image. Perhaps fulfilled one way on the stage and another way off the stage. Some may speculate or relate this to her heavy drinking and her attempts at oblivion through drugs, but it is safe to assume that the roots were watered way back in Port Arthur where being "odd" put her at odds with the world.

Big Brother and Little Sister toddled along until the First Monterey International Pop Festival in August of 1967. Janis with her hair flying and her body flailing brought the show to a stop with *Love Is Like a Ball and Chain*. The audience never knew what hit them. Janis screamed and stomped and they, the audience, reacted by screaming, and stomping, up and down the aisles. This sensation was repeated three months later at the Monterey Jazz Festival and along with it came the salary hike of $10,000 per performance from the $1,500 they had been receiving. Big Brother went into Big Business. To complement their new image, they were able to amicably dismiss Helms and become a part of the Albert Grossman stage of top rock performers: he was the top manager in the business, with

Bob Dylan leading the way as one of Grossman's clients.

UPI

Janis sang about her pain and from her pain. Women understood it, men grooved on it. Circa 1967.

Janis' new life style began with her own apartment shared by a new friend, Linda Gravenites. Ms. Gravenites taught Janis how to dress, designed Janis' clothes, managed to get her to slim down, taught her how to present herself in the new star image, and became her lifelong friend, as well as her adviser.

Grossman began to book them and even managed to get them out of a hastily signed recording contract with Mainstream, which had been a mistake from their early beginnings. Columbia Records was their newest asset and their first recording *Cheap Thrills* was set after their New York debut. It sold millions of copies but the results did not please Janis. The critics' reviews, mainly of the musicians, did not please her either and by 1968, after the Fillmore East concert, Janis Joplin went out on her own.

Joplin's drinking, at the time of the now surfaced drug culture, was in itself unusual. Except for Jim Morrison, most performers were on drugs not booze. The combination was rare but she persisted in comforting herself with Southern Comfort. Her $200 a day heroin habit was common knowledge as well as her trips with am-

Janis on the slim side. She always battled weight, losing the battle more times than winning it. Circa 1968.

phetamines and barbituates. Her excesses seemed to have a mesmerizing effect on her audiences. Sloppy, drunk, and drugged, she was cheered on by them not too unlike the Garland audiences. They rooted for her, as did Garland's flocks, but it was always for more, then more, after these stars had struggled back from the pits.

Janis on Janis: "On stage I make love to 25,000 people. Then I go home alone." Circa 1967.

Her first group, out on her own, was *The No-Name Band* and in a sense it really went No-where. It had a nine musician group, could command $20,000 per performance, which seems to indicate that it was successful, but rock was big, the name of Joplin was big, only the audience response to the music was not big. Although the group toured and was in demand, the audiences wanted Janis' old things, days of Big Brother and The Holding Company. Janis retaliated with, trying to get audience participation, get them involved with her, get them to riot if necessary, and she would go to any demonstrative exhibition to bring this about. She stooped once to exposing herself by lifting her skirt and baring her bare lower self. She was trying to get her act together and was constantly frustrated by the lack of audience approval . . . unless she incited them into rioting. "Pearl" her onstage, and later offstage, personality evolved from the crisis. Writer, Gary Carey, in his biography of Janis* described "Pearl" this way: "tough-talking waterfront tart who liked her 'likker' quick and her men quicker." But despite all of this, the handwriting was on the wall . . . the bottom of the sixties rock wave was coming to an end. There was only one Woodstock . . . it could never have been repeated.

Janis embraces David Rup, promoter of the Palm Beach Rock Festival, in November 1969. During her performance she denounced Florida's Gov. Claude Kirk and the Palm Beach County Sheriff who opposed the festival.

Janis disbanded The No-Name and suffering from physical pain, gonorrhea, alcoholism, and drug addiction went on methadone. She had a few mildly serious male relationships; one with David Niehaus, a law student, and another with up and coming star, Kris Kristofferson. She finally moved out of the small apartment and bought a house, in a middle-class neighborhood in Larkspur County, California. She began to form a new group, Full-Tilt Boogie, and was high on the hope of finding not only a new group, but a new way to make inroads into the music and times of the seventies. She also had a new boy friend, Seth Morgan, a 21-year-old handsome and rich college student. Morgan said that they would be married. Joplin called him her "old man,"

*Lenny, Janis & Jimi, Pocket Books, New York City

UPI

but didn't acknowledge the marriage plans.

She had in fact resumed an old girl-type love affair and saw Morgan mostly on weekends when he would fly down to Los Angeles from San Francisco to see her. In LA she was cutting a new album, *Pearl*, which would be her last. When she was not there, she was touring with Full-Tilt. Her last performance was at Harvard the day before her death, led anyone to believe that it was suicide. Coroner Thomas Nuguchi confirmed this with his report: "Acute heroin morphine intoxication, due to an injection of an overdose, was the cause of death." Her death was ruled accidental. Janis Joplin had started committing suicide years before. She tragically was the product of the sixties and the product of her life's goal.

She sang/cried on her last album. "Oh, Lord won't you please buy me a Mercedes Benz." All she had to do was write a personal check. Check?

Stadium, August 12, before 40,000 fans. She was, by now, back on drugs, and booze, and all of her other habits. She had also, strangely enough, gone back to Port Arthur for her tenth high school reunion. Although the press reported it as a "successful return," biographers disagree; Janis had made it big in the world, but in Port Arthur, maybe for different reasons, she was still odd . . . different.

On her return to Los Angeles after the reunion, she was hard at work on her album, *Pearl*, when she died. Her body was discovered one morning in her motel room. Nothing that she had done or said,

According to her wishes, she was cremated and her ashes were strewn along the coastline of Northern California. Another wish was granted: she had set aside $2,500 for her own wake. The Grateful Dead and others provided the music for the wake which was attended by 200 invited guests. The invitation read: "Drinks are on Pearl."

JANIS JOPLIN
Died: October 4, 1970, Hollywood, California

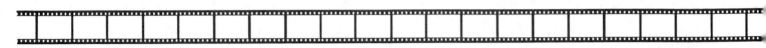

FILMS

1969 MONTEREY POP — Leacock-Pennebaker
with Otis Redding, Jimi Hendrix, The Mamas
and The Papas
1973 KEEP ON ROCKIN' — Pennebaker
with Jimi Hendrix

JANIS JOPLIN
RIAA GOLD RECORD AWARDS

Albums: (Columbia)
1968 CHEAP THRILLS (with Big Brother and the
Holding Company)
1968 KOZMIC BLUES
1970 PEARL
1972 JOPLIN IN CONCERT

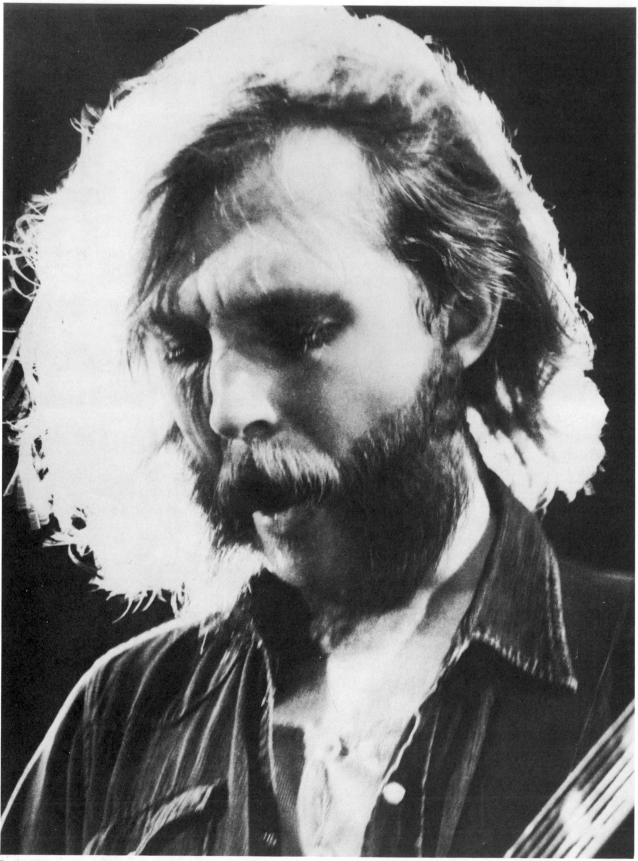

Duane Allman, "In order to talk about music, you gotta play music" and he did. Circa 1970.

Duane Allman

Born: November 20, 1946, Nashville, Tennessee

Howard Duane had two loves, his motorcycle and his guitar; one gave him life, the other took away his life.

He spent his early years in Tennessee, with not too much music in his life. His brother, Gregory Lenoir, was born 13 months after Duane and it was the two of them who later conceived and formed the Allman Brothers Band.

Their father died when they were young, leaving their mother, Geraldine, as the sole support of the family. In 1959, she moved them to Daytona Beach, Florida, in the hope of securing a better job. In 1960, Gregg received a guitar and Duane a motorcycle as Christmas presents. Gregg learned to play while Duane wrecked his motorcycle: a vision of what was to come. Duane traded the damaged motorcycle parts for another guitar and his music career began.

For the next few years Duane and his brother spent their time "building their chops" — gaining technique and strength — as they listened nightly to R&B late radio shows. They loved what they were doing, loved the blues, especially the tunes of Chuck Berry, and mastered the harmonies of the Beatles.

By '61, they had started their own band, playing at Y-Teens dances, or for anyone who would listen. But by now they knew music was going to be their way of life. Around 1963, having played in a succession of bands, one of which was the House Rockers, they formed another Allman group known as the Allman Joys. They played throughout the south, places such as bars and go-go joints, wherever work was available. They cut their first single, on the Dial label, for Buddy Killen, who told them that they were "never gonna make it" and "the worst I ever heard."

The second half of the sixties found them in Los Angeles: there among other assorted musical movements, they became a part of a studio group called Hourglass. Although they cut two albums on the Liberty label, they lacked control of the material and were very dissatisfied with the outcome. So they packed up and returned to Florida.

A record executive, Rick Hall, who ran Fame Studios, knew of and had respect for Duane's playing, so it was no accident that Duane went to Muscle Shoals, Alabama to do some playing. His work on *Hey Jude* and behind artists such as Wilson Pickett was so extraordinary that Hall convinced Duane to move to Muscle Shoals. For the next eight months Duane went back and forth between Alabama and Florida, but a new band, a band of his own, was still uppermost in his mind. In the Muscle Shoals' studio he worked with Aretha Franklin, King Curtis, Arthur Conley and others.

By the spring of 1969, the Allman Brothers Band, the great band with bassist Berry Oakley, two drummers, Jai Johanny Johanson and Butch Trucks, and guitarist Dicky Betts was formed. Manager Phil Walden hired them, the Capricorn label, distributed by Atlantic Records, gave them a contract, and the first album, *The Allman Brothers Band* was released. The reviews were excellent, their reputation spread to national proportions, and road tours followed. By 1970, the band's reputation was "one of the best in the rock and blues field." Their second L.P. *Idlewild South* became a chart hit. Work was plentiful, money poured in, and their third L.P., *The Allman Brothers Band At Fillmore East* reached the million dollar sales level, and earned a RIAA gold record certificate.

"The Allman Brothers Band," a long way from the "Hourglass" and the "Allman Joys."

Wide World

Writer Harper Barnes* makes two musical references: "At its best, the band [Allman Brothers] sounded like a more disciplined version of the Grateful Dead." It is interesting to note, that the Grateful Dead and the Allman Brothers appeared together in the summer of 1973 at a festival in Watkins Glen, New York. Ron "Pigpen" McKernan of the "Dead" had died on March 8, 1973 in California. The son of a white R&B disc jockey, he quit high school to have a musical career play-ing organ, harmonica, doing vocals, and then became a member of the Grateful Dead, so named in 1966; the name was picked from a dictionary, after the group had already performed first, as (1964) *Mother McCree's Uptown Jug Champions* and second, as (1965) *The Warlocks*. Pig-pen was born in San Bernadino, California, September 8, 1946 just one month prior to Duane's birth. He died in 1973 of a liver ailment a short two years after the death of Allman.

*The Rolling Stone Illustrated History of Rock & Roll, Rolling Stone Press, Random House, New York

The band onstage at the Watkins Glen Festival, minus Duane, summer of 1973.

The Grateful Dead, a family of existentialists; offsprings of the Mad Chemist, Owsley of LSD fame; carried twenty-three tons of equipment; put on two shows with each performance . . . one, as they tuned up, and two, as they decided what to play. They disbanded in 1974. Pigpen (4th from left) died in March of 1973, shortly after this photo was taken.

Harper Barnes, writing about the Allman Brothers Band, second musical reference: "It spawned a whole school of similar-sounding Southern bands—most prominently Lynyrd Skynyrd—which even now continue to troupe northward like dazed fire ants." Its leader Ronnie Van Zant died in 1977 at the age of twenty-eight. The untimely deaths of these three leaders is notable for other reasons: these three groups were growing musically at an unbelievable pace; the leaders were rapidly maturing as adults; the groups were gaining in the sort of popularity that promises superstardom. Individually, they have not fully recovered from the deaths of Allman, Pigpen, or Van Zant.

Duane Allman quit school in the tenth grade. He played pool, dug chicks, dug dope, and rode bikes too fast for him. He had two common-law wives: the first, Donna, the second Mrs. Dixie Meadows. Although Mrs. Meadows was living with Allman at the time of his death, the State Court refused to recognize her as a beneficiary because her previous marriage was undissolved. The court, on the other hand, recognized the previous common-law marriage of Duane and Donna, as it ended in a legal divorce. Their daughter, Galadrielle, inherited Allman's entire estate.

Allman was a gifted, natural, and dedicated musician. He once said: "In order to talk about music, you gotta play music." He played his music without gimmicks or tricks and is considered to be one of the greatest guitarists of modern rock. *Duane Allman: An Anthology,* Capricorn Records, will attest to this statement.

Duane Allman loved what he did and became one of the all time great modern rock guitarists. Circa 1970

In the fall of '71, Duane Allman was in the middle of his first vacation in two years. The band had a communal home in Macon, Georgia, called the "Big House," and after a brief visit there to wish Linda Oakley, wife of bassist Berry Oakley, a happy birthday, he took off on his motorcycle. To avoid a truck at an intersection Allman swerved and then was pinned under the cycle as it kept going another fifty feet. He was rushed to the Macon Medical Center but despite hours of surgery, he died just a month before his twenty-fifth birthday.

Hundreds of friends and family members crowded into the Macon Memorial Chapel for the services. The band's equipment was set up with Duane's guitar case in front of his casket. The band entered and played. Brother Gregg, wearing dark glasses, sang, "The sky is crying, look at the tears roll down my cheeks." Jerry Wexler, Atlantic Records executive delivered the eulogy. Johnny Sandlin, former member of Hourglass and an A&R man at Capricorn Records, said: "More than anyone else, Duane Allman is responsible for the musical revolution in the South."

The Allman Brothers Band was not only their name, for in real live they lived and loved one another as brothers. Berry Oakley, bassist, was the one who insisted on the name for the group. A year and two weeks later, three blocks away from the scene of Duane Allman's fatal crash, Berry Oakley died in a motorcycle accident.

The Allman Brothers Band sadly and heartbreakingly had to bury two brothers.

DUANE ALLMAN
Died: October 29, 1971, Macon, Georgia

DUANE ALLMAN
RIAA GOLD RECORD AWARDS

Albums:
1971 THE ALLMAN BROTHERS BAND AT
     FILLMORE EAST (Capricorn)
1972 EAT A PEACH — The Allman Brothers
     Band (Capricorn)
1972 AN ANTHOLOGY — Duane Allman (Cap-
     ricorn)
1973 BEGINNINGS — The Allman Brothers
     Band (Atco—double album)

Bruce Lee, Hero of Chinese Hong Kong.

Bruce Lee

Born: November 27, 1940, San Francisco, California

Li Yuen Kam means Protector of San Francisco. It was the name Bruce Lee's Eurasian mother Grace bestowed on him at birth. When Li Yuen arrived there were three older children staying with relatives in Hong Kong, but his Shanghai-born mother was alone in the United States. His father Li Hoi-chuen was working a few hundred miles away. The family had come to the United States, not as poor Chinese seeking refuge, but were the product of the Cantonese Opera, comparable to our vaudeville. His father was a stand-up comedian and a leading singer. Bruce Lee's future had its roots firmly planted in the soil of the theatre.

Within three years the family moved back to Hong Kong, and again not part of the starving Chinese populace, but there they lived quite comfortably and securely in one of Hong Kong's exclusive sections. Before becoming Bruce Lee, he had one other name Li Siu-lung, Little Dragon. By the time he was eight years old, he was the Oriental Andy Hardy, playing in Chinese versions of the role Mickey Rooney had made famous in America. But that part of his career was short-lived and Lee began to grow up. As a school boy, he was extremely proud of his body and good looks. As a teen-ager, living in the thirty square miles that comprise Hong Kong, with a population that boasts more than four million, he found himself in the inevitable crime ridden streets. He headed his own gang and together they sought out the crime areas where they could fight and defend themselves. In the beginning, Lee was not interested in the refined art of fighting, but more in how to protect himself against any onslaught. As he grew older, he settled down for three years at the Saint Francis Xavier College. There he became serious about the art of self-defense. Also, he began to wonder what would happen if he no longer had a gang to back him? He was most fortunate to find one of the grand masters in the lethal Chinese martial art of Kung-Fu. The origin of Kung-Fu dates back to around the year AD 600, and produced an enormous range of Chinese fighting techniques. Lee's master, Yip Man, brought his technique, Wing Chun (means Beautiful Springtime) to Hong Kong from behind the Bamboo Curtain. Yip Man had spent his life refining his art and Bruce Lee was to spend his life further refining it, and bringing it up-to-date . . . to be of use in the Twentieth Century. Those who studied Kung-Fu with ulterior motives, soon dropped out. The rigid basic training became boring and only those who could see the full potential of the art remained. Bruce Lee was one who remained. He left the back alley fighting behind and started not only a career, but a way of life that demanded inexhaustible physical and mental discipline.

According to Bruce Lee: "One great cause of failure is lack of concentration."

Author's Collection

In 1958, his parents shipped him to the United States with a hundred dollars in his pocket. First, he went to San Francisco's Chinatown and then to Seattle where he enrolled in the Edison Vocational School. After graduation he attended Washington University. It was there he met his future wife Linda Emery, a medical student. To augment his income he began teaching Kung-Fu, then dropped out of school and opened one of his own . . . the first Kung-Fu school in the United States. For only fifteen dollars a month, a student could receive instruction from the future martial arts champion. But Bruce Lee, like so many others, always felt the tug of Hollywood and slowly started his journey to the land of fame and fortune. He and Linda left Seattle, left the school in the hands of a friend Taky Kimura, and opened another school in Oakland. But how to expose his art was the problem. At that time, Karate was the number one fad in the U.S. and Lee decided to introduce Kung-Fu by entering major martial arts tournaments. At the Longbeach, Calif. International Karate Tournament, Lee's technique, peppered with speed and flash, caught the eye of famous hairdresser, Jay Sebring*, who in turn, mentioned Lee to William Dozier. Dozier had had success with his Batman series, so he placed Lee under option for $180 per week in the Green Hornet, a spin-off from the old radio serial. The series failed but the role of Kato, played by Lee, brought many offers to open schools plus other money making schemes. When the Green Hornet was dubbed in Mandarin Kato became a cult hero in the Eastern World. His twin fighting sticks, which he used for the first time in Hornet became his trademark. The "nanchukkas," as they were called, were sold in Hong Kong as the hula hoops were sold in the U.S. The studio 20th-Century Fox sent him on tour and he became the hero of Hong-Kong . . . local boy makes good. While in Hong Kong, Lee was approached

*Sebring was one of the victims killed by the Charles Manson gang at the home of actress Sharon Tate, 1969.

by Raymond Chow, who was just starting a film company, Golden Harvest. But Lee, still dreaming of glory in Hollywood, rejected Chow's offer and returned to Los Angeles. He opened his third Kung-Fu school when he discovered that *Hornet* had not brought the fame he thought would be his. But screen stars involved in the martial arts soon flocked to his school for private lessons. Lee raised his prices accordingly, and made lasting friendships with pupils Steve McQueen, James Coburn, and James Garner. It was Garner who got Lee his role in *Marlowe* and writer Sterling Silliphant, also a pupil, wrote Lee into the script he was writing for James Franciscus' series, *Longstreet*. Quick to praise him were the critics, but a not so quick Warner Brothers signed on David Carradine for their series featuring an exponent of Kung-Fu called, *The Warrior*. Lee wanted the role more than anything in life but he would have to wait a few years before Warner Brothers came to him. *The Warrior* was changed to *Kung-Fu* and catapulted Carradine into stardom, even though the star never believed in Kung-Fu. Meanwhile back in Hong Kong, Raymond Chow came through with another offer, this time for a lot more money plus starring roles, and Lee accepted.

Van Williams (right) star of "The Green Hornet" TV series is shown with "Batman" Adam West (left) and Bruce Lee in center, 1966. The "Hornet" series ran for only thirty episodes.

Wide World

Bruce Lee as Kato in "The Green Hornet" episode entitled, "May The Best Man Lose" on ABC-TV, 1966. Lee once told an interviewer: "The reason I got the job was because I was the only Chinese boy in California who could pronounce the name of the hero in the series ... Brit Reed!"

Wide World

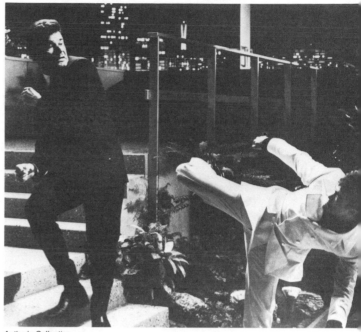

Author's Collection

Lee with James Garner (left) in "The Little Sister" 1969.

The first film, *The Big Boss*, broke all attendance records in Hong Kong and Lee was on his way. Unlike Carradine, Lee did all of his own fighting and no one ever challenged the authenticity of his work. He was a devout student/practitioner of his art and spent his life developing his art and maintaining the physicality of his body. He studied every other form of self-protection (Thai kick boxing, French boxing, Western wrestling and boxing, Judo, Karate) and when he had refined his art, he challenged and beat champion after champion in all of the other fields. To define what he did he said: "My movement is the result of your movement; my technique is the result of your technique." For example, in the movie *Way of the Dragon*, when U.S. Karate champ Chuck Norris beats Lee to the floor, Lee counters with something Norris can't handle ... the dancing toe work of a boxer. Lee always said: "Total fighting freedom is what my style is all about. It's actually no style." His schools of Kung-Fu were called Jeet Kune-Do—The Way of the Intercepting Fist. In other words "it is not punching someone before he punches you but reacting to what he does." Lee did not believe in self-imposed rules but in freedom of expression. Like his ancestors in Kung-Fu, he took the movements of animals and birds. For tempo he used music as a dancer does and then combined all in his

fighting technique. What he had more than anyone else was speed and absolute control. According to Bob Wall: "He was pound for pound unbeatable."

Bruce Lee was always ready, whether it was rehearsal or shooting. He always demanded more of himself than anyone else. Shown here in a scene from "The Big Boss" 1971, which was released in the U.S. as "Fists of Fury."

Author's Collection

Bruce Lee in "Fists of Fury," 1972. Strip down to basics in your movements, get rid of the non-essentials, the basis of Jeet Kune-Do. "Fists of Fury" was released in the U.S. as "The Chinese Connection."

Author's Collection

East Meets West as Bruce Lee and John Saxon confer in "Enter The Dragon," 1973.

Shown here is Bruce Lee and a buckling Chuck Norris in "Return of the Dragon," 1974 which was released in the U.S. as "Way Of The Dragon"——which was made before "Enter The Dragon" but released afterwards!

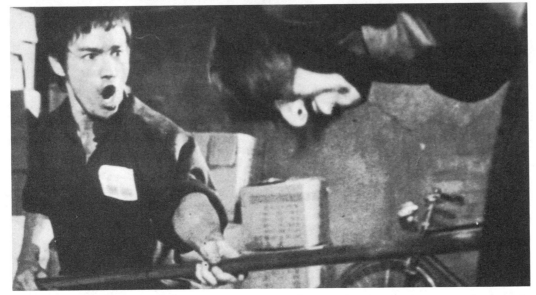

Although Bruce Lee movies became the hottest piece of property in the Eastern world, the Western world was slow to accept the Chinese hero. Just as Valentino had to wait for the world to think of the Latin as a lover, so did Lee have to wait for the world to accept a Chinese as something more than a waiter or laundry man. Chow's competitor, movie magnate Run Run Shaw, was responsible for starting the craze in the Western world. Shaw had offered Lee a contract about the same time Chow had approached him, but Lee turned Shaw down. Shaw produced movies like a Detroit factory assembly line and afforded his star performers very little leeway and very minimum contractual offers. Bruce Lee demanded better terms, considered Shaw's offer an insult, and signed with Chow, who agreed to his terms. Lee opened the door for future Chinese movie stars and eventually Shaw had to follow suit. Whatever the Eastern stars claim today as their right, they have Bruce Lee to thank for the foresight and courage to stick to what he believed. His film, *Fists of Fury,* grossed over 3 million dollars in the United States and finally Warner Brothers, along with other studios, began to see the light. Lee accepted Warner's offer which carried with it a salary for life, and a deal was set with Golden Harvest to shoot, in America, the film, *Enter the Dragon.*

TOP LEFT: First Bruce Lee changed his own life. Then he was ready to help others change theirs.

TOP RIGHT: Bruce Lee kicks out at basketball player, Kareem Abdul-Jabbar while filming his last movie, "Game of Death." The shooting of this sequence took over three weeks and it was the film debut of Jabbar. The film was finished five years after Lee's death and was scheduled to be released in the fall of 1978.

Bruce Lee became a movie star all over the world. He also became a movie star in life-style. He owned a mansion in Hong Kong where he lived with Linda and their two children, Brandon and Shannon. He owned a scarlet Mercedes and a Rolls Royce and although he was not a partying man (neither smoked nor drank), he did entertain Hollywood's visiting royalty in Hong Kong. As a star, he also acquired its hang-up restrictions and its lack of freedom. Many times he fought with the press and constantly he fought for his privacy. He made back-to-back movies and trained for each fight as if it were his last. Vanity, another hang-up, forced him to have his underarm sweat glands removed so he would look better on camera. In May of 1973, he got his first warning about his health when he collapsed on the set. Doctors agreed that he had had a mild seizure, a convulsion disorder, and prescribed Dilantin used by epileptics. One evening two months later, he complained of a headache as he sat in the apartment of Taiwanese actress, Betty Ting Pei, with his producer Raymond Chow. They were going over a deal for his next film when his head started bothering him. Miss Pei gave him a prescribed drug for the pain, Equagesic . . . nothing more than an aspirin compound and a drug, meprobamate. Lee decided to lie down and rest, Chow departed. Later when Miss Pei could not rouse Lee she called Chow, who returned and phoned for a doctor. Lee was rushed to a hospital but he could not be saved.

His Hong Kong funeral on July 25th was reminiscent of Valentino's. The Chinese had lost their hero. They had lost the man who had given them back their pride. They were bent on giving him a proper funeral, proper respect, and a proper send-off to the United States, where he was to be buried in Seattle six days later. As he lay in the open bronze coffin in a white Chinese suit, thousands streamed by blocking the streets, many fainted, many cried, and a banner overhead read: "A Star Sinks In A Sea Of Art." In Seattle, he was buried at the Lake View Cemetery in the dark blue suit he wore in *Fists of Fury*. Steve McQueen and James Coburn served as pallbearers. Coburn said: "Farewell brother. As a friend and teacher you brought my physical, spiritual, and psychological being together. Thank you and peace be with you."

Mrs. Lee Hoi Cheun, mother of Bruce Lee, being assisted at airport by Ruby Chow (foreground) and Mrs. William Ho, sister of Bruce Lee (at right).

Casket, bearing the body of Bruce Lee, is unloaded at Seattle airport after trip from Hong Kong.

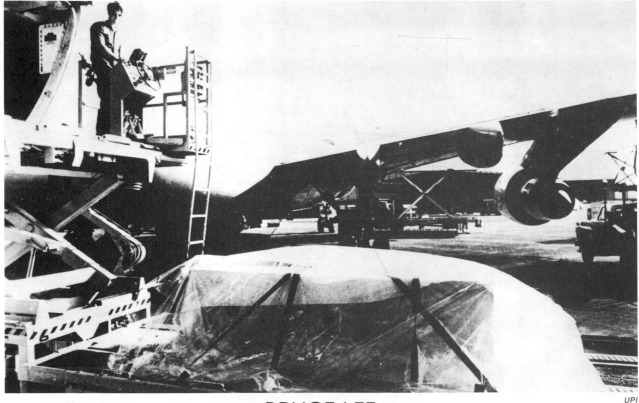

BRUCE LEE
Died: July 20, 1973, Hong Kong, British Crown Colony

BRUCE LEE
MAJOR TELEVISION APPEARANCES

1966 series: THE GREEN HORNET — Warner
-67 Bros.
    with Van Williams

FILMS

As a child in Hong Kong:
1946 THE BIRTH OF MANKIND
1948 KID CHEUNG
    This was one of a popular series starring
    Bruce Lee as Kid Cheung, a sort of martial-
    arts Andy Hardy character
    Adult films:
1969 MARLOWE — MGM
    with James Garner, Rita Moreno
1972 THE BIG BOSS, released in the U.S. as
    FIST OF FURY — Golden Harvest Pictures
    with Ken Hsiu, James Tien, Robert Baker
1973 FISTS OF FURY, released in the U.S. as
    THE CHINESE CONNECTION — Golden
    Harvest Pictures
    with Maria Yi, Hang Ying Chieh, Tony Liu
    Lee was co-director and co-author
    ENTER THE DRAGON — Concorde,
    Sequoia Productions, & Warner Bros.
    with John Saxon, Anna Capri, Angela
    Mao-Yung, Jim Kelly Lee co-produced

1974 WAY OF THE DRAGON, released in the
    U.S. as RETURN OF THE DRAGON —
    Concorde, with Golden Harvest Pictures
    (made before ENTER THE DRAGON)
    with Chuck Norris, Nora Miao, Robert Wall
    Lee wrote, directed, starred, co-produced
    KATO AND THE GREEN HORNET — 20th
    Century-Fox
    with Van Williams
    Three episodes from the TV series, plus
    footage from Lee's screen test
1975 BRUCE LEE AND I — Pacific Grove
    Sheau Chyi Lin, Tsang T. B. Jau, Jin Fei
1976 GOODBYE BRUCE LEE: HIS LAST GAME
    OF DEATH — Aquarius
    A Robert Chow/Atals International Produc-
    tion
    Kareem Abdul Jabbar, Lee Roy, Ronald
    Brown, Johnny "Big" Floyd
    Containing footage from his last, un-
    finished film

Jim Croce as he appeared on LP ABC - Dunhill, "You Don't Mess Around With Jim," his first solo album.

Jim Croce

Born: January 10, 1943, Philadelphia, Pa.

Jim Croce's first claim to musical accomplishment was his rendition of *Lady of Spain* on the accordion . . . a far cry from *Leroy Brown*. He grew up on the outskirts of Philadelphia, in a middle class Italian family. He attended Villanova College, where in his junior year as a cultural exchange student, he went overseas on tour taking in such places as: Turkey, Lebanon, Yugoslavia, Nigeria, and Tunisia. Back home, music making resumed with college bands playing up and down fraternity row. Two lasting things were being established: his love of music and his love of people. Both continued after graduation, as he taught music to children in a Philadelphia high school and worked for three or four years in a hospital. He was always in touch with people, he studied them, and later wrote about them.

With his wife Ingrid he went into the music business full time in New York City. Together they worked coffeehouses, from 1968 to 1969 made one album* together, but as he said later: "I lived there about a year and I never once felt at home." Before they returned to Pennsylvania, an old college pal, Tommy West, lured him "west" to Los Angeles. Together with his musical partner, Terry Cashman, West was able to convince Capitol Records to make an album, *Croce*, but discouraged by lack of sales, Croce and his wife returned to the east and settled down. He drove a truck, she worked as a potter, and together they produced a son, Adrian. In 1970, West and Cashman reappeared, and once again persuaded him to return to the business of making music. He accepted an offer from guitarist Maury Muehleisen, working behind him. He turned his attention to writing his own music, sent a cassette to West, who sold it to Phillips label in England.

Although Jim Croce died before realizing the fame that eventually was his, it was not his death that accounted for it. He was destined for fame, the time was right for him, he just didn't live long enough to see it. He was a musicologist who knew and understood all facets of American music. He wrote about and sang about the people he knew . . . the years of working with them, and being one of them. He was not a rock 'n roller, but a cigar smoking, thirty-year old folkie, "a tough guy with a warm heart." Seated on stage in his workshirt and boots, he sang about the slice of life he knew first hand . . . the young working class of Middle America. He said of himself: "I'm a kind of musical psychologist, or a musical bouncer, or a live juke box; it depends on the audience." But what he really was—was a performer who could size-up his audience and then give them what they wanted. Under the outward guise of a joking man, there lay the serious and diligent one who wrote: "Hey tomorrow you've gotta believe that I'm through wastin' what's left of me. 'Cause night is fallin' and the dawn is callin'. I'll have a new day if she'll have me."

*Another Day Another Time, Capitol Records

Jim Croce performing his own music, but he loved to quote Fats Waller singing: "You're not the only oyster in the stew."

After his death, his first solo LP, *You Don't Mess Around With Jim* (ABC Records) tripled in sales. It became number one on Billboard's chart, as *I Got A Name*, recorded a week before his death, took the number two spot. His third album, *Life and Times*, released January 1973, was already twenty-two on the chart. And of course, his biggest commercial hits, *Bad, Bad Leroy Brown* and *Operator* made this star's star even brighter.

He was doing a series of one-nighters, on a college tour, when his chartered plane crashed into a tree on take off from Natchitoches Municipal airport. He had just finished a concert at Northwestern Louisiana University with only a seventy mile hop to the next town. Five others were killed in the crash, among whom was Maury Muehleisen, now playing backup to Croce.

Almost predicting his own fate, he once said: "There never seems to be enough time to do the things you want to do once you find them."

Wreckage of plane in which Jim Croce and five others were killed, after plane crashed into a tree on takeoff.

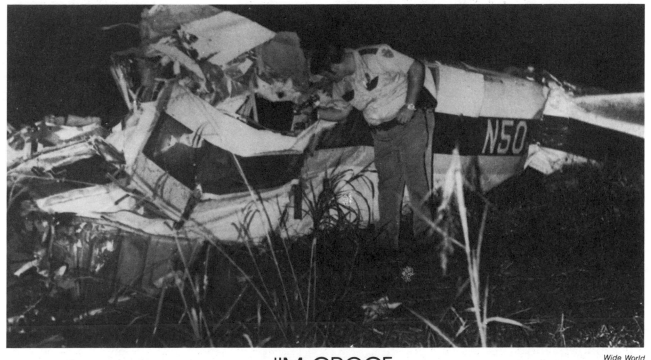

JIM CROCE
Died: September 20, 1973, Natchitoches, Louisiana

JIM CROCE
RIAA GOLD RECORD AWARDS

1973 BAD, BAD LEROY BROWN (single) (ABC-Dunhill)

1973 LIFE AND TIMES (album) (ABC)

1973 YOU DON'T MESS AROUND WITH JIM (album) (ABC-Dunhill)

1973 I GOT A NAME (album) (ABC-Dunhill)

1973 TIME IN A BOTTLE (single) (ABC)

FILM

1973 THE LAST AMERICAN HERO — 20th Century-Fox
with Jeff Bridges, Valerie Perrine
Croce sang "I Got a Name" on the soundtrack

Bobby Darin as he looked in 1964 during the filming of Universal Pictures, "Captain Newman, M.D." with Gregory Peck, Tony Curtis, and Angie Dickinson.

Bobby Darin

Born: May 14, 1936, New York, New York

Sammy Davis, Jr. called him "the shtarker," which means in Yiddish, the strong one. He was half right. For Walden Robert Cassotto had to be strong to overcome his ghetto background. But the other half, his health, was weak. As a child, he suffered from rheumatic fever, which left him with heart damage and eventually was the cause of his early death. The strong part of him enabled him to fight his way from the Bronx streets to the Beverly Hills streets; from poverty to millions.

His cabinet-maker father Saverio, according to Darin, was "a small time gangster, who died before I was born." His mother Vivian Ferne Walden had tried her hand in vaudeville, but gave it up for marriage. They lived on welfare and later received some additional support when Bobby's older sister, Vanina married Charles Maffia. The young Bobby, a sickly child, was in and out of school and was always in need of attention. Later in life, when he stated that he would be a legend by the time he was twenty-five, one wonders if he anticipated his early death. He was always in a hurry.

He attended the Bronx High School of Science, known for its high academic standing, but the already brash, "notice me," Bobby was evolving and it did not sit well with his schoolmates. He did graduate in 1953, and for a short while tried college, but dropped out after one semester. His summers were spent in the Catskills either playing in bands or as a busboy or as a master of ceremonies. He was an energetic entertainer who would try anything. He could play piano, guitar, and drums. And even learned to play the bongos in order to get a job with a dancer, who was about to go on tour. When the tour ended several months later, Walden Robert was disillusioned, unhappy, and unemployed. His new image began with a new name, one he picked at random from a phone book . . . Darin. For a while he shared a flat with with another up-and-coming star, Don Kirshner, where he wrote music, played music, and earned money doing musical commercials. In 1957, he was signed by Atco Records, but it wasn't until 1958, when Ahmet Ertegun, president of the parent company, Atlantic Records decided to produce him. Darin finally made the splash in the big time with his own tune and his recording of *Splish, Splash*. In about three weeks the record sold more than 100,000 copies to the teen-age rock'n roll rioters. Music had become his life.

Bobby Darin . . . songwriter, entertainer, musician, recording artist, movie star, television personality . . .

Author's Collection

But to Darin life meant more than the rock 'n roll market, so he adroitly and wisely took his earnings and made an album, *That's All*, which included most of his favorite songs, plus the one track that became a single seller in the millions . . . *Mack The Knife*. As Darin put it: "*Mack The Knife* allowed me into the adult world." It also allowed him to pick up two Grammies: Best Single Record of the Year and Best New Performer of 1959. He was now 23, just two years away from his impossible goal, "becoming a legend at 25." But he was by now a million years away from the skinny, sickly kid from East 135th Street. Unfortunately Mrs. Cassotto, Bobby's mother, died in 1959, before the release of *Mack The Knife*, and before she could enjoy her son's rapid success.

Bobby Darin, **then** called "the newest singing rage," with Jo-Ann Campbell, his then fiancée, about to go out on-the-town in New York City, 1960.

Darin missed his goal "to become a legend" at twenty-five but aimed instead for thirty. Circa 1961.

Bobby Darin with his friend and press agent Harriet Wasser.   *Cinemabilia*

270

The next several years became a series of successes, from the Las Vegas stages to New York's Copacabana, to movies and TV appearances. The great comedian George Burns became his sponsor and launched him in Las Vegas and ultimately they developed a father-son relationship: something the young Darin had been cheated out of in his early life. His first film was released in 1961, *Come September*, for which he composed both the title theme and the title song. While on location in Rome, Italy, Darin met an 18-year old actress, Sandra Douvan, who like her future husband, had also changed her name to Sandra Dee. They were married December 1, 1960, rather suddenly at 3: a.m. in a friend's apartment in Elizabeth, New Jersey. By December 1961 they had a son Dodd Mitchell Cassotto. In 1963 they broke up, tried a reconciliation, but were finally divorced in 1966.

Darin and Pamela Tiffin in "State Fair" released 1962. It was his third movie.

Darin coaching his costar in the film "Pressure Point," 1962.

Bobby Darin, at right with pipe in his mouth, age twenty-five, buys his dream car. The car, valued at $150,000, represented more than six years of planning by Darin and Andrew Di Dia, who built the vehicle. Crushed diamond dust was used in the paint applied in 30 coats to the car. March 1961.

Darin and his leading lady, whom he married, Sandra Dee, in their film "If A Man Answers," 1962.

Dodd Darin, age 4, made a surprise appearance with his father onstage in Las Vegas in his first tuxedo. His mother, Sandra Dee Darin, watches as Dad Bobby coaches young Dodd. January 1966.

By 1964 Darin had received an Academy Award nomination for his performance in *Captain Newman, M.D.*, had $2,000,000 worth of movie contracts, and was drawing upward of $20,000 a week for nightclub and Vegas performances. It was time to join the ranks of Hobart Inc. (Sinatra), Cooga Mooga Inc. (Boone), Ramrod Inc. (Fisher), so Darin self-incorporated and became King Kong Inc. He also, by now, had come to realize that one cannot become a legend in two and a half years. There just hadn't been enough "exposure time." But he did know that in his age category, there wasn't a contender for the throne. Singer/entertainers such as Dean Martin, Sammy Davis, Jr., even Eddie Fisher were older and the slot ten years beneath them was empty except for Darin. He was a good entertainer, he had style, and class, and he had nerve. He always spoke out and fought for his beliefs. In 1967 he was booed from the stage of the Sahara Hotel in Las Vegas, where he sang freedom songs, protest ballads, used terms like "Slicky Dick" and "Zero Agnew", and appeared in scruffy blue jeans. Darin praised the Sahara for having the guts to allow him his freedom and they

were paying him $40,000-a-week to boot —unlike CBS who had refused him the right to sing a song on the air during the Jackie Gleason Show. It was a song he had written about the discovery of bodies at an Arkansas prison farm. It was Gleason with whom he fought and ironically, it had been Gleason, only thirteen years before, who had given Darin a spot on his TV show. That spot was caught by Atco Records who were the ones to sign him in 1957. Darin had been a friend of Robert Kennedy's, believed in Kennedy, and freaked out when Kennedy was assassinated. He sold all of his possessions, bought a trailer, and went to Big Sur in northern California to live. There he hoped to get his head together, his perspective in focus, and to emerge with an inner peace. Perhaps when he stopped battling himself he learned to stop battling the world. When he returned to his old world of performing, he brought a new peaceful performer.

Bobby Darin and wife Sandra Dee arriving for the 36th Annual Academy Awards. Darin was nominated for Best Actor in a Supporting Role for his part in "Captain Newman, M.D.," April 1964.

Sidney Poitier reacting to Darin's congratulations at a post-Academy Award party. Actor Poitier had just become the first Negro (actor) to win an "Oscar," for the top acting award. April 1964

Courtesy of Doug McClelland

Darin and Dee in "That Funny Feeling" released a year before their divorce, 1965.

Darin, between marriages, escorts singer Bobbie Gentry to the gala premier of "Dr. Dolittle" in New York City, December 1967.

Darin (right, with mustache) with Jean Simmons (l) and Shirley Jones (r) in his next to last film, "The Happy Ending," released 1969.

Courtesy of Doug McClelland

Darin and Debbie Reynolds on NBC-TV's "Dean Martin Presents the Bobby Darin Amusement Co." July 1972.

Courtesy of Doug McClelland

274

Bobby Darin, 1969, had matured in looks, grown in performance, developed his own style and was on his way to becoming the legend he had promised himself.

In June of 1973 he married a legal secretary, Andrea Joy Yeager, but the marriage lasted only a few months. His career had faltered but now the Vietnam War was over and Darin's comeback on the Vegas stages was assured, with a brand new contract for $2,000,000, over a three year period, from MGM's Grand Hotel. He was Dean Martin's summer replacement on his TV show in 1972 and was soon to have his own TV show. But all of these plans were cut short. For in 1971 surgeons had implanted two artificial valves in his heart and by December 1973 the valves were malfunctioning. At Cedars of Lebanon Hospital in Los Angeles, a four-surgeon team, in a six hour struggle, fought in vain to save his life. One of the doctors said: "He was just too weak to recover." There was no funeral because Darin had left instructions for his body to be used for medical research. His wishes were fulfilled as his body was sent to the UCLA* research department.

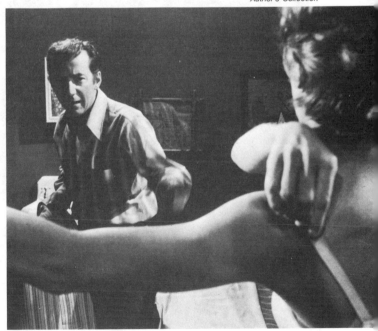

Darin in his last film "Happy Mother's Day, Love George," with Patricia Neal, released 1973.

Darin and his second wife, Andrea Yeager. They were married June 26th 1973, and separated a few months later.

*University of California, Los Angeles.

275

TV star Dick Clark summed it all up when he said: "I used to laugh when people told me how Bobby was an arrogant little son-of-a-bitch. But if you knew him, he was the kindest and gentlest person I knew. He had a great native intellect and if he were only healthy physically, he probably could have gone on to be a legend."

"All the arrogance you read about, stems from those days in high school. It all stems from a desire to be nobody's fool again," said Darin in 1961 in an interview for the Saturday Evening Post. And he never was again.

Courtesy of Doug McClelland

BOBBY DARIN
Died: December 20, 1973, Los Angeles, California

BOBBY DARIN
MAJOR FILMS

1960 PEPE — Sidney, Columbia
with Cantinflas, Dan Dailey

1961 COME SEPTEMBER — Universal-International
with Rock Hudson, Gina Lollobrigida

1962 TOO LATE BLUES — Paramount
with Stella Stevens

1962 STATE FAIR — 20th Century-Fox
with Pat Boone, Pamela Tiffin, Tom Ewell

1962 HELL IS FOR HEROES — Paramount
with Steve McQueen, Fess Parker

1962 PRESSURE POINT — Stanley Kramer
with Sidney Poitier, Peter Falk

1962 IF A MAN ANSWERS — Universal-International
with Sandra Dee, Micheline Presle, John Lund, Cesar Romero

1964 CAPTAIN NEWMAN, M.D. — Universal
with Gregory Peck, Tony Curtis, Eddie Albert, Angie Dickinson

1965 THAT FUNNY FEELING — Universal
with Sandra Dee, Donald O'Connor, Nita Talbot, Larry Storch

1965 THAT DARN CAT — Buena Vista
with Hayley Mills, Dean Jones
Darin sang the title song, but did not appear in the film

1967 GUNFIGHT IN ABILENE — Universal
with Emily Banks, Leslie Nielsen
Darin did the music for this film, as well as appearing in it

1967 STRANGER IN THE HOUSE — de Grunewald, Rank
with James Mason, Geraldine Chaplin

1968 COP-OUT — Cinerama
with James Mason, Geraldine Chaplin

1969 THE HAPPY ENDING — United Artists
with Jean Simmons, John Forsythe, Lloyd Bridges, Shirley Jones

1973 HAPPY MOTHER'S DAY — LOVE, GEORGE — Cinema 5
with Patricia Neal, Cloris Leachman

GRAMMY AWARDS

1969 Record of the Year: MACK THE KNIFE (Atco)

1969 Best New Artist of the Year

RECORDING

Recorded for Atco, Capitol

Ellen Naomi Cohen to Mama Cass to CASS ELLIOT.

Cass Elliot

Born: September 19, 1941, Baltimore, Maryland

Ellen Naomi Cohen was given the nickname "Cass" by her restaurateur father. He named her for the Trojan princess, Cassandra, daughter of Priam and Hecuba, who was given the power of prophecy by Apollo. But the Greek Cass rejected Apollo as her lover and he countered with a curse: All of her prophecies were never believed.

Cass Elliot bore somewhat of a curse herself. She weighed double what she should have for her five-foot five-inch frame, and to herself she was not beautiful. She did manage to prove to herself (and to the world) that one could become idolized and that one could live in splendor and luxury without being beautiful or thin. Unlike her Greek namesake, Cass' prophecy came true.

She was raised first in Baltimore, Maryland—then in Arlington, Virginia. After a little bit of college at American University, she decided that New York's Greenwich Village was more to her liking, so at age nineteen she packed up and started on her career. New York pianist/singer Ronny Whyte remembers her as a hatcheck girl in the Village and he remembers her "sitting in" with him one night at the Showplace: "Cass sang *Melancholy Baby* and wiped out the so-called sophisticated New Yorkers who have 'heard everything'. I saw them crying from her rendition of the song. She might have thought she was being 'camp' but she was singing from the depths of her soul."

Cass continued to sing and became a member of several different groups. One group was the Big Three and included in the group was her future husband, James Hendricks. Another group was the Mugwumps, (1962) which didn't go far but did include Dennis Doherty. Together they founded the Mamas and the Papas . . . and that group hit the moon.

The Mamas and the Papas were considered autobiographical in their work/music/lyrics. They observed themselves and put themselves into their music. *Sitting in our mansions, guarded by expansion,/ Questioning our motives and our means . . . / Wondering why this isn't quite the dream —* Whatever you thought of them, they did have style in life and in their work. And they became rich hippie superstars. Mama Cass was the shiningest star of them all.

*Wingate Music Corp./Honest John Music (ASCAP)

"The Papas and The Mamas." Cass (rear) looking like Mother Earth/Earth Mother. Circa 1965.

Cass (right) being escorted by plainclothes policeman and policewoman on arrival at Waterloo Station, London, England. She was arrested as she debarked from the liner, "France" at Southampton on a warrant issued in London alleging larceny, 1967.

Mama Cass freed of charges "taking blankets and keys from a London hotel," to which she pleaded "not guilty." Shown here as she rejoins The Papas and,The Mamas. (l-r) Denny Doherty, Michelle Gilliam, flower singer Scott McKenzie, and John Phillips. British boy fans look on. 1967.

The Mamas and The Papas at the height of their career together. Cass split soon afterwards. Circa 1965

She and Hendricks were divorced in 1969 after a six-year marriage, during which time they had a daughter, Owen Vanessa. Cass admitted to taking acid five times during her pregnancy and admitted to doing everything the doctors told her not to do. Perhaps what was at first called "observation of self," turned to pure self-ishness: *Go where you wanna go. Do what you wanna do,*** and *Live life exactly as you please.** Despite the fact that the Mamas and the Papas became the Fantastic Four, adored for their wit and sophistication, they were hedonistic. And despite the fact that they had their freedom, had their art — any art — demands discipline. The Mamas and the Papas split in 1967. They tried to go back together about three years later but it didn't work anymore. In 1972 Cass married Baron Donald von Weidenman, a German nobleman and later they were divorced. After the split of the Mamas and the Papas, she tried another union, a professional union, with English singer/instrumentalist Dave Mason, but that didn't work either.

Cass split with the singing group to do her own thing. Shown her doing her thing from a bathtub scene from "Pufnstuff" for Universal, 1970.

*Wingate Music Corp./Honest John Music (ASCAP)

**Trousdale Music Publisher, Inc. (BMI)

"Americans Abroad for McGovern" (Senator George) jamboree in London in 1972. (l-r) Cass, actor Tony Curtis and his wife, Leslie. *UPI*

When Cass left the Mamas and the Papas she said she wanted to do her own stuff . . . her own thing. Career-wise, she did many guest spots on television and did her own TV special in 1969. She became a leading female singer in the "top 10" lists of Record World and Cash Box. And in 1971 RCA Records signed her. She toured Europe, Canada, and the U.S. Philosophy-wise she stated: "I think we should fight to keep bad things from happening. We should work from within, not criticize from the outside. But as a white liberal I am afraid. Afraid that the blacks won't know that I was always what I am." She said that: "The summer '68 Chicago Democratic Convention really turned my head around." Lifestyle-wise in her Los Angeles home, she was called "The Queen of Pop Society." There she held court to musicians, performers, and composers: One of whom was singer/composer, Joni Mitchell, who supposedly wrote some of her songs at Chez Cass. Music-wise, Cass was a singer who felt the meaning of a good lyric. Her earlier solo rendition of *Dream a Little Dream of Me* was the first step back to the impact of her hatcheck rendition of *Melancholy*

Baby. In her last solo album, *Don't Call Me Mama Anymore* (RCA), she does a torch song medley so full of tenderness and warmth that Ronny Whyte . . . from her Village days said: "I felt this recording was the way back for her. That she was going to do what she was meant to do musically."

Ronny Whyte, pianist/composer/singer/recording artist, knew Cass during her Greenwich Village days and later sublet his apartment to her just prior to the formation of The Mamas and The Papas. 1978

In the album, recorded at Mr. Kelly's in Chicago, there is something reminiscent of Billie Holiday. Cass, like Billie, puts her feelings on the line—and shares these feelings with the world. But while she's breaking your heart, she's making you laugh. She talks about working in Chicago in the early lean years at "basket houses": "After a performance a basket is passed and if you're lucky you might make six dollars a night." She points out that her hotel room at that time cost six dollars a week. All of the time she's sharing these intimacies with the audience, she jokes about a cane she's using from a fall sustained in her own kitchen-!: "Why couldn't it have been Howard Hughes' kitchen or even Howard Johnson's?" And then in true Cass style, she belts, *I'm Coming to the Best Part of My Life.*

But before she could have or would have come to the best part, she died suddenly. The first report from her physician said that she probably choked on a sandwich. But an autopsy revealed that she succumbed to a heart attack brought about by overweight. Her Greek namesake, Cassandra, became a slave of Agamemnon and Clytemnestra. Cass became a slave of food. Clytemnestra killed Agamemnon and Cassandra. Food killed Cass. Both deaths were indeed a tragedy.

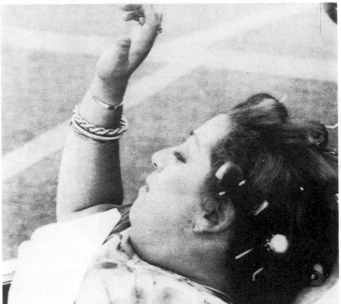

UPI

Just three months before her death Cass collapsed on the set of "The Johnny Carson Tonight Show." She was suffering from chronic overweight and exhaustion.

Memorial services were held in Hollywood, California at Hollywood Memorial Park. (l-r) Leaving the services Leah Cunkel, Cass' sister and her husband, Joseph Cunkel who is holding Vanessa, age 7, daughter of Cass Elliot.

UPI

CASS ELLIOT
Died: July 24, 1974, London, England

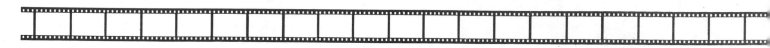

CASS ELLIOT
GRAMMY AWARD

1966 Best R & B Performance by a Group (Vocal or Instrumental): MONDAY, MONDAY (Dunhill) (with The Mamas and The Papas)

RIAA GOLD RECORD AWARDS

With The Mamas and The Papas (Dunhill)
1966 CALIFORNIA DREAMIN' (single)
1966 MONDAY, MONDAY (single)
1966 IF YOU CAN BELIEVE YOUR EYES AND EARS (album)
1967 THE MAMAS AND THE PAPAS DELIVER (album)
1968 FAREWELL TO THE FIRST GOLDEN ERA (album)

FILMS

1969 MONTEREY POP — Leacock-Pennebaker with Otis Redding, Janis Joplin, Jimi Hendrix, Elliott appeared with group, The Mamas and The Papas
1973 L'AMOUR — Altura with Elliot sang the soundtrack by Ben Weisman and Michael Sklar

"I'll never be mistaken for Pat Boone," said Sal Mineo about himself. Circa 1975

Sal Mineo

Born: January 10, 1939, New York, New York.

Salvatore Mineo, Junior was raised in a tough Bronx neighborhood at 217th Street. He had two brothers, Michael and Victor, and one sister, Sarina. His parents were Sicilian immigrants from the town of Mineo. His father Salvatore, Senior carved out a living by making caskets. His mother, Josephine, was a tiny fragile woman who had her hands full with the four children. Sal made it very clear from the beginning that he would be a child with whom they had to reckon.

At age 8, he was a member of a street gang, a trouble-maker who was dismissed from parochial school. His mother, in an attempt to keep him off of the streets, enrolled him in dancing school when he was 9. This made him a target for his street friends, who bullied and taunted him about his "sissy school," but the young Mineo squared himself by beating them to the ground. By the time he was 10, he had become an underground hero in his own right and in his own way. He planned a $5,000 heist of gym equipment from his Bronx school and stashed it in his father's caskets. But upon delivery of the caskets to a funeral home the robbery was uncovered, the authorities stepped in, and gave him two choices. One, he could go to a home for delinquents or two, he could attend a professional high school for stage aspirants. Sal, Jr. wisely took the latter. According to him: "The idea was to make me so tired that I couldn't get into trouble. But I really got hung up on the theatre." He not only got "hung up" but stayed there until his death. He never finished high school but went on the stage by the time he was 11.

Producer/director Cheryl Crawford was looking around for two Italian-American children for her production of Tennessee William's *The Rose Tattoo*, starring Maureen Stapleton and Eli Wallach. Ms. Crawford spotted the young Mineo in dancing school and asked him to say one line: "The goat is in the yard." So for the next year, saying his one line, Sal led a goat across the stage. His next job was in *The King and I*, starring Gertrude Lawrence and Yul Brynner. For a short while he was just an understudy, but later went into the role as a young prince. He stayed with *The King* for two years, but in the short span of three years he had appeared in two Broadway productions.

Mineo looks over a script as sister Sarina looks in. Circa 1948

Cinemabilia

287

Mamaroneck, New York in 1956. He made over twenty movies and again in 1960 received another Academy Award nomination for his part in *Exodus*. He lost one role that he wanted very badly in *Lawrence of Arabia* after *Exodus*. According to Mineo: "I lost because I had appeared in a pro-Jewish picture, played a sympathetic Jewish boy, and shot four Arabs." The Jordanian government would not allow him in the country where the desert scenes for *Lawrence* were being shot.

Away from the streets and street fighting Mineo keeps in shape at the Gotham Health Club, N.Y.C. Circa 1949

Mineo "tinkering" with his 1949 automobile. He raced them "for kicks" as he said. Circa 1956.

In 1950, when his movie idols were all making records, he decided to try his hand at that and actually did a big selling one, *Start Moving*. By 1955, age 16, he had made his first movie playing Tony Curtis as a young boy in *Seven Bridges to Cross*. Then came the big role as Plato with James Dean in *Rebel Without a Cause*, released in 1955, also. He became a teenage idol and as the idol received an Academy Award nomination for his role as Plato. And he was only 17.

With his Hollywood success he purchased a $200,000 home for his family in

Mineo age 17 surrounded by fans, returns to Manhattan to promote his film, "Crime In The Streets," released 1956.

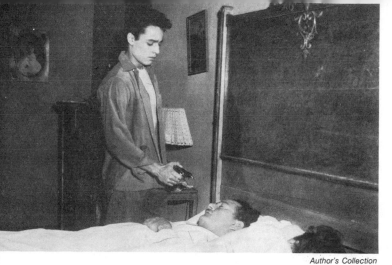

Mineo in "Dino" with Joseph DeSantis released in 1957.

Mineo arriving back in New York after a promotion tour for "The Young Don't Cry" released 1957. At age 18 he had already done eight movies and three plays.

Four of the five candidates for the 1957 "Emmys" for Best Single Performance in a television show (l-r) Red Skelton, Mineo, for "Dino," which was first a feature film then adapted for TV, Lloyd Bridges, and Jack Palance. The missing fifth was Frederic March. California 1957.

Mineo as he appeared in "Tonka" age 19, released in 1959. Here White Bull, his name in the film, gets a makeup retouch.

Mineo portrayed an Israeli terrorist, Dov Landau, in "Exodus" released 1960. He received his second Academy nomination for his performance.

289

TOP LEFT: Mineo, at right, appeared at the Cannes Film Festival with (l-r) Mrs. Otto Preminger, director Otto Preminger and English 15-year-old Jill Haworth, who also appeared in the film, "Exodus." Circa 1961

Mineo and actress Tuesday Weld at the Academy Awards. Sal lost the award for his performance in "Exodus" to British actor Peter Ustinov, 1961.

Martha Hyer congratulates Sal Mineo after he received the Golden Globe Award statuette for Best Supporting Actor in "Exodus." California 1961.

As a young man in California he was always considered a loner and although he had a few close friends in the movie colony, he avoided the typical Hollywood scene. Later he would hang out with the motorcyclist group known as Hell's Angels. As a young man he said his hobby was girls and although he dated a lot, he claimed he was never serious about any one special girl. In 1967 one girl must have been serious about him, or thought he was about her, because when he tried to break up with her she took an overdose of tranquilizers. He loved jazz, thought Gene Krupa was "one of the greatest artists," so when the role of Krupa for the film of the famous drummer's life came along, Mineo fell into it quite naturally. Perry Como gave Mineo a set of drums. It was one of his prize possessions.

TOP LEFT: Mineo entertains costars (l-r) Barbara Eden, Terry Moore, and French actress Christine Carere, all in "A Private Affair." Mineo was preparing for his next film, drummer Gene Krupa's life, as he was finishing this one. 1959.

TOP RIGHT: Mineo with drummer Gene Krupa. Mineo said that as a kid he used to sneak into N.Y.'s Paramount Theatre to hear Krupa play and in 1959 he portrayed his idol on the screen.

Mineo dated many girls but "not any one seriously" according to him. Here he is shown with Joey Heatherton at the Foreign Press Golden Globe Awards in 1964.

As he began to grow older he tried to shake the image of the teen-age idol, always remembering though the famous Bob Hope episode. Hope jokingly on TV once said: "All the schools in the Bronx will be closed tomorrow because it's Sal Mineo's birthday." The next day the schools were empty in honor or their hero. This was the image Mineo set about to change.

Sal Mineo is aided by actor Yul Brynner (r) after he and co-star Madlyn Rhue (l) were accidentally injured during the filming of "Escape From Zahrain" while on location in Barstow, California. They stumbled and fell, during an escape scene, upon a string of detonating caps being exploded to simulate machine gun fire. 1961

Mineo, 22 years old, had to turn in his driver's license in New York after three speeding violations in eighteen months. The black patch over his eye was for an inflammation not an imitation of Moishe Dyan. Circa 1962

MIDDLE LEFT: "Patty Meets a Celebrity" was the title of the episode in Patty Duke's TV show on ABC. Here Patty talks to makeup man Peter Garofalo as guest Mineo studies his script. 1965.

Wide World

At age 30, 1969, through his own choice he turned from actor to director. He spent a lot of time researching the play *Fortune And Men's Eyes.** In an unprecedented fashion he cast the players as teen-agers, not thirty-year-olds, and promised the audience that if they had come to see the play for its nudity, they would leave with

Fortune first opened in 1967 and has been on one stage or another since it was first seen.

something else. He would greet the actors who auditioned with: "Welcome to our prison. I've been imprisoned, as success came too early for me." He was using its "prison" as an analogy to movie-making with its lack of privacy, its programming of one's life, and the censuring sometimes of one's attitudes and beliefs.** His production of *Fortune* first played in Los Angeles and then in New York. Both met with reasonable success.

**Mineo spoke out on TV against the Warren Commission's findings.

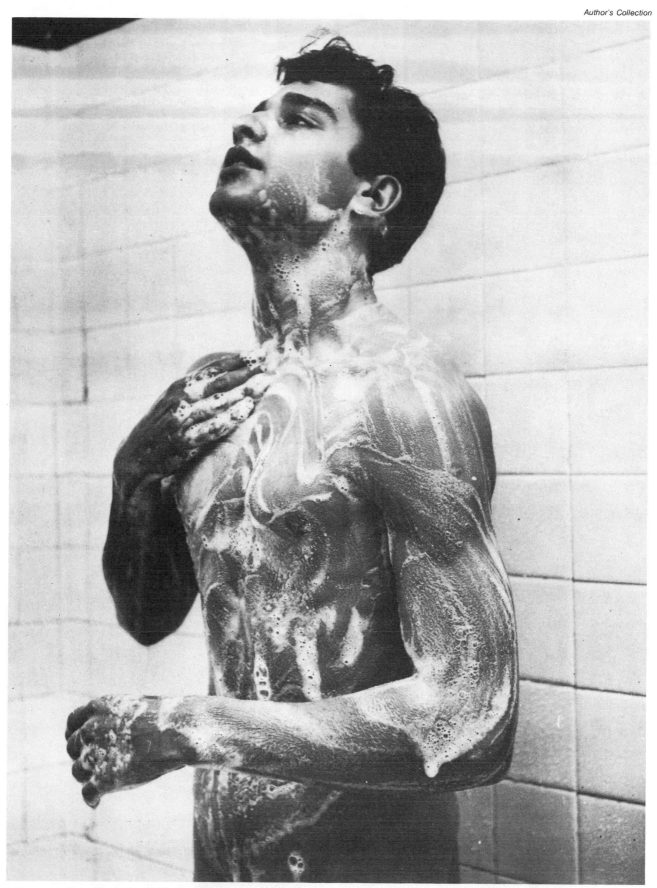

Mineo age 30 as he appeared in ''Fortune And Men's Eyes'' in 1969. He also directed the play in California and New York.

In the sixties, Mineo's movie career lagged badly and his money began to sag, along with his career, as his attempted financial deals fell through. In 1961 he was reduced to playing one of the simians in *Escape From the Planet of the Apes*, which was his last film. At the time of his death his estate had dwindled to a paltry $8,500.00. Back in Mamaroneck, his mother moved into an apartment with her son Michael, and together they operated a health food store. Mineo never married and by then his reputation had grown to that of a bisexual . . . a person attracted to both sexes. At the time of James Dean's death, Mineo was quoted as saying: "We never became lovers, but we could have—like that." He was reported to have had a fondness for sadomasochistic ritual and according to director Peter Bogdanovich: "Sal had some strange tastes." It is possible that "all of this", could have played a part in his unsavory death, was the rampant rumor heard around Hollywood.

Courtesy of Doug McClelland

Courtesy of Doug McClelland

Sal Mineo and Rossano Brazzi in "Krakatoa, East of Java" 1969. It was Mineo's next to last film.

Wide World

Mineo in character for his role as Taggart in "80 Steps to Jonah" released in 1969. It was one of his last films which starred Wayne Newton, Jo Van Fleet, and Keenan Wynn. Mickey Rooney also did a guest spot in the film.

BOTTOM LEFT: Sal Mineo and Laurie Prange on NBC-TV's "The Name of the Game," 1970.

Sal Mineo (right) gets makeup to simulate simian (left) for his last film "Escape From The Planet of the Apes" 1971.

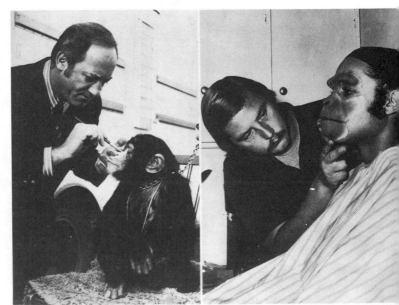

Author's Collection

(l-r) Ben Gazzara, James Farentino, and Sal Mineo as CBS-TV's "The Family Rico" 1972.

One night after rehearsal of *P.S. Your Cat is Dead*, still with his script in hand, Mineo returned home and as he emerged from his car was ambushed by an unknown and unidentified assailant. A neighbor, Raymond Evans heard him cry out: "Help! Help! Oh, my God." Evans rushed to his aid, gave him mouth-to-

Bill Jones, Mineo's neighbor, heard him yell "Help, Help, Oh, My God" but when he reached Mineo it was too late. Jones also reported that he saw a man running away. Los Angeles, February 1976.
BOTTOM RIGHT: Sheriff's deputies are shown photographing the sheet-covered body of Sal Mineo. 1976

mouth resuscitation, but he was beyond help when the paramedics arrived. He had been stabbed in the chest, one thrust, and according to the coroner's report: "He died of a massive hemorrhage, due to the stab wound of the chest which penetrated the heart." Don Drynan, the assistant coroner said: "It was a heavy-type knife." At first the police thought it was possibly robbery, until his wallet was found still on his person. Then a report came in from a boy who was walking his dog at the time. The boy said that he saw "a white male with long hair, dressed in dark clothes running away from the scene." Then the police thought that perhaps Mineo had resisted robbery. Others felt that his death had to do with his companions and his way of life. Hundreds of leads came to the police but the motive was missing.

Police floodlights light the scene as a Sheriff's deputy examines Mineo's body which is seen face up on the ground. Mineo's West Hollywood apartment is at top left. 1976

Sal Mineo's funeral took place at the Holy Trinity Roman Catholic Church in Mamaroneck and he was buried at the Gate of Heaven Cemetery in Valhalla. Nicholas Ray, director of *Rebel Without A Cause* attended along with Mineo's friends, Michael Greer and Desi Arnaz, Jr. Charles Myers, husband of Mineo's sister Sarina, delivered the eulogy: "He was a rare and very special person, a gentle man whose sensitivity and understanding affected everyone he met." And referring to his tough guy roles: "It was a happy irony of his life that he was so different a person than the roles he created. Those who loved him knew that he loved life, that he lived his life with courage, with abandon, with humor, and with grace."

British actress Jill Haworth (center) attended Mineo's funeral in Mamaroneck, New York. 1976. They met in 1959 when both played in "Exodus."

Mrs. Josephine Mineo is aided at the funeral of her son, Salvatore, Junior. 1976

SAL MINEO
Died: February 12, 1976, Hollywood, California

SAL MINEO
FILMS

1955 SIX BRIDGES TO CROSS — Universal-International
with Tony Curtis, George Nader, Julie Adams, Jay C. Flippen

1955 THE PRIVATE WAR OF MAJOR BENSON — Universal-International
with Charlton Heston, Julie Adams, William Demarest

1955 *REBEL WITHOUT A CAUSE — Warner Bros.
with James Dean, Natalie Wood
*Mineo was nominated for an Oscar as "Best Supporting Actor"

1956 CRIME IN THE STREETS — Allied Artists
with James Whitmore, John Cassavetes, Mark Rydell

1956 SOMEBODY UP THERE LIKES ME — MGM
with Pier Angeli, Paul Newman, Everett Sloane, Eileen Heckart

1956 GIANT — Stevens & Gilsberg, Warner Bros.
with James Dean, Elizabeth Taylor, Rock Hudson

1957 DINO — Block-Kamarsky Productions
with Brian Keith, Susan Kohner, Joseph Desantis

1957 THE YOUNG DON'T CRY — Waxman, Columbia
with James Whitmore, J. Carroll Naish

1959 TONKA — Pratt, Disney, Buena Vista
with Philip Carey, H. M. Wynant, Jerome Courtland

1959 A PRIVATE'S AFFAIR — 20th Century-Fox
with Christine Carrere, Barry Coe, Barbara Eden

1959 THE GENE KRUPA STORY — Waxman, Columbia
with Susan Kohner, James Darren, Susan Oliver

1960 *EXODUS — Otto Preminger
with Paul Newman, Eva Marie Saint, Ralph Richardson
*Mineo was nominated for an Academy Award as Best Supporting Actor

1962 ESCAPE FROM ZAHRAIN — Paramount
with James Mason, Yul Brynner, Madlyn Rhue

1962 THE LONGEST DAY — 20th Century-Fox
with John Wayne, Henry Fonda, Robert Mitchum

1964 CHEYENNE AUTUMN — Warner Bros.
with Richard Widmark, Carroll Baker, James Stewart, Edward G. Robinson

1965 THE GREATEST STORY EVER TOLD — United Artists
with Max Von Sydow, Dorothy McGuire, Charlton Heston

1965 WHO KILLED TEDDY BEAR? — Magna
with Juliet Prowse, Jan Murray, Elaine Stritch

1969 80 STEPS TO JONAH — Warner Bros.
with Wayne Newton, Jo Van Fleet, Keenan Wynn
KRAKATOA, EAST OF JAVA — Cinerama
with Maximilian Schell, Diane Baker, Rossano Brazzi

1971 ESCAPE FROM THE PLANET OF THE APES — 20th Century-Fox
with Roddy McDowell, Kim Hunter, Bradford Dillman

Flo Ballard, one of the original Supremes, which was one of the most famous and most popular black singing groups in the history of the recording business. Circa 1969.

Flo Ballard

Born: January 30, 1943, Detroit, Michigan

Four little girls from school were they, Flo, Betty, Mary, and Diana. Raised in Detroit's Brewster housing project—it was no wonder they all wanted out—singing was the way. Flo Ballard spearheaded the group, who as high school students were told by Motown founder Berry Gordy, Jr. to come back and see him after they graduated. At first the girls were called the Primettes, sister group of the Primes. Otis Williams and Melvin Franklin had been part of the singing group, The Distants for about three years before they joined Paul Williams, no relation to Otis, and Eddie Kendricks who were Primes, and Elbridge Bryand . . . these five became the original Temptations. Bryant was replaced by David Ruffin shortly before their first big hit. As the Distants and the Primes merged into the Temptations so did the girls, as Primettes, merge into the Supremes—minus Betty: they were Flo Ballard, Mary Wilson, and Diana Ross . . . the original Supremes.

UPI

Initially Flo Ballard was assigned as lead singer of the group and was given credit for its name. But Motown's chief, Gordy and his fellow associates, Lamont Dozier, Brian and Eddie Holland, wished to further refine their product. The end result was a new lead singer, Diana Ross, backed up by Flo Ballard and Mary Wilson.

Of all of Berry Gordy's supreme efforts as the mighty mogul of Motown, the Supremes reigned as his royalty. Royalties of another sort were reaped by and from their unbelievable twelve Number One pop hits, five of which were consecutive . . . a feat still unparalleled. The Supremes' first effort for Motown in 1963, *When the Lovelight Starts Shining Through His Eyes*, didn't shine, but by June 1964 with Ross leading the way, *Where Did Our Love Go* climbed to numero uno on the pop charts in just five weeks. The Supremes traveled across the nation, to the Far East, and to Europe, cut eight gold records, which sold a million copies as they racked up fame and fortune—at least that is what Flo Ballard was led to believe. She stated in an interview, after she left the Supremes, that she had "received an allowance of $225.00 a week during the seven years she was a Supreme" and that "the rest of her money was being banked for her."

The Temptations, the first big skilled black singing group who pleased the eye, as well as the ear. Paul Williams (upper right) born July 2, 1939, left the group in 1971. At the age of 34 (August 1973) he died of a bullet wound in the head, apparently self-inflicted. He was the father of five children and divorced from his wife Mary.

The Primettes . . . (l-r) Mary Wilson, Flo Ballard, Diana Ross . . . 1964.

Courtesy of William Ewald

Ballard left the Supremes in 1967. She had risen from poverty and obscurity to security and stardom. But why did she leave? Again a quote from her: "I left the Supremes under pressure from Berry Gordy, Jr. and from Diana Ross. They were critical of my singing and that Gordy repeatedly urged me to quit. Gordy said," she continued, "You're a millionaire at twenty-four—you can leave anytime now." However, somewhere deep down inside she must have harbored a grudge about being pushed aside for Diana Ross and for the new name of the group, Diana Ross and The Supremes. Whatever the reason or reasons she terminated her contract with a $160,000 release and went out on her own.

In 1968, February 29th, she married Thomas Chapman, a former employee of Motown and chauffeur to singer Etta James. As a solo artist, Flo Ballard signed with ABC Records, she did two singles, but for lack of promotion or lack of interest the records went nowhere. In 1969 she had twin daughters, Michelle and Nicole, and later separated from her husband. He paid child support until he lost his job, she lost her home through foreclosure, and then was forced to live with her mother, Mrs. Laura Lee Wilson.

She had gone from high living to what she thought was financial security for life, to ADC (Aid to Families with Dependents) which paid her $135.00 every two weeks. She was also hospitalized twice for nerve strain and once for exhaustion. Her last public appearance was in 1969.

In 1971 she filed a suit for $8.7 million dollars against Gordy and other Motown officials, Diana Ross, and Mary Wilson, charging that "they had conspired for her to leave under a fraudulent settlement." In signing the '68 release for $160,000 she gave up all rights to any future income from the Supremes, Motown, or International Management. Miss Ballard claimed that the release should now be declared void. The opposing attorney Donald Barris told the court that the release signed by Ballard, which took eight months to negotiate, was legal and that the reason she had been fired was "because of her conduct and because of the fact that she wasn't performing well." Ballard also brought charges against Cindy Birdsong, who had replaced her and against Jean Terrell, who had replaced Diana Ross. Ballard's attorney argued that: "the release should be declared void because the Supremes made huge amounts of money and the $160,000 Miss Ballard received was greatly disproportionate to those earnings." The case was dismissed by the Wayne County Circuit Court but in 1973 the Michigan Court of Appeals overturned the ruling.

The Appeals Court said that "it agreed with the defendants' contention to challenge the release agreements but Miss Ballard must give back the amount paid her. Since she did not, the release agreement will be permitted to stand." The court went on to state however, that "Miss Ballard may bring a case in lower court asking for damages for alleged mental and emotional distress suffered by her after signing the agreement. Whether the injuries alleged were in fact suffered by the plaintiff must be determined by a lower court proceeding."

And then there were none . . . Mary Wilson (l) became The Supremes, Mary Wilson; Flo Ballard (r) tried to make it solo; Diana Ross (center) went on to fame and further fortune as an actress. Circa 1967

After her rags to riches story was printed from coast-to-coast, job offers be-

gan to filter in and Flo Ballard felt her life was on the upswing again. She and her husband had a reconciliation and with it another daughter, Lisa, born in 1973. Diana Ross had gone on to superstardom as a fine solo artist and as an actress in *Lady Sings The Blues*, the inaccurate life story of Billie Holiday. Mary Wilson instituted her own lawsuit against Motown and went to Europe where she performed as The Supremes, Mary Wilson. Eventually Ballard was in a position to buy a new house and a new car. The exact terms of the final settlement are not known but she must have received some money. *Detroit Free Press*

Flo Ballard's seven-year-old twins, Nicole and Michelle, sit with their father Tommy Chapman and Diana Ross (l) through the service for their mother. February 1976.

But it was all too late and too much strain. Florence Ballard was "alert but suffering from paralysis of the lower body" when she was admitted to Mt. Carmel Mercy Hospital. She died there the following day of cardiac arrest. A police report stated that: "She ingested an unknown amount of pills and consumed alcohol." The pills were for overweight and high blood pressure. The bitterest pill of all . . . the one she could not swallow . . . must have been her own bitterness. She had gotten out of the housing project life for a brief time, only to be thrust back again through fate, bad judgment, circumstances, and the grinding machinery of the American Dream.

Diana Ross, wearing hot pants, shown with Motown chief Berry Gordy (right) arriving for the Clay-Frazier fight. Ross was the remaining Supreme who went on to further fame and fortune as an actress/singer. 1971.

Down the street from the New Bethel Baptist Church, Judy's Record Shop blasted *Where Did Our Love Go* as a tribute to Flo Ballard Chapman, as a thousand people lined both sides of the street to view celebrities arriving in sleek limousines. Inside the church Rev. C. L. Franklin, father of singer Aretha Franklin, had to ask the 2,200 people, some attired in evening dresses and mink, others in house dresses, to "quiet down and have respect for the dead." Gladys Knight and The Pips sent a floral arrangement; Stevie Wonder and The Four Tops were there; the light blue coffin was flanked with a huge heart-shaped floral arrangement of white and blue carnations from Diana Ross, crossed by a ribbon that read: "I love you, Blondie, Diana."

After the service Mary Wilson, who had arrived in a Rolls Royce, and Diana Ross, flanked by men who spirited her down the aisle, stood beside the closed coffin for a few minutes of silent prayer . . . as flashbulbs popped like champagne corks. Then as the coffin was carried out of the church the crowd went wild shoving and pushing and tearing the floral arrangements apart leaving the police helpless and the arrangements in shreds.

Left amid the choatic and disarray of the final tribute to Florence Ballard, are her daughters, husband, mother, five sisters, four brothers, and the words of Rev. Franklin: "We have experiences that are not always good and true, sometimes frustrating and crushing, but positive good grows out of negative situations."

FLO BALLARD
Died: February 22, 1976, Detroit, Michigan

FLO BALLARD

(Motown, the company for which Flo Ballard recorded with The Supremes, has never joined the Recording Industry Association of America, so there is no official listing of Gold Records. The following are some of the greatest hit singles of The Supremes.)

HIT RECORDS

1963 BABY LOVE
1964 WHERE DID OUR LOVE GO?
1965 COME SEE ABOUT ME
1965 I HEAR A SYMPHONY
1965 NOTHING BUT HEARTACHES
1965 STOP! IN THE NAME OF LOVE
1965 BACK IN MY ARMS AGAIN
1966 LOVE IS LIKE AN ITCHING IN MY HEART
1966 MY WORLD IS EMPTY WITHOUT YOU
1966 YOU CAN'T HURRY LOVE
1966 YOU KEEP ME HANGIN' ON
1967 REFLECTIONS
1967 THE HAPPENING
1967 LOVE'S HERE AND NOW YOU'RE GONE

Jack Cassidy . . . he worked hard to achieve his success. Circa 1971.

Jack Cassidy

Born: March 5, 1927, Long Island, New York.

Richmond Hill, Queens, where John Edward Cassidy grew up, is only a short eight miles from Broadway...if you drive. But if you plan to make it there as a star the road is long, the going is tough, and the detours are many. Jack Cassidy not only made it there but he made it in Europe, in California, and on the television screen which made him "there" all around the world.

By the time he was eleven he had abandoned his thought of becoming a priest: a thought that perhaps crosses the mind of every young Irish-American. Instead he worked part time on a coal and ice truck, delivered circulars, whipped up sundaes and milk shakes as a soda jerk, and even managed to attend parochial school. John Edward, the youngest of five children, whose father was a railroad engineer, became dedicated to his career and never lost sight of his goal. He never had time for games but worked diligently on developing his young boy soprano voice which later became a full theatre voice. He was fortunate in having an uncle, Ben Dora of Music Hall fame, to guide him and to steer him in the right direction.

In 1943 producer Mike Todd ran an ad in *Variety* announcing the call for chorus boys, ages 16-17 or 4F, for his new show *Something For The Boys* starring Ethel Merman. Cassidy, age 16, applied and got his first job on Broadway. Another first appeared at the same time . . . "withholding tax." The $45.00 a week minimum that the chorus boys and girls were earning was barely enough for their rent and food. The thought of having to chip in for the new tax gambit from their meager salary was more than they intended to do. As they were preparing to walk out, word

reached them that their employer, Todd had known about this and was trying desperately to get the War Stabilization Board to agree to a raise for his chorus. As in most Hollywood/Broadway stories, "the boy gets the girl" and all ends happily; this was no exception. The chorus boys and girls got a salary raise to $50.00, instead of each other, and *Something For The Boys* opened on time with Jack Cassidy singing and dancing. When the show closed Cassidy took interim jobs as a chauffeur, bell-hop, stable boy, and hotel clerk. Theatrically his next role was a bit part in *Small World* in 1948.

He married his first wife, actress Evelyn Ward and in 1951, their son David was born. David, unlike his father, had overnight superstardom as the teeny-bopper idol on the TV series, *The Partridge Family* and then as a rock singer. His father, spawned from a battery of musicals and nightclubs, reached his stardom slowly and assiduously. He sang and danced his way through *Sadie Thompson* and *South Pacific* and in 1952 appeared in *Wish You Were Here*.

By 1955, at age 28, Jack Cassidy was beginning to travel an even tougher road than the one from Richmond Hill to Broadway. The search for self . . . the tortuous inner soul searching of where, how, and why. He was cast in a dramatic musical, *Sandhog*, in a serious role. According to his own words: "This turned me around and in order to sort it out, I attempted an autobiography, to get it all out." Writing it down has served as a most effective catharsis for many and for many years. Cassidy not only had to battle his inner war but had to battle his image. He appeared cocky and also appeared as a dimpled pretty chorus boy. He went to work on his image and he went to work on his life.

As Curley in ANTA's government sponsored production of *Oklahoma!* he went to Europe. With him, playing the lead, Laurey, was his future wife, Shirley Jones, whom he had previously met in New York City. Cassidy, now divorced from his first wife, and with his guts spilled out onto paper, was now ready to take the giant

TOP: He played "Curley" and she played "Laurie" in the European government sponsored ANTA's production of "Oklahoma!," Shown here in Rome, Italy 1956.

RIGHT: A closer look at the engaged and happy couple, Jack Cassidy and Shirley Jones, as they appeared during their European tour. Circa July 1956

steps in his career and in his personal life. In an interview with the *New York Times* in May 1966, he explained it this way: "When I met Shirley everything positive seemed to fall into place. She was dead honest and unafraid and she had an abundance of patience. I'd always been attracted to the erratic, but Shirley was complete. She had no neurotic fusions going on inside her."

They were married August 5, 1956 in Cambridge, Massachusetts at the Church

of the New Jerusalem. Just across the street from the church they were appearing together in *The Beggar's Opera*. They were young, talented, beautiful, and in love. The marriage lasted eighteen years and produced three children, Shaun, Patrick, and Ryan. Together they toured in a supper club act and separately they pursued their careers. Shirley Jones Cassidy, known for her musical talent in such

movies as *Oklahoma!*-1955, *Carousel*-1956 and *Music Man*-1962 turned it all around when she won the Oscar for best supporting dramatic actress in 1960 for her role in *Elmer Gantry*. Later of course she was seen with her stepson in the TV series, *The Partridge Family*.

Just across the street from the church the newlyweds were performing together in the "Beggar's Opera," August 1956.

Shirley and Jack, married August 5, 1956 in Cambridge, Massachusetts.

Shirley Jones Cassidy and proud husband Jack after she won an "Oscar" for best supporting actress in "Elmer Gantry," California 1961.

Just "Shirley and me and baby makes three." Their first of three sons, Shaun, born 1959.

The Cassidys moved to California in 1958, where they worked, when work was available, in movies and/or television. For Jack Cassidy the big breaks started around 1962. He began being seen on all the major television shows which culminated in 1970 with the national success of Saul Levitt's *The Andersonville Trial* directed by George C. Scott. Cassidy, playing the role of the civilian defense counsel, won an Emmy for "a single performance by a leading man."

TOP: Jack Cassidy with wife Shirley and oldest son David (from a previous marriage) shown arriving at the Emmy Awards in California, 1971. Cassidy won his Emmy for The Best Performance by a Leading Man in "The Andersonville Trial."

LEFT: The Cassidy careers grow. Shown here she is en route to Italy to begin a film while he remained in New York to do a play. The family has grown, too . . . another son Patrick, age 1 and brother Shaun, age 4. Circa 1963.

During the intervening years between the move to California and the Emmy winning performance, Jack Cassidy kept his fingers in the Broadway pie. In 1963 he won a Tony for his portrayal of the dashing wandering Hungarian lover, Mr. Kodaly, in *She Loves Me*. He returned to Broadway again briefly with Carol Burnett in 1964 in the musical, *Fade Out, Fade In*. And if his fans missed him in any of these performances he could always be seen as a regular on television's talk or game shows.

Broadway bound from the beginning Jack Cassidy scores in "Fade Out-Fade In" with co-star Carol Burnett, 1964.

Cassidy (directly behind him) wife Shirley Jones and Carol Burnett at recording session for "Fade Out-Fade In," 1964.

Jack Cassidy represented the textbook profile of what an actor should be and how an actor reaches his goal. Hard work, determination, humor, wit, introspection crossed with the necessary outer layer of extraversion. He looked in the mirror, harnessed his dimpled cocky Irish-American face to his acting ability, and produced the thoroughbred thespian so aptly described by writer Wolfgang Saxon: "His specialty was to play leading men who caricatured leading men as preening, yet crafty, fops."

Gallant Jack Cassidy escorts actress Tammy Grimes to the premier of the movie "Tom Jones," New York City, 1963.

"IT'S A BIRD . . . IT'S A PLANE . . . IT'S SUPERMAN" . . . it's superstar Jack Cassidy on Broadway, 1966. He received a Tony nomination for Best Performance by an Actor in a Musical.

Shown here in a scene from "Wait Until Dark" the Cassidys toured with the production, both playing straight roles. Not one note of music. Circa January 1967.

Jack Cassidy models a dinner jacket for
After Six Formals.

Jack Cassidy and Diane Baker on TV's "Bonanza," 1971.

Cassidy with actress Nanette Fabray and actor Joel
Gray as they appeared in CBS-TV Show, "George
M."

Jack Cassidy and Shirley Jones were married eighteen years. Shown here in 1974.

TOP: The real John Barrymore is at right. Jack Cassidy who portrayed the famed "profile" in Universal's "W.C. Fields and Me" is at left. The only facet of Cassidy's appearance that had to be altered was his hair, which had to be darkened. At this time Cassidy lived across the street from the old Barrymore mansion in Hollywood. Circa 1975.
BOTTOM: Jack Cassidy (left) as Barrymore in "W.C. Fields and Me." (l-r) Rod Steiger as Fields, Harold Gould, unidentified player, Frank De Vol, and Milt Kamen. 1976

Courtesy of Doug McClelland

A year before his death he returned to Broadway to play the role, "his specialty", a self-admiring arrogant actor in *Murder Among Friends*, a comedy-mystery co-starring Janet Leigh. Critic Clive Barnes called him: "Stormily brilliant" and "Marvelous" and "His timing impeccable" and "He takes the most harmless lines and makes them sound wickedly and bizarrely funny." The kid from Richmond Hill, Queens, had been crowned Broadway's King.

RIGHT: Jack Cassidy from Queens (New York) became a King (of the entertainment world). He died just before his fiftieth birthday, 1976.
BOTTOM: Fire swept through the four-story building in West Hollywood as residents were evacuated. The fire truck ladder reaches to the appartment where the unidentified body was found.

UPI

Apparently touched off by a smouldering cigarette on or under the couch, a fire swept through his penthouse apartment. His car was missing from the garage, and as friends and family waited for the charred body found in the living room to be identified, they hoped that he had gone to Palm Springs as planned. It took five Fire Department units to put out the blaze, 100 residents had to be evacuated, and the total damage was in the vicinity of $150,000.

The intensity of the blaze is shown in this view of the Cassidy living room. The Los Angeles Coroner's office identified the charred body of Jack Cassidy through dental records. December 13, 1976.

But the fears of his family and friends became a reality when dental charts disclosed the identity of the badly burned body and when agent Rowland Perkins identified jewelry known to belong to Jack Cassidy. The missing automobile had just been borrowed by a friend. Cassidy was buried in Los Angeles just a few months before his fiftieth birthday. Former wife and devoted friend Shirley Jones wrote the following final tribute.

"He was an extraordinary man with an uncanny sense of humor and a gifted talent. He was one of a kind and the world suffers a great loss that he was taken from it so soon."

At right, son David Cassidy with his mother, actress Evelyn Ward, first wife of Jack Cassidy shown leaving the chapel after services for the famous actor were held.

Shirley Jones (center), son Shaun, 17, (to her right) are shown leaving the chapel after services for her former husband Jack Cassidy. She is being assisted by her husband, performer Marty Engels. California, December 1976.

JACK CASSIDY
Died: December 12, 1976, Los Angeles, California

JACK CASSIDY
SMALL ROLES OR CHORUS IN BROADWAY SHOWS

1943 SOMETHING FOR THE BOYS, by Cole Porter, produced by Michael Todd

1945 SADIE THOMPSON, by Vernon Duke and Howard Dietz

1945 MARINKA, by Emerich Kalman and George Marion, Jr.

1945 THE RED MILL (revival), by Sigmund Romberg

1945 BILLION DOLLAR BABY, by Morton Gould, Betty Comden, Adolph Green

1946 AROUND THE WORLD IN 80 DAYS, by Cole Porter, co-produced by Michael Todd

1947 MUSIC IN MY HEART

1948 INSIDE U.S.A., By Arthur Schwartz, and Howard Dietz

1949 SOUTH PACIFIC

MAJOR BROADWAY SHOWS

1948 SMALL WONDER, with Tom Ewell, Alice Pearce, Mary McCarty

1950 ALIVE AND KICKING, with Bobby Van, Carl Reiner, Jack Cole, Gwen Verdon

1952 WISH YOU WERE HERE, with Sheila Bond, Larry Blyden, Patricia Marand

1954 SANDHOG, with Leon Bibb, Michael Kermoyan, Alice Ghostley, Betty Oakes

1956 SHANGRI-LA, with Martyn Green, Alice Ghostley, Harold Lang, Dennis King

1957 THE BEGGAR'S OPERA, with Peter Turgeon, Shirley Jones, George S. Irving

1963 *SHE LOVES ME, with Barbara Cook, Barbara Baxley
*see Awards, Below

1964 *FADE OUT — FADE IN, with Carol Burnett
*Cassidy was nominated for an Antoinette Perry (Tony) Award for Best Performance by a Supporting or Featured Actor in a Musical

1966 *IT'S A BIRD. . . IT'S A PLANE. . . IT'S SUPERMAN!, with Patricia Marand, Bob Holiday, Linda Lavin
*Cassidy was nominated for an Antoinette Perry (Tony) Award for Best Performance by an Actor in a Musical

1968 *MAGGIE FLYNN, with Shirley Jones
*Cassidy was nominated for an Antoinette Perry (Tony) Award for Best Performance by an Actor in a Musical

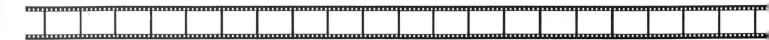

1960 THE MUNDY SCHEME, with Dorothy Stickney

AWARDS

1963 Cassidy won an Antoinette Perry (Tony) Award for Best Performance by a Supporting or Featured Actor in a Musical for his role in SHE LOVES ME.
This performance also won an award from *Variety*, the New York Drama Critics' Poll, and the *Saturday Review* Critics' Poll.

1970 Cassidy won an Emmy for Best Single Performance by a Leading Man in THE ANDERSONVILLE TRIAL.

MAJOR FILMS

1961 LOOK IN ANY WINDOW, Allied Artists
with Ruth Roman, Alex Nicol, Gigi Perreau, Paul Anka

1962 THE CHAPMAN REPORT, Warner Bros.
with Jane Fonda, Claire Bloom, Glynis Johns, Shelley Winters

1964 FBI CODE 98, Warner Bros.
with Jack Kelly, Ray Danton, Peggy McKay

1970 THE COCKEYED COWBOYS OF CALICO COUNTY — Universal
with Dan Blocker, Nanette Fabray, Jim Backus, Wally Cox

1971 BUNNY O'HARE — American International
with Bette Davis, Ernest Borgnine

1975 THE EIGER SANCTION — Universal
with Clint Eastwood, George Kennedy, Vonetta McGee

1976 W.C. FIELDS AND ME — Universal
with Rod Steiger, Valerie Perrine, Bernadette Peters

Señor Chico—Freddie (Preutzel) Prinze.

Freddie Prinze

Born: June 22, 1954, New York, New York

Freddie Prinze, nee Preutzel, an only child, was born in New York's Hell's Kitchen, moved to Spanish Harlem, and then to Southern California's Hall of Fame: All in a brief twenty-two years. It was too fast a trip to be safe. Comedian David Brenner said it this way: "There was no transition in Freddie's life. It was an explosion. It's tough to walk off a subway at age 19 and then step out of a Rolls-Royce the next day. He was in a life-style that's very unusual for a 22-year-old."

His mother Mary, a devout Catholic Puerto Rican housewife, barely spoke English. She adored her only child Freddie, who grew into a six-foot-two inch handsome white man, who spoke beautiful English. His gypsy father Karl was a, partly Jewish, Hungarian tool and die maker, who was fluent in three languages. Karl, forty years old when his son was born, moved the family to Apt. 64 at 550 West 157th Street in Washington Heights . . . a Spanish Ghetto. Prinze described himself as a "Hungarican." He turned his mixed-up heritage into comedy as he delivered lines like: "My Puerto Rican mother met my Hungarian father on a subway when they were picking each other's pockets." But as with all great comedians, the underlying theme is always sadness.

The building where Freddie Prinze grew up in the poor area of Washington Heights.

Prinze's mother, Maria Preutzel, standing in front of giant poster which hangs in the hall of the home her son purchased for her and his father in California. Circa 1977.

was heavy into cocaine." Although he hated fighting, he studied karate and the art of self-defense. But it was his fantasy life that proved to be his best self-defense from a life he could barely tolerate, much less understand. As a child he could entertain with imitations and would talk about people who were his idols. He would say of idol Joe Namath: "I just came back from Joe's house—" Friends wondered if he really believed it. He'd do his Nixon and Rockefeller imitations at Hornstein's Stationery store at 3764 Broadway until employee Louis Calderon would throw him out. There he also read, never bought, movie magazines or anything else he could get his hands on: stories and pictures that showed the "Let's get away from it" other side of life. As the young "fish out of water," he took his imaginary trips through the magazine's pages, but as he grew older, he began to swim into the mainstream of life.

A young Freddie Prinze—he didn't have enough time to adjust to his "rags to riches" life. Circa 1974

The young Freddie attended Catholic mass every Sunday at his mother's insistence, while his father enrolled him in a Lutheran elementary school. In lieu of friends, he had the only piano in the neighborhood. Instead of fighting, he preferred to drop water bombs, made from wet toilet paper, on the heads of subway passengers who exited under his window from New York's underground transportation system. As a kid he was fat and "fantasy-ful." One of his friends said: "He was a chubby little white kid that everyone beat up on." His mother enrolled him in ballet school and there he slimmed down. She was against fighting and as much as he always tried to do what his mother told him, he knew he had to protect himself in the rough neighborhood streets. By the time he was twelve, he had already been mugged. He dealt "grass" to make money, worked as an usher in a movie house, and by his own admission, had "almost overdosed on Valium, and

He graduated from New York's High School for Performing Arts and worked in the New York City Street Theatre productions of *West Side Story* and *Bye Bye Birdie*. Soon he abandoned singing and dancing for comedy. At the Improvisation Club, a showcase for new talent, he would sometimes wait until 2:00 or 3:00 a.m. for his turn to try out his comedy routines. Instead of carrying a switchblade, he turned his tongue into a rapier, he reached into his ethnic grab bag, and made its background work for him: "Our roaches are so big they eat at the dinner table."

In 1972, a talent scout caught his act at "Improv" and this led him to a booking on one of Jack Paar's final TV shows. The videotape of the Paar broadcast was what convinced Johnny Carson and his staff to put Prinze on The Tonight Show, only one year later. An unbelievable step in such a short time from the gutter to the glitter. Then in December 1973, Jimmie Komack, producer of the NBC-TV series *Chico and the Man*, saw the young stand-up comic on television and thought "here's a kid who might be able to argue with a crank:" Veteran star Jack Albertson played "the Man", a cranky, grumpy, garage owner who never won an argument from the smart hip Chicano, "Chico." The series started in September 1974, and from the beginning was a smash . . . a hit . . . a sensation. Freddie Prinze, half Puerto Rican, half Hungarian, who was thought by many to be an Italian, was now playing a Chicano, a Mexican-American. His bitter life had become better . . . or had it?

UPI

Winners all in Hollywood Women's Press Club 34th Annual Golden Apple Awards. (l-r) Prinze won as male Newcomer of the Year, Kate Jackson won as female Newcomer of the Year, and Alan Alda won as male Star of the Year. 1974.

Freddie Prinze and Jack Albertson, "Chico and The Man."

Wide World

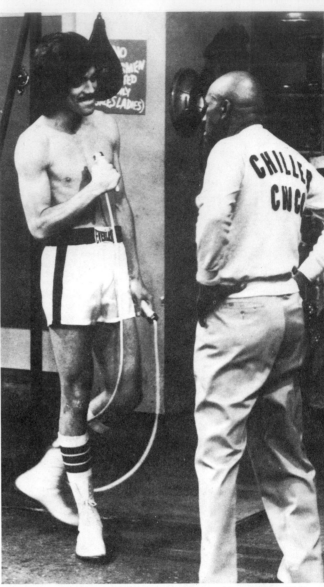

TOP: Guest star Caesar Romero on "Chico and the Man." Romero seen here as Chico's father, Gilberto Rodriguez, has just told Chico that he is his father, who was presumed dead by Chico. 1977.

RIGHT: Louie, played by Scatman Crothers on the series "Chico and the Man" tells Chico how to make a fortune as a fighter. In real life Prinze made a fortune fighting his way up from his humble beginnings. 1977

BOTTOM: Costars Jack Albertson and Freddie Prinze seen in one of their episodes from their successful "Chico and the Man."

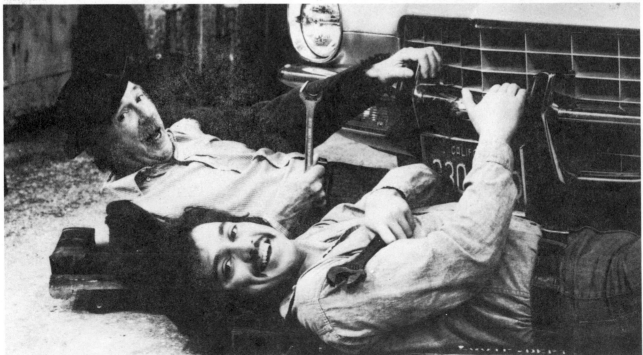

After the first season on the air, Prinze went on the road with a nightclub comedy act. He was a first-class mime, who wrote all of his own material, and who won the hearts of all with his super imitation of the Puerto Rican super "Mr. 'Ees-not-my-job' Rivera." While vacationing in Jackson Hole, Wyoming, he met travel agent employee Katherine Elaine Cochran, four years his senior. They were married in Las Vegas, October 1975. Their son, Fred James Prinze arrived March 1976. The first year was a stellar one for the first successful Latin-American comic.

Chico takes a bride. Prinze and his wife Katherine Elaine Cochran in Las Vegas after the ceremony. "Mrs. Chico" is being kissed by "The Man," Jack Albertson. 1975

Chico hit the road after the first season with a very successful nightclub act, 1975.

The following year, Prinze had his choice of many parts, but chose to remain with the series and develop as an actor. He told an interviewer: "I feel I am growing as an actor — a Puerto Rican, to be sure — but an actor. I still love comedians, but I'd rather act than be funny." The series remained in the top ratings but the bottom began to fall out for its superstar. The happy-go-lucky Chico faced an expensive lawsuit, which he eventually lost, to an ex-manager David Jones. He moved his parents to a house in the San Fernando Valley, while Kathy sued for divorce. Although they were "not in love" when they married, Prinze told Komack that "they fell in love after the marriage." He was arrested for reckless driving while under the influence of drugs. Wine, drugs, hypnosis, therapy, all became a way of life. He was searching for happiness and losing it as quickly as it appeared. He knew full well who Chico was but who was Freddie? Few of his friends knew his past history of depression and very few believed him when he would pull out his gun, point it at his head, then pull the trigger as he would say: "Life isn't worth living." The safety device on the gun prevented it from going off. His publicity agent, Paul Wasserman, said: "The people who saw it (the gun pointing) didn't take it quite as seriously as perhaps they might. They thought it was an attention-getter, or maybe, an overdramatic act." Everyone agreed that Freddie Prinze had everything to live for. Co-star Jack Albertson put it another way: "He was a strange boy. He was a barrel of laughs. A real good kid, but at 22 he may have run into problems he just couldn't handle." TV America saw him handle the guest host spot on the Carson show . . . just a hop, skip, jump, and leap from the three minute stand-up comic routine that had launched him on the show, to Carson's very own chair. He epitomized the American Dream.

UPI

Prinze and his wife attended a "Friend Raising Party" for President Ford. May 1976.

Prinze in makeup for his first dramatic role as an electronic genius/ex-jailbird for NBC's "The Million Dollar Rip-Off," 1976.

Wide World

324

Carol Novak, his personal secretary for two years, was with him the night before he died. He had received a copy of the restraining order from his estranged wife, forbidding him to "harass her." The papers also charged that he hid his earnings from her and didn't provide enough money for her and for their son. People who knew him well never considered him stingy and if Freddie had known the Hollywood scene well, he would have known that this was just a lot of Hollywood legalize lingo. Instead it made him nutty. Ms. Novak said he was "calling his attorneys, dancing around the apartment, swallowing Quaaludes, loading and unloading his gun, putting it in his mouth and holding it to his head." He scared her to death when the gun went off in another room, as he said: "Well, I'm gonna do it." Finally, she went home exhausted from the mental strain of the evening. He apparently called her the next morning to check and double-check arrangements for his move into his own luxury apartment, just across the street from the apartment/hotel where he was then living. He kept all his appointments that day including a date with Suzanna Martin in the evening and another one, with his psychiatrist Dr. William Kroger. Kroger, according to Ms. Novak said to Prinze: "You're a little boy with masochistic tendencies." Prinze's reply: "Pseudomasochistic tendencies." Prinze should have believed Dr. Kroger.

Freddie Prinze had a new $6,000,000 five-year contract with NBC. He had a $1,000,000 deal with Caesar's Palace, Las Vegas' plush hotel. A few weeks before he had made an appearance at the Inaugural celebration for President Carter. With all he had achieved, he was quoted as saying: "Is this what it is? Is this what it's all about?" He never gave himself the chance to sort "it" out. After a phone call to his personal manager Ron De Blasio, whose office worker earlier in the day had spent time trying to cheer the depressed star, he then phoned his estranged wife. As his manager Marvin "Dusty" Snyder walked into his suite, Prinze hung up the phone, reached for the gun under a pillow on the sofa, and put it to his head. Snyder couldn't get to him fast enough. This time the gun went off.

Thirty-three hours after he shot himself in the temple, despite the efforts of a team of experts at UCLA's Medical Center, "he succumbed to his self-inflicted wounds . . . massive brain damage." In his hotel suite he had left a note: "I cannot go on any longer."

Wide World

Karl Prinze, (right) father of Freddie, Tony Orlando (center) and Jose Ortiz (left) both close friends, wait for the elevator in the UCLA Medical Center after a hospital spokesman announced that Prinze had died. 1977

Back in New York on 157th Street, friends managed to raise $65.00 to send flowers. In Charlie's Bar there's an inscribed photo which reads: "To Jaime and the bunch at Charley's, Love, Freddie." A memento from Prinze's trip back to the old neighborhood with wife Kathy. Someone in the bar said: "Those small setbacks shouldn't have bothered him that much. He should have been used to being heckled." Over at Hornstein's Stationery Store, Louis Calderon put it into dollars and cents: "He lived in a $695.00 a month apartment. It must have been very big, when he [Snyder] couldn't get across the room in time."

Wide World

Prinze's friends from the early days (l) store clerk Tyronne Peek, (r) Chico Sagain and in the center Luis Calderon.

Freddie Prinze was buried far from Spanish Harlem, in Southern California's famous Forest Lawn Cemetery. His death may not have been in vain, for months later, his dearest friend, singer Tony Orlando, feeling the same pressures that besieged Freddie, put down his microphone and walked away. He said: "You can quit. You can walk away from it all, including the money, when your own survival is at stake. You can seek help, take time off. You just cannot take the path of least resistance. You must fight back."

Wide World

UPI

Jack Albertson (right) accompanied by his wife are shown arriving for Freddie Prinze's funeral. California 1977.

Grief-stricken estranged wife Kathy Prinze shown leaving Old North Church at Forest Lawn Cemetery in California.

Singer Tony Orlando is followed by songwriter Paul Williams as they help carry the casket bearing the body of friend Freddie Prinze.

UPI

Close friend Tony Orlando (left) cradled Prinze's head for thirty-seven tortuous hours as Prinze fought to live. They looked alike and felt like brothers. Orlando promised Prinze "a great funeral," but said: "It was the hardest thing I've ever done." They are shown here when Orlando made a guest appearance on "Chico and the Man," 1976.

FREDDIE PRINZE
Died: January 29, 1977, Los Angeles, California

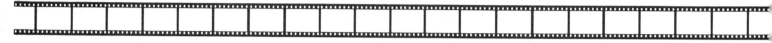

FREDDIE PRINZE
TELEVISION

1973 JACK PAAR SHOW — ABC
1973 & 1974 TONIGHT SHOW — NBC (5 appearances)
1974-75 & 1975-76 CHICO AND THE MAN — NBC (series)
1974 THE FLIP WILSON SPECIAL — NBC

1975 ENTERTAINMENT HALL OF FAME AWARDS SHOW — NBC
1976 DEAN MARTIN CELEBRITY ROAST: MUHAMMAD ALI — NBC
1976 JOYS! — NBC
1976 FROM MONTREAL, TEXACO PRESENTS THE BOB HOPE OLYMPIC BENEFIT — NBC
1976 THE GREAT NBC SMILIN' SATURDAY MORNING PARADE — NBC
1976 THE MILLION DOLLAR RIP-OFF — NBC

PERSONAL APPEARANCES

1974 THE BITTER END (New York)
1975 CAESAR'S PALACE (Las Vegas)
1975 MR. KELLY'S (Chicago)
1976 FONTAINEBLEAU HOTEL (Miami)
1976 WESTBURY MUSIC FAIR (Long Island)

RECORD ALBUM

1975 LOOKIN' GOOD — Columbia (recorded live at Mr. Kelly's)

AWARD

1974 GOLDEN APPLE AWARD — Hollywood Women's Press Club "Newcomer of the Year"

Wide World

329

He wasn't just the eye of the tornado, he was the total tornado . . . Elvis Presley.

Elvis Presley

Born: January 8, 1935, East Tupelo, Mississippi

Gladys Smith Presley, a sewing machine operator, knew she was carrying twins. Her doctor did not agree and so when Elvis Aron was delivered the doctor turned away and began cleaning up. But Gladys was still in pain . . . labor pain . . . and a few minutes later, Jesse Garon, Elvis' identical twin, was born dead. Elvis grew up as an only child, completely devoted to his mother, and she, to him. She spoiled him as much as the family budget would allow. She was, also, very over-protective of him, taking him everywhere she went. Or when he was out of her sight, it would be only minutes before she would check up on him. His father Vernon Elvis Presley worked at any-thing that would bring in money. Mainly he was a farmer-sharecropper, carpenter, factory worker, and at one time he had a milk route. They attended the Assembly Church of God and it was there that Elvis heard music for the first time. Certainly the roots of his music were well watered by the gospel sounds and the gyrations of the preacher. As a student, he was considered average. Although spoiled, he was always considered polite . . . something his mother insisted on. Years later, Elvis still retained his "Yes, Ma'am" or "No, sir" training. His first award for singing was at a county fair, where he placed second and won five dollars.

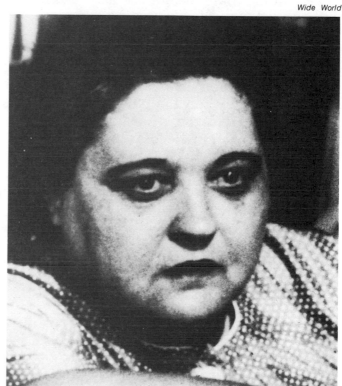

Wide World

Elvis' mother, Gladys, who taught him to always be polite and walked him to school until he was a teen-ager.

The family moved to Memphis hoping their income could be enlarged, but life continued to be a struggle. They were abjectly poor and in a strange way it worked in their favor: For when Elvis longed for a bike, he had to content himself with a guitar. The instrument was all the family could afford. Elvis taught himself to play it and learned tunes by listening to blues and country music on the radio. He continued learning through the revival music at church. In high school he acquired his love of football, which stayed with him his entire life. Even then he wore long hair, which distinguished him from his boyhood pals, and later grew his famous sideburns. He was shy and didn't enjoy performing in public, but in his senior year he did perform at the high school, and later when he joined a local boys' club, he would play at hospitals and benefits. There was never any doubt that Elvis "dug" girls, always young ones, and that girls were attracted to this shy, heavy lidded, polite, handsome young man.

When he graduated from high school, he secured a job at the Precision Tool Company driving a truck, for $41.00 a week. On his route he became acquainted with the Memphis Recording Service, where you could make your own record for four dollars, *two* songs. Elvis did just that, cutting the Ink Spot's *My Happiness,* on one side, and *That's Where Your Heartache Begins,* on the other side. Sam Phillips, who ran the recording service, had a sideline, Sun Records, and a very enterprising assistant, Marion Keisker. She was very impressed with Elvis and every time her boss was looking for a singer she would mention Elvis' name. Finally Sam Phillips paid attention and Elvis' career was underway. He [Elvis] was put together with Scotty Moore, a guitarist, and Bill Black, a bassist, and together they had a hillbilly band, known as The Starlight Wranglers. But the actual birth of the Elvis sound and movement came about in the studio one day, when just the three of them were taping. Not content with what they were doing, Elvis started moving about the small room, swinging the guitar up, down, and around, as Bill Black started hitting his bass, and generally clowning around the studio. But they were making music . . . their kind. It was as if someone had hit their release button . . . shy Elvis put his *real* feelings into his music. It was a wild and crazy sound. Sam Phillips took the tape to various DJ's, as was the custom in those days, and when the tape was played people started calling in for more. The first record order was for five thousand discs. On the Memphis country and western charts, *That's All Right, Mama* climbed to number 3, by July of 1954. Billboard called Elvis "a potential chanter." But their popularity was only regional . . . just a little known in Nashville and New Orleans. But the teen-agers began going crazy over Elvis as he and the boys started performing in night spots or any other place they could get work. This mild confusion started just a year before the death of the teen-agers' hero, James Dean. And it would be Elvis, who would take over the throne vacated by the young movie star.

Nashville's *Grand Ole Opry,* which was built in 1892, the same time as New York's Carnegie Hall, and Shreveport's *Louisiana Hayride* were the show spots to make and Elvis with the boys made their appearance shortly after the release of their first record. They "hit" on *Hayride,* and were given a contract to appear weekly for a year. Announcer Frank Page is given the credit for recognizing their talent. But *Opry* talent co-ordinator Jim Benny thought Elvis should go back to driving a truck! Instead, the group renamed themselves, Blue Moon Boys, signed a contract with local DJ Bob Neal of Memphis's WMPS, and started doing more and more concerts. Their next record didn't sell so well, but still the fans flocked. Then enter one Colonel Tom Parker who knew what and how to handle herds of flocking fans. As the Colonel put it: "You stay talented and sexy and I'll make amazing deals that'll make us both rich as rajahs."

TOP: Grand Ole Opry House, of Nashville, Tennessee, built in 1892, the same year as New York's Carnegie Hall. Both concert halls mean the pinnacle of success to performers.

RIGHT: Elvis first appeared at the Louisiana Hayride in Shreveport, La. December 18, 1954.

Col. Tom Parker (l) beams at his "virtuoso of the mobile hips." Said Parker of the then 21-year old Presley: "We've been good for each other. He's like most other 21-year old fellows. He has a few dates, takes care of his folks, and tries hard to live right."

The Colonel could have been joined at the hip of P. T. Barnum, for he had all the ingenuity and showmanship of the circus owner. He was right out of carnival/sideshow business, a clever wheeler-dealer, who knew what show biz packaging was all about. He managed Eddy Arnold and Hank Snow and in less than a month, from the time DJ Bob Neal took over for Presley, The Colonel had his share of the pie. The first concert he set for The Blue Moon Boys, was in February 1953, in Carlsbad, New Mexico. Eventually The Colonel owned Elvis and they formed Jamboree Attractions, their own company. It was in Jacksonville, Florida where the handwriting on the wall took shape. For it was there that the teen-agers for the first time, ripped off Elvis' clothes after one of his wriggling performances.

That was the beginning of something the world had not seen, since the teen-agers screamed, and fainted, in front of a skinny youth, Frank Sinatra at the Paramount Theater in New York City.

Elvis' fourth record made the national charts and The Colonel sold his recording contract to RCA-Victor, who released his first record [for them] in 1956. About the same time, Elvis was booked on the Tommy and Jimmy Dorsey Show which preceded the Jackie Gleason Show, The Honeymooners, on CBS-TV. New Yorkers didn't know who he was and the rest of the country was just as much in the dark, but when he sang *Heartbreak Hotel*, the country sat up and took notice. Whatever name you want to attach to him, The King, Elvis the Pelvis, Creole City Chanter, Guitar Playing Brando—there he was, rolling to the top with the libido of the teen-agers charting his course. They had found their hero and they were going to keep him.

TOP : The Colonel told him to stay talented, and sexy, but here with his dog, Sweet Pea, he's gentle and sweet. Circa 1956.

BOTTOM LEFT: Elvis and Sherlock, a basset hound, supplied by a press agent. This doggie he didn't "kick out the window" . . . just the song.

BOTTOM: Elvis, Brazilian singer, Leny Eversong, and Ed Sullivan (died 1974) prepare for the TV "Ed Sullivan Show" in 1957.

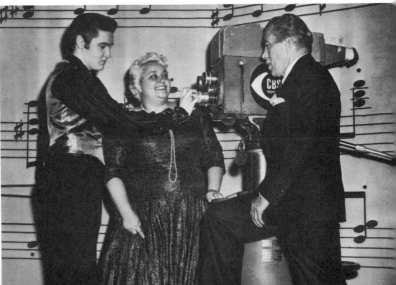

By the time he was twenty-one, his contract with Neal had expired and The Colonel took over. He marketed his product with things like: Presley blue jeans, Bermuda shorts, charm bracelets, T-shirts, bobbysocks, guitars, anything that could carry the Elvis name or carried the Elvis name. Any manufacturer who produced a Presley item, paid back 4 to 11% of their wholesale price, to Parker/Presley. Elvis became a millionaire and continued to amass millions, and millions, throughout his lifetime. He reportedly received one million for each of his three engagements in 1970 in Las Vegas. His records sold over 500 million; single personal appearance fee was $100,000.00, plus a percentage of the gate; his income was estimated to be about three to five million a year. One point worth mentioning is that neither he nor The Colonel played tricks with the Internal Revenue Service. They paid up honestly. Fan clubs also erupted, with about 250,000 members in the United States and about 150,000 elsewhere. The Colonel had all kinds of packages ready for them, which they bought and bought. So extreme was their idolatry that in later years the fans would place flowers on the grave of Elvis' mother, celebrate his birthday, his wedding anniversary, and even the birthday of his daughter. After his death, fans continued to commemorate his birthday.

A box was placed outside of Elvis' home on his birthday, so fans could drop off their cards. Seen here is Stephen Marsh, age 6, and his mother, songwriter Tina Marsh, inserting birthday wishes.

One year after his death, visitors still acknowledged the anniversary of his birthday. Elvis would have been forty-three. This shot shows visitors outside of his Graceland home in Memphis, Tenn. in 1978.

Elvis started a whole new career when he entered the movies. His film debut in *Love Me Tender*, for 20th-Century Fox and his recording of the title tune, sold over two million copies. He was an instant box office success. Those who labeled him a "flash-in-the-pan" would eat crow in a pan of their own.

Elvis, Walter Matthau and Carolyn Jones in an early film, "King Creole," 1958.

In 1958, Elvis received a draft notice from Uncle Sam and a physical examination that revealed he was 1-A. He was about to start filming *King Creole* but when the studios raised a fuss about their investment, the draft board gave him a deferment until March. Obviously people be-

gan to dispute the preferential treatment, but when Elvis publicly announced that he wanted "to protect his country" and "do his share" he was readily re-instated. In fact, he was more than re-instated, he gained the respect and love of the adult population, something he had had only from the youth of the country. When he reported in March for his two-year-tour-of-duty, his salary dropped from $100,000 a month to $78.00 a month. And when he became No. US 53310761, Colonel Parker issued simulated dog tags for the fans to wear. Parker was not about to let the world forget about Elvis. Reissues of back records came out, anything of Elvis' that had fallen by the wayside was dug up and recorded. His mother died in August of 1958, so it was his father and grandmother, who, according to Army regulations, were allowed to accompany him to Germany where he was stationed after completion of basic training in the U.S. The army post's post office was happy to see him depart, as approximately 15,000 fan letters arrived a week! Both Elvis and his father met their future wives while in Germany, although they did not marry at that time.

Elvis and his parents, Mr. and Mrs. Vernon Presley, on the eve of his induction into the army, 1958.

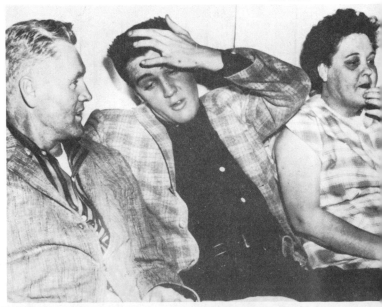

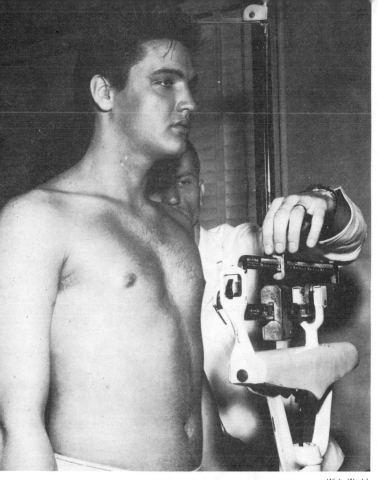

Wide World

Elvis weighs in for his two year stint in the army, 1958.

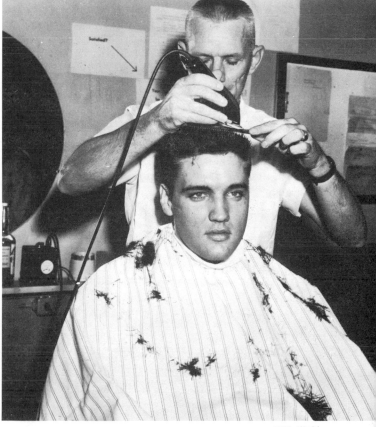

Wide World

Elvis quipped on the occasion of his being clipped: "Hair today, gone tomorrow." Fort Chaffee, Arkansas 1958. Barber, James B. Peterson.

Home on emergency leave, Elvis and his father, visit Mrs. Presley in Memphis hospital. Gladys Presley died in August of 1958, shortly before Elvis was sent overseas.

Wide World

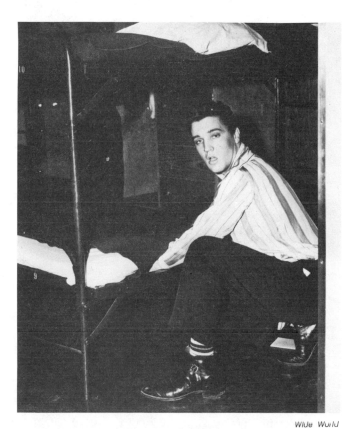

Wide World

Private Elvis Presley, No. US 53310761, tucks in a blanket, in his new bed, in his new home . . . the US army.

"Willkommen," German style, to Elvis, as the transport ship arrives in Bremerhaven, West Germany. Military police had their hands full. October 1958.

Elvis checks out a borrowed guitar in the hotel room of his father and grandmother, who joined him in Germany.

Wide World

Wide World

Business as usual. Hal B. Wallis, Paramount Pictures' producer, discusses with Elvis his next film, "GI-Blues" to be filmed after Elvis is discharged from the army. Germany 1959.

Wide World

Elvis as he appeared in "GI-Blues" for Paramount Studios, just as planned two years ago, in Germany, when Hal Wallis flew over there to discuss the movie.

Wide World

1960 rolled around and with it the anticipated discharge of Sergeant Presley (he started as a private). Parker had done his share of keeping Elvis' name before the public, but no one really knew what was going to happen when Elvis re-appeared. Actually, what had happened was that: Elvis had left, leaving his fans wanting more; Bobby Darin, Frankie Avalon, Ricky Nelson, etc. had come and gone—no one had replaced Elvis; his Army record had been good and to ice the cake, Senator Estes Kefauver of Tennessee, wrote a tribute to Elvis, which went into the *Congressional Record*. Elvis became a civilian on March 5, 1960 and as a civilian he appeared on Sinatra's TV show, in a tuxedo, for six minutes for . . . $125,000.00. He sang Ole Blue Eyes' special, *Witchcraft* and Sinatra sang the Elvis special, *Love Me Tender*, while two generations swooned, fell apart, became unglued, and loved every minute of it.

BOTTOM: "They knew he was comin' and they baked a cake," in the shape of a guitar, with Elvis' recorded song titles around the sides, and "Welcome Home" on the top. In back yard of Elvis' Memphis mansion. March 1958.

BOTTOM RIGHT: Elvis gets a stepmother, whom his father met, while living with his son, in Germany. Mr. and Mrs. Presley were married July 3, 1960, and are seen here honeymooning in Panama City, Florida.

"MR." Presley once again, Elvis displays his mustering out pay, and envelope containing his discharge, from the U.S. Army. March 1960.

From the spring of '61 to the summer of '68 Elvis made twenty-one films and about five million dollars. He hovered between his Memphis mansion, Graceland, which he had purchased before the army stint, and various houses he rented or owned in plush West Los Angeles. He kept a group of buddies around, referred to as the "Memphis Mafia," who kept him company, kept him out of trouble, fetched, and "go-ferred," offered him security, threw around his football, and *all* enjoyed the company of girls. Then in May of 1967, in a double ring ceremony, Elvis married the girl he had met in Germany, twenty-one year old Priscilla Beaulieu. They were married in Las Vegas and nine months later their daughter, Lisa Marie, was born. He opened up his career even wider, when he agreed to work in Las Vegas and after one month, the tabulation of audience goers was 161,500. He broke all Vegas attendance records. The Memphis Mafia fell apart, except for one or two of its members, and unfortunately Elvis' marriage ended in divorce in 1973.

Graceland, the Memphis mansion of Elvis, where his new bride would reside, as the Memphis Mafia, his bodyguards/boyfriends, moved out.   *Wide World*

Wide World

Elvis, 32, takes a wife. He met Priscilla Ann Beaulieu, while he was stationed in Germany. Her father, Lt. Col. Joseph Beaulieu, was an officer in the Air Force, also stationed in Germany.

341

The new Mrs. Presley, age 21, receives a kiss from her famous husband, after the ceremony in Las Vegas, Nevada.

After a champagne breakfast, the newlyweds cut the cake. It is a first marriage for both. May 1, 1967.

Wide World

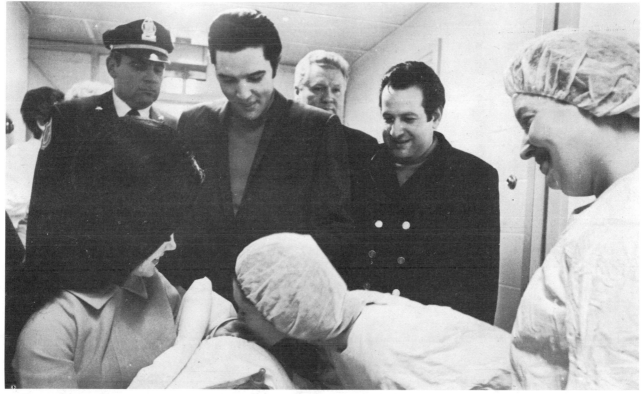

TOP: Lisa Marie Presley was born nine months, to the day, after the marriage. Nurse Mary Dunaway, seen kissing Lisa Marie, took care of the baby in the Memphis hospital. Directly behind the proud papa, is the equally proud grandfather, Vernon Presley, and to Elvis' left is Joe Esposito, his personal secretary.

BOTTOM: Baby Presley goes home to Graceland, in 1968. The Presleys were divorced in 1973.

Wide World

Two vocal eras come together, each a legend in his time. On the set of "Live A Little, Love A Little," Elvis displays his trademark, the guitar, while Rudy Vallee displays the megaphone that was his trademark. Hollywood 1968.

Elvis' stepmother, Mrs. Dee Presley, eleven years since her marriage, is shown here as she launches her own musical career. After only three months of writing, two of her songs have been recorded.

The ensuing years found Elvis aging. Worried constantly about his weight, he dieted and took pills. Worried about his image, he started dyeing his hair. His eating habits had not always been the best and his habit of staying up all night, sleeping all day, continued giving his life no real pattern, or structure. Linda Thompson, Miss Tennessee, became his "live-in" girlfriend and stayed with him until a few months before his death. Although Ginger Alden was in the house when he died, it was Linda who was called on the phone by Elvis' daughter Lisa Marie. Linda affectionately called him "Button" and he called her "Precious." Linda said: "We would wrestle together, or read the Bible together." When it was disclosed that Elvis had been lying in the bathroom for 3 hours before his body was discovered, Linda said: "Someone should have been watching over him. I never let him out of my sight for more than five minutes."

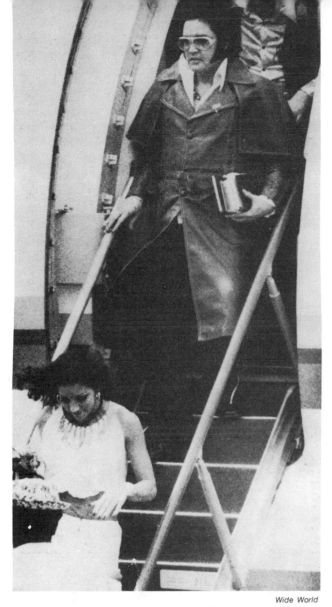

TOP LEFT: Elvis in May 1975 . . . aging and heavier than the public was used to seeing him. Nevertheless, he is seen here arriving in Jackson, Mississippi) where he did a benefit performance to aid tornado victims. Elvis gave Gov. Bill Waller a $109,000. check for the victims, proceeds from the sale of tickets in the 10,000-seat Mississippi Coliseum.

TOP: Ginger Alden, the new girl in Elvis' life, was living in Graceland when Elvis died.

BOTTOM LEFT: Ray Morgan of Forest Hill Cemeteries, of Memphis, checks the crypt in the Mausoleum, final resting spot for Elvis, prior to the funeral.

All attempts to revive Elvis were futile. His personal physician Dr. George Nichopoulos pronounced him dead at 3:30 p.m. in a Memphis hospital. Elvis had been a patient there five times before his death. He was treated for hypertension, an enlarged colon, gastroenteritis, a liver condition . . . all afflictions of the trade. No evidence of any illegal drug was found: only drugs, and there were many, prescribed for him by his doctors were in evidence. Although Elvis had been called a "walking medicine chest," he was known to be afraid of "hard stuff." He suffered "cardiac arrythmia" (irregular heartbeat) brought about by "undetermined causes." It was ruled "death by natural causes." He lived fast and he died quickly.

Tens of thousands of people poured into Memphis for his funeral. Elvis Presley Boulevard, named for him in 1972, was packed with fans, who "just *had* to be there." A hundred vans delivered 3,166 floral arrangements, one from the Soviet Union. Colonel Parker and Elvis' father decided the flowers should go to his fans. The confusion was so overwhelming that unfortunately two mourners were run over by a car and both died.

Wide World

Thousands of people arrived in Memphis for the funeral, and to pay final respects to their idol. Crowds poured through the gate to Graceland as it opened, to allow the public one last view.

Wide World

Many of the mourners were overcome by heat, as thousands wait outside of gate of Elvis' home.

An unidentified woman at right shouts, "Oh God, let her be alive!" as she looks at a young woman, who had just been struck by an automobile, in front of Elvis Presley's mansion. The automobile crashed into the crowd, and drove away.

Wide World

The car that crashed into the crowd, killed two Presley fans (left) Alice Hovarter, (right) Juanita Johnson. Both girls traveled from Monroe, Louisiana to Memphis, to attend the funeral.

Trestise Wheeler 11, (right) listens as a Memphis judge orders him held without bond, after he was accused by police of running down, and killing the two women, outside of the Elvis Presley mansion. One of the several charges against him was second-degree murder. At left is Sgt. W. E. Cantrell of the Memphis police.

Inside Graceland Elvis lay in state in the foyer, while in the music room a simple and plain ceremony took place with family and close friends in attendance. His body was placed inside a white marble mausoleum, in a six-crypt family chamber at the Forest Hill Cemetery.

347

TOP: During the funeral procession a young woman tried to reach the hearse, bearing the body of Elvis. A Memphis policeman is seen carrying her away.

BOTTOM: The last trip for Elvis moves down Elvis Presley Blvd.

TOP: Flower arrangements completely covered the ground, around the Mausoleum, where Elvis was entombed. A florist (shown here) carries more to another area.

TOP RIGHT: Pallbearers carrying the flower covered casket into the mausoleum.

He stayed "talented and sexy," and The Colonel did make them both, "richer than rajahs." He always remained "polite," as his mother had raised him. He remained close to his family, close to his religion, yet always very much alone, no matter how many of the Memphis Mafia milled about. It was his music that liberated him—that propelled him from poverty to wealth. It was, also, his music that liberated an era, allowed performers to express their feelings musically and in appearance, and nothing will ever be the same.

Vernon Presley, father of Elvis, is being helped from services by road manager, Joe Esposito. Mr. Presley is the white haired gentleman, Mr. Esposito is on his left.

ELVIS PRESLEY
Died: August 16, 1977, Memphis, Tennessee

ELVIS PRESLEY
FILMS

1956 LOVE ME TENDER — 20th Century-Fox
with Richard Egan, Mildred Dunnock, Debra Paget

1957 LOVING YOU — Paramount
with Lizabeth Scott, Wendell Corey

1957 JAILHOUSE ROCK — MGM
with Mickey Shaughnessy, Judy Tyler

1958 KING CREOLE — Paramount
with Carolyn Jones, Walter Matthau, Vic Morrow, Delores Hart

1960 G. I. BLUES — Paramount
with Juliet Prowse

1960 FLAMING STAR — 20th Century-Fox
with Dolores Del Rio, John McIntyre

1961 WILD IN THE COUNTRY — 20th Century-Fox
with Tuesday Weld, Gary Lockwood, Hope Lange, William Mims

1962 BLUE HAWAII — Paramount
with Angela Lansbury, Joan Blackman, Nancy Walters

1962 FOLLOW THAT DREAM — United Artists
with Arthur O'Connell, Simon Oakland, Joanna Moore, Anne Helm

1962 GIRLS! GIRLS! GIRLS! — Paramount
with Stella Stevens, Laurel Goodwin

1963 KID GALAHAD — United Artists
with Joan Blackman, Gig Young

1963 IT HAPPENED AT THE WORLD'S FAIR — MGM
with Gary Lockwood, Yvonne Craig, Ginny Tui, Joan O'Brien

1964 FUN IN ACAPULCO — Paramount
with Larry Tomasin, Ursula Andress, Elsa Cardenas

1964 KISSIN' COUSINS — MGM
with Arthur O'Connell, Glenda Farrell, Yvonne Craig, Pam Austin

1964 VIVA LAS VEGAS — MGM
with Ann Margret, Cesare Danova

1964 ROUSTABOUT — Paramount
with Barbara Stanwyck, Joan Freeman, Leif Erickson

1965 GIRL HAPPY — MGM
with Gary Crosby, Jody Baker, Jimmy Hawkins, Shelley Fabares

1965 TICKLE ME — Allied Artists
with Jocelyn Lane, Julie Adams

1965 HARUM SCARUM — MGM
with Mary Ann Mobley

1966 PARADISE HAWAIIAN STYLE — Paramount
with James Shigeta, Suzanna Lee

1966 FRANKIE AND JOHNNY — United Artists
with Donna Douglas, Nancy Novack

1966 SPINOUT — MGM
with Deborah Walley, Diane McBain, Shelley Fabares

1967 DOUBLE TROUBLE — MGM
with Yvonne Romaine, Annette Day

1967 EASY COME, EASY GO — Paramount
with Dody Marshall, Pat Priest, Elsa Lanchester

1967 CLAMBAKE — United Artists
with Shelley Fabares, Will Hutchins, Bill Bixby

1968 SPEEDWAY — MGM
with Bill Bixby, Gale Gordon, Nancy Sinatra

1968 STAY AWAY, JOE — MGM
with Burgess Meredith, Joan Blondell, Quentin Dean

1968 LIVE A LITTLE, LOVE A LITTLE — MGM
with Don Porter, Rudy Vallee, Michele Carey

1969 CHARRO — National General Corporation with Gary Lockwood, Yvonne Craig, Ginny Tui, Joan O'Brien
1969 THE TROUBLE WITH GIRLS (AND HOW TO GET INTO IT) — MGM
with Marylyn Mason, Nicole Jaffe, Vincent Price, John Carradine
1969 CHANGE OF HABIT — NBC-Universal
with Mary Tyler Moore, Jane Elliott, Barbara McNair
1970 ELVIS: THAT'S THE WAY IT IS — MGM
Documentary
1972 ELVIS ON TOUR — MGM
Documentary

GRAMMY AWARDS

1967 Best Sacred Performance: HOW GREAT THOU ART (RCA Victor)
1972 Best Inspirational Performance: HE TOUCHED ME (RCA Victor)
1974 Best Inspirational Performance: HOW GREAT THOU ART (RCA Victor)

RIAA PLATINUM RECORD AWARDS

Albums: (RCA Victor)
1977 ELVIS SINGS THE WONDERFUL WORLD OF CHRISTMAS
1977 MOODY BLUE
1977 IN CONCERT

RIAA GOLD RECORD AWARDS

Albums, unless designated as single: (RCA Victor)
1958 HARD HEADED WOMAN (single)
1960 ELVIS
1961 ELVIS' GOLDEN RECORDS
1961 BLUE HAWAII
1962 CAN'T HELP FALLING IN LOVE (single)
1963 G. I. BLUES
1963 ELVIS CHRISTMAS ALBUM
1963 GIRLS! GIRLS! GIRLS!
1966 ELVIS PRESLEY
1966 ELVIS' GOLD RECORDS VOL. 2
1966 ELVIS' GOLD RECORDS VOL. 3
1968 HOW GREAT THOU ART
1968 LOVING YOU
1969 HIS HAND IN MINE
1969 IN THE GHETTO (single)
1969 ELVIS' TV SPECIAL
1969 SUSPICIOUS MINDS
1969 FROM MEMPHIS TO VEGAS, FROM VEGAS TO MEMPHIS (2-record set)
1970 DON'T CRY, DADDY (single)
1970 FROM ELVIS IN MEMPHIS
1970 THE WONDER OF YOU (single)
1971 ON STAGE, FEBRUARY 1970
1972 BURNING LOVE (single)
1972 ELVIS AS RECORDED AT MADISON SQUARE GARDEN
1973 WORLDWIDE 50 GOLD AWARD HITS, VOL. 1
1973 ELVIS — ALOHA FROM HAWAII VIA SATELLITE
1973 ELVIS — THAT'S THE WAY IT IS
1975 ELVIS — A LEGENDARY PERFORMER, VOL. 1
1977 PURE GOLD
1977 WELCOME TO MY WORLD
1977 FROM ELVIS PRESLEY BOULEVARD, MEMPHIS, TENNESSEE
1977 ELVIS — A LEGENDARY PERFORMER, VOL. II
1977 ELVIS SINGS THE WONDERFUL WORLD OF CHRISTMAS
1977 HIS HAND IN MINE
1977 ELVIS COUNTRY

And into the Eighties

John Lennon

Born: October 9, 1940, Woolton, England

John Lennon wasn't born when John Lomax and his son, Alan, sat transfixed in a rural black church, in 1934, listening to a raspy-voiced leader shouting one-line, singsong phrases as several dancers stamped a steady rocking beat—a shuffle-like motion—across the floor. Lennon was only 14 when *Rock Around the Clock,* a movie theme, became the international anthem of rock and roll. Yet his roots were rock as he was connected to the history of it. Rock was a long time developing and would not take its place alongside jazz, country, folk, and the contributors until someone could shape it; give it true definition. Once having absorbed its history, Lennon developed mastery over it. As the driving force behind the Beatles, the shape of the music would be reshaped forever.

To quote Bob Dylan: "The Beatles had staying power. I knew they were pointing the direction where music had to go."

In the history of music, rock had some of the most overrated, undertalented writ-

ers and performers. By comparison, these were in the kindergarten; John Lennon was an adult. He introduced a new way of listening to music. In his droll and satirical way, never predictable, always creative and diversified, he led the listeners from the fury of the streets to nursery songs: songs sometimes puzzling, occasionally mystical, and often heartrendering. By 1967, (Sergeant Pepper) rock had unbelievably passed over a cultural barrier once thought impossible. As Lennon began to emerge in the new decade, the Eighties, one wondered where he would go. All that remains is what he gave from his own learning experience for the 40 years of his life.

Born into a working-class family in a suburb of Liverpool, he was sent to live with an aunt at the age of four. His father, a porter, abandoned the family during WW II when John was three. His mother could not cope with wartime life and her only child. And so, John went to her sister's house, although Julia, the mother,

John and his Aunt Mimi   *London Express*

Paul McCartney and John Lennon, considered by many, the greatest songwriting team in the history of music. Paul brought the humor and melody; John, the social consciousness. Circa, mid-Sixties.

Courtesy of Doug McCle

353

lived just 15 minutes away. She was killed in a traffic accident in 1956. Fourteen years later, as John tried to unshackle his emotions, one hears: *"Julia you had me/You were all I had/"* and *"Father I needed you/You didn't need me."* Finally, the coda on the last track of the last song: *"My mummy's dead."* Later, he went on to reinvestigate his background with *Working Class Hero.*

At age 15, with four others, he started "The Quarrymen." Their music was rock and skiffle—"a tame brand of pop folk music." Two months later, he met Paul McCartney, age 13, and the nucleus of the future Beatles was formed. Although rock 'n roll (formerly called "race music") began its breakthrough into white America when Lennon was 13, and even though Bill Haley's *Shake, Rattle and Roll* had hit the British charts in 1955, Lennon said: "Nothing affected me until I heard Elvis." McCartney favored Little Richard. Together they would work as a duo, "The Nurk Twins."

John and Paul fumbled along until 1958 when George Harrison, 15, joined them and then they disbanded "The Quarrymen," becoming "Johnny and the Moondrops." Harrison, influenced by Buddy Holly and Chet Atkins, brought still another voice to the formation of the group. And taking the lead from "Buddy Holly and the Crickets," they became

John Julian Lennon, first son of John, and the first Mrs. Lennon, Cynthia Powell. London, 1970.

"The Silver Beatles." For two years, they shuffled between Hamburg and Liverpool, adding art student, Stu Sutcliffe, on bass in 1959. Drummer, Pete Best, was added in 1960. But it was in 1961, when future manager, Brian Epstein, stepped in, that the future course of the Beatles was set. (see pp. 198-205)

Stu Sutcliffe left the group to return to painting in 1961 and died the next year of a brain tumor. The same year, 1962, Epstein made his famous announcement, which came true, that "his group would some day be bigger than Elvis." Ringo (Richard Starkey) Starr, a drummer with the group, "Rory Storm and the Hurricanes," had "sat in" with the Beatles in Hamburg. No reasonable explanation was ever offered as to why he replaced Pete Best, but he did, and the Beatles were set. Later Storm died in what was called "a double suicide with his mother." In 1963, *Please Please Me* was released, reached the number one spot on the charts, and Beatlemania was unleashed in the United Kingdom. In 1964, by way of the (television) "Ed Sullivan Show," the British invaded America for the first time since 1775.

The Beatles in "A Hard Day's Night," 1964.

Courtesy of Doug McClelland

The Beatles in "HELP!" 1965.

Mrs. Ringo Starr, Ringo Starr, John Lennon, Paul McCartney, and Jane Asher at party to mark the Beatles' TV-film, "Magical Mystery Tour." London, 1967.

But where was John Lennon, the individual, all these years? He finished secondary school, failed his high school exams, and entered the Liverpool Art College. He was never proud of his nonscholastic record and urged others not to follow in his footsteps. He met Cynthia Powell, a classmate, was married, had one child, John Julian, and the couple was divorced six years later, 1968.

1966 was a big year in his life. In August, the Beatles made their last concert appearance in San Francisco; they had to meet their competition head-on, as Dylan and "The Rolling Stones" were taking aim; Lennon wanted to leave the Beatles but as he said: "I didn't have the guts;" and he met Yoko Ono, an avant-garde artist, marching and speaking for peace.

Although Lennon knew in his heart that things were over, he wasn't able to make the break. Fellow Beatles blamed Yoko; they thought she put a spell on him. She jocularly said in a Playboy interview: "I sort of went to bed with this guy that I liked and suddenly the next morning I see these three in-laws standing there." Obviously, George, Ringo, and Paul.

Lennon was correct, for in 1967, *Magical Mystery Tour* was the first Beatle failure. John and Yoko were married in 1969 and faced severe criticism for their lifestyle. Nude photographs, their famous "bed-in" five days after their marriage, and their vigorous anti-war stance: this at a time when the prevailing public attitude did not favor anti-war themes. But the former "cheeky" attitude was gone, and the political arena became fair game for them and for rock. Looking for answers, the Beatles went into Eastern religion but soon the search that had begun with the Maharishi Mahesh Yogi, ended. Psychedelic trips took them and their listeners dangerously to the fringes. But unlike Janis Joplin, Jimi Hendrix, and Brian Jones, John Lennon survived. He did not go over that emotional cliff as so many did and then died in this time. With founding father, Arthur Janov, Lennon went into Primal Scream therapy and then set it all down on discs. "I don't believe in Elvis . . . I don't believe in the Beatles . . . The dream is over . . . I was the Walrus, but now I'm John."

Apparently his nightmare came during the 18 months of separation from Yoko. In Los Angeles, on booze and drugs, he couldn't produce. He also faced deportation from the United States on a British drug charge. Each time he sat down to produce, he said: "A cloud was between me and the source; a cloud that hadn't been there before." (Los Angeles Times interview 12/80)

The turnabout came for him when he and Yoko were reunited. She convinced him that he, John Lennon, did exist. Not as a Beatle, not just a rock star, but as a person.

They moved to New York City, first settling in Greenwich Village, and then later in their spacious West Side apartment. Yoko had been told that she could not have any more children; that they couldn't. One doctor told them that if they gave up drugs and started taking care of their bodies, as well as their minds, that a child was possible. Sean, their son, now five, was born.

355

John and second wife, Yoko Ono, staged a weeklong "bed-in" for peace, five days after their marriage. "It's a plea for peace among young people," they stated from their Hilton Hotel bedroom. Amsterdam, 1969.

The Beatles in feature film documentary, "Let It Be," 1970.

John and Yoko in the recording studio before their five-year retreat from the "business." 1970.

Although Lennon and his wife dropped out of the recording limelight from 1975-1980, they did not drop out of the glitter of opening nights. Shown here at the Merce Cunningham's Dance Company opening in New York City, 1977.

Honolulu resident, Mark David Chapman, with his head covered, is being escorted by police to maximum security cell. The Texas-born youth fatally shot John Lennon, after requesting an autograph. NYC, 1980.

Doorman, at the gate of the apartment house where John Lennon lived, watches as another fan adds her contribution to the memory of the slain Beatle. Flowers, album covers, photos adorned the gate while hundreds stood at a distance singing and lighting candles. NYC, 1980.

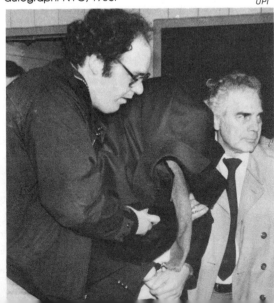

From 1975 until 1980, they lived quietly in the city of their choice. They could move about, not unnoticed, but unhassled. They could be seen walking through Central Park or shopping at the local fruit store. They reversed the customary marriage roles: John took care of Sean; Yoko took care of business. Their estimated fortune, according to the New Standard of London, is in excess of 235 million dollars.

John Lennon, musician, househusband, spokesman, surfaced in 1980 with his first album, *Double Fantasy*. At the time of his death, he had just about completed another, *Starting Over*.

As he and his wife of 11 years, stepped from their car, having spent the evening at work on the new album, an unemployed security officer, former printer, Honolulu resident, stepped forward and said: "Mr. Lennon . . ." Then in a military stance,

fired four bullets into John Lennon. He died almost immediately. Two days later, his body was cremated. To honor her husband, Yoko Ono requested a ten-minute silence be observed to pray for his soul.

Six days after his death, throughout the world, people of all generations honored her request in one of the saddest tributes ever staged. His assassin, under 24 hour police guard, sat on Rikers Island fearing for *his* life.

By the Eighties, John Lennon, child of the streets, multimillionaire, the conscience of his generation, had words for his followers. He stressed self-reliance and told them to "think for yourselves." In his last interview, hours before the fatal shooting, he told three reporters from the RKO Radio Network: "I am going into an unknown future, but we're still all here. We're still wild about life, there's hope!" His final legacy.

JOHN LENNON
Died: December 8, 1980 New York, New York.

BEATLES' RIAA GOLD & PLATINUM RECORD AWARDS
(* Denotes Platinum) (1968 through 1977)
(see p. 205 for 1964 through 1967)

1968 THE BEATLES (album)
1968 LADY MADONNA (single)
1969 YELLOW SUBMARINE (album)
1969 ABBEY ROAD (album)
1969 GET BACK (single)
1969 BALLAD OF JOHN & YOKO (single)
1969 SOMETHING (single)
1970 HEY JUDE (album)
1970 LET IT BE (album)
1973 THE BEATLES '62-'66 (album)
1973 THE BEATLES '67-'70 (album)
1974 THE EARLY BEATLES (album)
1976 *ROCK 'N' ROLL MUSIC (album)
1977 *THE BEATLES AT THE HOLLYWOOD BOWL (album)
1977 LOVE SONGS (album)

LENNON'S GRAMMY AWARDS
(through 1970)
1966 Song of the Year: MICHELLE
1970 Best Original Score, Motion Picture: LET IT BE

LENNON: (* Denotes Gold Record Awards)

1969 TWO VIRGINS
1969 UNFINISHED MUSIC #2; MUSIC WITH THE LIONS
1969 WEDDING ALBUM
1970 *THE PLASTIC ONO BAND LIVE PEACE—IN TORONTO
1970 *INSTANT KARMA (single)
1970 *PLASTIC ONO BAND
1971 *IMAGINE
1972 SOMETIME IN NEW YORK CITY
1973 *MIND GAMES
1974 *WALLS & BRIDGES
1975 ROCK & ROLL
1975 SHAVED FISH
1980 DOUBLE FANTASY
       STARTING OVER

The first motion picture studio, Nestor Film Company was housed in this building in Hollywood, Fall of 1911.

Some could handle it, some could not.
Some could cope, some copped out.
Some had no choice.

The Capitol Records' Tower (left) seen from Hollywood's famous Sunset Strip as the equally famous kleig lights emblazoned the sky; the ultimate.

All died trying . . .

John R. Adler

PATRICIA FOX-SHEINWOLD, Baltimore-born, lived in Beverly Hills, California for many years. Presently she lives in New York City where she works as a free-lance writer.